Drugtakers in an English Town

Drugtakers in an English Town

Martin A. Plant

Tavistock Publications

First published in 1975
by Tavistock Publications Limited
11 New Fetter Lane, London EC4
Typeset in Great Britain by
Preface Limited, Salisbury, Wilts
and printed in Great Britain
at The University Printing House, Cambridge

ISBN 0 422 74650 9(hardback)
ISBN 0 422 74660 6(paperback)

Distributed in the USA by
HARPER & ROW PUBLISHERS, INC
BARNES & NOBLE IMPORT DIVISION

'We are obviously demanding a new method of collecting evidence. The anthropologist must relinquish his comfortable position in the long chair on the veranda of the missionary compound, Government station, or planter's bungalow where, armed with pencil and notebook and at times with a whisky and soda, he has been accustomed to collect statements from informants, write down stories and fill out sheets of paper with savage texts. He must go out into the villages, and see the natives at work in gardens, on the beach, in the jungle . . . Information must come to him full-flavoured from his own observations . . . Field work can be done first or second hand even amongst the savages, in the middle of pile dwellings, not far from actual cannibalism and head hunting. Open-air anthropology, as opposed to hearsay note-taking is hard work, but it is also great fun. Only such anthropology can give us the all-round vision of primitive man and primitive culture.'

B. Malinowski *Magic, Science, and Religion*

Contents

Preface

Between August 1970 and August 1972 I was employed by Cheltenham Youth Trust to undertake a research project concerned with the social problems of young people in the 17–24 age group in Cheltenham. It was during this work that I made my first encounters with drugtakers, and my ideas of an observation study developed.

This book is based upon a PhD thesis prepared in the Department of Social Administration and Social Work, University of Bristol. I would like to thank Professor Roy Parker and David Peryer for their help and advice throughout this study. I am indebted to Charles Reeves for his encouragement and to David Downes, Gethin Morgan, and Jock Young for criticism of the original draft. I am grateful to Cheltenham Youth Trust for initiating the original research from which this study grew. My work was financed by the Home Office, Cheltenham Youth Trust, Cheltenham Education Department, and by a Social Science Research Council grant. My thanks go to Mrs Barbara Smith for typing the manuscript so efficiently.

My main debt is to the subjects of this study, the drugtakers. Without their kindness, friendship, and co-operation the whole exercise would have been impossible. Thanks also to Cheltenham Mountaineering Club for keeping me (almost) sane throughout.

I dedicate this book to Moira.

Note

In order to preserve the anonymity and to protect the interests of respondents and other individuals mentioned in this study, pseudonyms are used in references to specific people. In addition, case histories and descriptions have in all cases been rearranged in order to conceal individual identities without changing details pertinent to this study. It is not, therefore, possible to identify any person by descriptions contained in this book, and any conclusions drawn about the 'real' identity of persons described are purely conjectural.

Introduction

Most societies use some form of consciousness-altering drug. Alcohol and tobacco are extensively used and accepted. Alcohol is a customary part of some of our most important social rituals. Births, anniversaries, marriages, and celebrations in general are frequently occasions for the communal consumption of alcohol, and tobacco use is tolerated virtually everywhere, even during work time.

Some drugs are acceptable in certain situations, but not in others. For example, amphetamines are considered valid if taken by troops in battle, but not by athletes in Olympic competitions. Although many middle-aged people receive amphetamines on prescription, it is illegal for their children to use them at parties. Drugs are not evaluated solely in terms of their pharmacological properties. Their legal status and the social context of use are also important considerations.

This is an empirical, rather than a theoretical study. Drugtaking is controversial, beset by myths, vested interests, and prejudice. Theories are needed, but these must be related to research. This book is an observation study of a group of people in a provincial town. It is intended to be a contribution to our knowledge of drugtaking as it is within society, rather than as depicted, in general, by theory or by folklore.

Cheltenham, Town with an Image

Cheltenham may seem to be a strange place for a study of drugtaking. To outsiders, it has a sedate image as a spa town beloved by retired army officers. Cheltenham is renowned for its public schools, literary festival, Regency terraces, and its attractive, tree-lined Promenade. It is, superficially, at least, an elegant and attractive town, with good road links to major cities and close to the Cotswolds. Cheltenham is traditionally a popular retirement town, and continues to be so. Its popular reputation owes much to this fact.

A closer investigation reveals that Cheltenham is neither exclusively affluent nor solely the preserve of the elderly. There are large council estates and about a third of the town's housing is municipal. In addition, Cheltenham is a higher education centre and there are over 3,000 full-time students at the four main colleges. Although largely a commercial town, there are light engineering factories and a large branch of the Civil Service. Cheltenham was an area of relatively low unemployment at the time of this study and the area attracts many young adults who come to the town to work or study.

Many of the Regency buildings are in poor repair and a large number have been converted into flats and bedsitters to meet the demands of the young temporary residents living in the town. Cheltenham has areas of poor housing and areas reputed for delinquency. The town is a gathering centre for young people from the surrounding countryside. Just before the study began, in the summer of 1970, national publicity was given to fights between local gangs of skinheads and Hell's Angels.

The 1966 10 per cent national sample Census showed that 19,950 of the population of 72,390, 23.5, per cent of the Municipal Borough of Cheltenham, were aged 15–29. More than two-thirds of those in this 15–29 age range were unmarried. The young people, many of whom are students and other new arrivals in the town, have had a considerable impact and are a visible section of the community.

Several of the older drugtakers I encountered stated that Cheltenham was one of the first places outside London to develop a 'drug scene'. This may be a partisan view, but some groups were certainly using cannabis and other drugs during the mid-1960s. Since 1967 members of the town's 'vice squad' have been performing the role of a drug squad on a part-time basis, and on a full-time basis since 1969. At present the vice squad is largely concerned with drug offences. Cheltenham has a youth advisory service, Contact, which has been in existence since 1967. This organization was expanded in co-operation with local detached youth workers during 1970–71, and offers confidential counselling. This agency operates in a broadly similar way to Release, the London counselling service. Like Release, it devotes much of its time to helping young drugtaking groups. Several shops sell hippy clothing and cater specifically for the 'underground', attracting young people from quite a wide area around Cheltenham.

Cheltenham is not an isolated community. Many of the drugtakers I encountered, like other young people, were born elsewhere and a large proportion of the students spent only part of each year in the town. While not being a 'representative' community in a rigorous statistical sense, Cheltenham is not, to my knowledge, too unlike other towns with large populations of young people. Thus while this study was carried out in a specific place at a specific time, my subsequent encounters with drugtakers elsewhere (Bristol, Edinburgh, Glasgow, London, and Southampton) indicate that many of the observations and conclusions made in relation to Cheltenham are broadly applicable to other areas of Britain.

Aims of the Research

The objectives of the research are:

1) to examine the differences between drugtakers in different social positions;
2) to examine the social characteristics, lifestyles, biographies, and general well-being of different individuals who have used drugs;
3) to examine the processes of changing values, beliefs, and social position involved in becoming, remaining, or ceasing to be, a drugtaker;
4) to compare the drugtaker's self-image and definition of his social position with the 'conventional' view that drugtaking is a social problem.

These objectives were selected after a review of the literature on deviance and drugtaking as well as protracted discussions with many drugtakers and people concerned with drugtaking as a social problem or research topic. Much of the literature on drugtaking has been related to individuals dependent upon opiate narcotics. It is often assumed that the opiate dependent or 'junkie' is typical of drugtakers in general, or that other drugtakers are incipient drug dependents. The literature has widely supported the view, based upon studies of in-patients at hospitals, that drugtaking is pathological, a form of individual disease. The 'medical model' of drugtaking as intrinsically and invariably harmful has been generally accepted. This model is consistent with the legal proscription of certain types of drugtaking. It ignores the possibility that drugtakers may regard their behaviour differently, and might view drugtaking as valuable within their own terms of reference. Little attempt has been made to understand or appreciate the drugtakers' own views, or to evaluate the significance to them of their drugtaking. For this reason, it is proposed to go beyond a mere statistical description of a group of people and to evaluate the general situation, lifestyle, and outlook of different groups of drugtakers.

1) To examine the differences between drugtakers in different social positions

It is popularly assumed that drugtakers are a homogeneous group. It is hypothesized in this research that this is not the case, and that drugtakers may differ in relation to their general social positions. This is assessed using survey data and the evidence of my observation of drugtakers.

2) To examine the social characteristics, lifestyles, biographies, and general well-being of different individuals who have used drugs

The 'conventional' image of the drugtaker depicts an individual who is distressed, inadequate, or under-privileged. This evaluation draws upon my subjective impressions, as well as survey data.

3) To examine the processes of changing values, beliefs, and social position involved in becoming, remaining, or ceasing to be a drugtaker

What are the changes a person must undertake to adopt a pattern of behaviour contrary to his earliest values or goals? This is a consideration of the dynamics of becoming a drugtaker.

4) To compare the drugtaker's self-image and definition of his social position with the 'conventional' view of

drugtaking, and to assess the view that drugtaking is a social problem

Do drugtakers share the outsider's view of their social situation? An assessment of the factors associated with drugtaking examines the effects on individuals, as they and others see them.

In order to approach this subject, it is necessary to consider the basic characteristics of the drugs involved, as well as existing research into deviance in general, and drugtaking in particular. These topics are discussed, together with the crucial issues of methodology, reliability and validity.

ONE Background Information

1. Methodology

My work in Cheltenham 1970–72, involved general discussions with youth leaders, probation officers, policemen, social workers, and others in daily contact with young people. In addition, I spent considerable time establishing friendly contacts with students and other young adults in the town. During this period I located a number of drugtakers on a friendly basis, and my interest in drugtaking as a research topic developed.

The first, casual, encounters convinced me that it was feasible to collect information from drugtakers. My experience suggested that it would be possible to carry out a 'consumer survey' amongst different groups of drugtakers. Personal experience, and discussions with a number of local people, both drugtakers and others, indicated that several hundred individuals in Cheltenham were using drugs and that there was scope for a study confined to the Cheltenham area.

It was hoped that my field-work during the two years of the original project on social problems would establish enough personal links with drugtakers to enable a survey to be carried out to examine variables that existing research and my observations suggested might be pertinent. It was also hoped that the field-work would enable me to make a general assessment of the lifestyles and orientations of different groups of drugtakers. In the end, the methodology selected was observation, reinforced by a survey of a group of drugtakers in the community.

Background Information

Some useful background information was provided by a 10.0 per cent sample survey of persons aged 17–24 living in six central wards of

Cheltenham (All Saints, Lansdown Park, Pittville, St Paul's and St Peter's) during 1971 (Plant 1973). This survey included a few questions about drugtaking, and sixty-two of the 302 people interviewed, a fifth, reported that they had tried drugs at least once. This indicated that there might be at least 600 young people with drugtaking experience in the six wards. My own experience indicated that there were many drugtakers outside the 17–24 age group, in addition to people such as vagrants, who were missed by the survey.

Observation

In normal usage the word 'observation' refers to the activity of watching. Observation is a useful scientific technique to the extent that it:

1) serves a formulated research purpose;
2) is planned systematically;
3) is recorded systematically and related to more general propositions, rather than being presented as a set of interesting curiosa;
4) is subjected to checks and controls upon its validity and reliability.

Observation is especially useful in studying small groups with reference to interaction and overt behaviour. This enables data to be compiled at the time of relevant events (or soon after if note-taking might disrupt group behaviour), thus reducing distortions and exaggeration. But unless the presence of the observer is concealed, he faces the problem of forming relationships with those he observes. The presence of the observer may change the nature of the group under scrutiny. Even so, an observer may gain insights not available from group members.

Observation will depend upon the ability and training of the observer, whose perception will be selective and may be strikingly biased. To some extent, bias may be limited by 'structuring' though this will depend upon the nature and purpose of the research. The main danger, acknowledged by Whyte (1966), is that during extended observation the researcher may begin to accept the norms and prejudices of the group he is observing and overlook factors which would be apparent to an external observer.

One major dilemma, which must be resolved early in the research, concerns *participation.* Is the researcher to become a participant observer, or merely an observer? In the context of deviance, this issue is particularly vexed. Many researchers would naturally shy away from some forms of participation, such as injecting drugs, sexual deviations, or violence, etc.

The participant observer faces great problems of preserving objectivity, since he becomes more involved than a non-participant. This may be partly resolved by full recording. The ethical problems are considerable and there are no generally accepted rules about these. Should a sociologist studying criminals drive their getaway car?

In practice, an observer may have to 'fit in' with those he observes to such an extent that he will adopt some of the behaviour of the group. In practical terms he is ill-advised to conceal his true identity but can increase his acceptability by being unobtrusive and tactful. Since a policy of openness was adopted, I was accepted as a researcher and little pressure was ever put on me to use drugs or assist in criminal activities. The extent of involvement is partly an ethical decision, partly a reflection of the degree of risk the researcher is willing to accept.

Krech, Crutchfield, and Ballachey define participant observation as: 'A method of studying the structure and functioning of groups in their natural settings in which the observer lives intimately with the members of the group, participates in their various activities, and makes a continuing record of the content and pattern of group interaction' (1962:421). Thus the observer is part of the context being observed, and both modifies and is influenced by this context.

Participant observation, then, is an attempt to understand by close contact, how a group works. As Bruyn (1966) points out, traditional empiricism, that is, experimental behaviour studies and participant observation studies, are two polar yet basic research orientations in social science. He argues that sociology must build up a comprehensive body of theory, consistent with the findings of these two orientations, traditional empiricism and participant observation. This rejects Weber's concern for 'causal adequacy' and 'human meaning' or '*verstehen*'. As Skolnick remarks; 'A participant observer . . . must genuinely be prepared to see the world through the eyes of his subjects' (1966:26). Participant observation is the favourite technique of anthropologists. Beattie (1965), for example, in his study of the Bunyoro, had to overcome great antipathy to whites. This is the first great problem of observation; gaining acceptance by those one hopes to study.

Polsky (1969) suggests that the best approach is to exploit one's particular talents. He was good at 'pool' (billiards) and gained acceptance through that. Thompson (1967), in his journalistic study of San Francisco Hell's Angels, used his knowledge of motor bicycles and his possession of a Harley-Davidson (the type of motor bicycle favoured by the Hell's Angels) to ease his entry into the milieu he wished to observe. William Whyte (1966) gained the acceptance of 'Doc', a key person in the gang he wished to study. In this way he was accredited and managed to enter the group with a minimum of explanation. James Patrick (1973) was introduced to the 'Young Team' a Glasgow gang he observed by Tim, one of the gang's key members.

Should the researcher conceal or reveal his identity? Festinger and his associates (1956), studying a group who believed that the world was about to end, managed to enter the group by posing as believers. This ploy was justified by the fervour and insularity of the group concerned, and was deemed the only feasible approach. Patrick in his participant observation study in Glasgow, posed as an ex-borstal boy, and dressed like the youths he wished to study, but discovered that this approach was difficult to carry out successfully:

> 'However within a short time it was established that I was an approved school boy, a fellow inmate of Tim's and a housebreaker. I saw from Baggy's face that this last claim had been a mistake. On our return to the school Tim told me that the gang, although convicted numerous times for shop-breaking, had never broken into a home: "It's yir ain people – people just like yersel." ' (Patrick 1973:27)

Polsky argues that in studying criminal groups the researcher had better reveal himself, otherwise he will be detected and rejected. He managed to enter groups of 'beats' and gamblers by frequenting their haunts and being unobtrusive. Charles Reeves (1973) used a similar approach to make contact with drugtakers in Southern Hampshire. He spent considerable time walking the streets and visiting cafes and public houses used by drugtakers in order to establish friendly contacts with them. Polsky and Reeves gradually developed acquaintanceships with individuals and were open about their research purposes. The details of observation will, in the last analysis, be the choice of the researcher in any given situation.

Participant observation is invaluable to the study of a group in its natural setting especially when little is known of the area being investigated. It is a particularly appropriate method of investigating the *meaning* that emerges from behaviour, of assessing the subjective significance of the acts of one's subjects.

In order to make a contribution to sociological theory, as much as possible must be done to ensure scientific validity. The effects of face-to-face relationships between the observer and the observed, both in the behaviour of the observed and in the bias of the observer, are impossible to quantify. Howard Becker suggests that the issue of bias, either in favour of the deviant, or against the deviant, is a problem: 'Perhaps the best surety . . . is close contact with the people we study' (1963:176).

There has been a major debate about the usefulness of field research in criminology. Generally, writers have preferred to avoid field-work, justifying this on the grounds that it is too subjective and unscientific. Polsky accuses criminologists of 'copping out' or failing to come to terms with the realities of their subject. He emphasizes the fact that the official crime statistics do not represent crime in general and advocates more frequent use of field-work to look beyond the statistics. He rejects Sutherland and Cressey's assertions that to observe criminals, one must 'associate with them as one of them'. Polsky maintains that it is fully possible to collect information from criminals without joining in with the commission of their crimes.

Polsky details the problems of interacting with criminal deviants, but is emphatic that successful observation is possible. He describes the technique he uses:

> 'In my experience, the most feasible technique for building one's sample is "*snowballing*": get an introduction to one criminal who will vouch for you with the others. (It is of course best to start at the top if possible, that is, with an introduction to the most prestigious person in the group you want to study.)' (Polsky 1969:129)

With regard to the ethical considerations of this approach, Polsky has this to say: 'You must draw the line between yourself and the criminal. Precisely where to draw it is a moral decision that each researcher must make for himself in each research situation' (1969:132). He adds that one must keep faith with one's informants and, of necessity, write more vaguely than one would prefer, in order to preserve anonymity. He comes to terms directly with *the* ethical issue of this type of approach to deviance:

> 'If one is effectively to study adult criminals in their natural setting, he must make the moral decision that in some ways, he will break the law himself. He need not be a "participant" observer and commit the criminal acts being studied, yet he has to witness such acts or be taken into confidence about them and not blow the whistle.' (1969:138)

Polsky's 'neutral' view is challenged by Yablonsky, who maintains that non-moralizing, accompanied by an interest in criminality, constitutes a romantic encouragement of the criminal. Polsky rejects this view, referring to Weber's precept of value-neutrality in social science, and suggests that there is a distinction between one's role as a citizen and as a researcher. My own view is that observation of criminal deviants, such as the users of proscribed drugs, necessitates the researcher being aware of illegal acts. The subjects of field research take a great risk in permitting their behaviour to be observed. The very least a researcher can do to repay this trust is not to rat on those who made the research possible, the deviants themselves.

Polsky's views are highly controversial. In Sutherland and Cressey's book *Criminology* the existence of *Hustlers, Beats and Others* is noted with this scathing comment:

> 'Few individuals can acquire the technique to pass as criminals, or even to be trusted by criminals. One individual cannot build upon the work of another to a very great extent, for precise, controlled techniques of observation can scarcely be employed. Moreover, when confidence men study confidence men by this method (field research), it is impossible to determine whether the published conclusions are social science or part of a confidence game. (Sutherland and Cressey 1970:68)

Becker's essay 'Becoming a Marihuana User' is based upon participant observation (Becker 1953:235–42). While working as a dance musician, Becker managed to befriend a number of marihuana (cannabis) smokers. As an accepted member of the group he was able to observe how people learn to use cannabis. His conclusions were based upon the reports of drugtakers themselves. Becker's examination of the exclusiveness of dance musicians, another participant observation study, provides a lot of rich data about the lifestyles and self-evaluations of this group. His theoretical conclusions are derived from close personal contact with his subjects.

In my view, the interactionist approach advocated by Polsky and expounded by Becker is a valuable way of examining social phenomena. Observation permits a controlled subjective approach to one's data, and while this is not a rigorously objective technique, enables the researcher to get so close to his subjects that it is possible to collect information, and to gain insights into lifestyles which would not otherwise be accessible. Observation is especially valuable as a means of obtaining qualitative information of the type usually missed by 'hit and run' surveys and clinical studies. Observation is especially useful when one wishes to investigate role performance, including expressed beliefs and values.

> 'In this way the scientist acquires some sense of the subjective side of events which he could less readily infer if he observed without taking part.' (McCall and Simmons 1969:4)

The 'war stories', myths, and rumours popularly circulating amongst deviant groups are valuable in helping to build up a picture of their values and self-images. In the present study I found that the folklore of the drugtaking groups was an interesting reflection of the nature of these groups and a useful guide to interpreting how drugtakers saw themselves and their peers.

There is a major divergence between the 'classical' approach of Sutherland and Cressey and that advocated by Polsky. Both methods have much to offer, but in the present study Polsky's methods are favoured since there was no reliable way of knowing the universe under study, or of establishing its structural characteristics, namely how many drugtakers there were in Cheltenham. It is my view that Polsky's methods are justified, if subjected to careful validation, and thus a whole new realm of data is accessible through field observation.

Observation, admittedly, has problems. The major obstacle to overcome is the problem that one might be misled by one's subjects. It is possible that one's subjects may play the 'roles' they believe are expected of them. They might accept the outsider's stereotype of the deviant, or try to live up to the researcher's expectations. The researcher just has to get to know his subjects very well indeed. I found a lot of data were available gratuitously from informal contacts. Lifestyles and demeanour are readily observable. If the researcher gets well established in the network he wishes to study, he should discover a lot of basic facts about them. Some deviants certainly lie or conceal information but in practice that need not alter one's general impression too much. Others within the group are likely to supply information about those one is curious about, and this is often a useful check. Observing people over time one has an opportunity to note inconsistencies and to test people out. This is a two-way process, and any researcher who pretends to be something other than he really is will soon be detected.

In the present study I developed contacts with several groups of drugtakers, in anticipation of eventually interviewing them. During this time I kept diary notes about some people. I made no attempt to conceal my identity and always supplied details of my research, but avoided discussion of any theories that might be influencing the behaviour or statements of those I was observing.

It is suggested that the field-work enabled me to gain insights into certain groups of drugtakers which enabled a richer interpretation of data collected later during the survey. In addition, field-work located a willing group of potential respondents and made the survey feasible. A good deal of effort was invested in creating and maintaining good 'public relations' with drugtakers, and I repeatedly reassured people about the confidentiality of the study. This permitted me to mix with a large number of regular drugtakers and to establish their trust. This was demonstrated by the eventual ease with which I managed to carry out the formal interviewing programme.

Location of Drugtakers and Collection of Data

During December 1970 I took a part-time job as a barman at a public house in Cheltenham. This enabled me to meet young people socially, and to be accepted as a research student with an interest in drugs. This succeeded, and one of the girls working with me soon told me that she used cannabis a lot. She introduced me to some of her friends, one of whom was a drug dealer. My brief period as a barman established my first contacts with a group of non-student drugtakers. I fostered these by frequenting some of the public houses favoured by this group, and spent a good deal of time in places such as folk clubs and cafes, where drug users were likely to be found.

My work as research assistant to a local charitable organization enabled me to meet many students and I developed friendly relationships with several who had used drugs, or had friends who were drugtakers. It took me a full year to know enough people sufficiently to feel confident that a 'consumer survey' of drugtakers in Cheltenham would be feasible. I discussed my general ideas with several of the drugtakers I knew and they were encouraging and indicated that they would be willing to introduce me to their friends if I did conduct a survey. In the meantime, I adopted a friendly, casual approach to most of the individuals I met, and tried to form natural friendships rather than researcher-subject relationships. I talked quite openly about some of the information I hoped to collect and received a great deal of technical advice and help from different individuals.

While working as a barman I met two girls whom I told about my proposed research. One of them had been an undergraduate, but had left university following her conviction for the possession of cannabis. She had used the drug for three years, and, at the time I met her, was smoking it daily. She bought £5 'deals' of the drug whenever she needed it. She had introduced her flatmate, another girl in her early twenties, to the drug three months earlier. Both girls appeared to be nervous extroverts, and talked openly about their turbulent love lives. They suggested that they should visit my flat one afternoon, and talk to me about their drugtaking.

I followed up these and other contacts and spent a good deal of time talking informally to drug users, often emphasizing my 'neutrality' or sympathy with their views. I avoided discussions of my own opinions, but did not conceal the fact that I had little knowledge of most of the drugs they had used. My naïveté was accepted, and I found individuals very helpful in describing drug-effects, and even pharmacology.

Whenever possible, I tried to be helpful to the drugtakers I knew. I put several in touch with legal advice and found accommodation for some who were without homes. In practical terms, this generally paid off by increasing my acceptability to those I intended to interview, and did a little to repay all the help I received from the drugtakers I observed and interviewed.

I piloted a questionnaire amongst a few drugtakers I knew well and began to interview people in August 1972. Most of my field-work was carried out during September and was completed in October. Altogether 200 people were interviewed. These were all members of the networks I had located during the preceding two years. There is little doubt that there were far more regular drugtakers in Cheltenham than I actually interviewed.

Many school pupils used drugs, yet few were contacted during my field-work, largely because they tended not to frequent the places where I made most of my contacts. In addition, some experienced drugtakers who had married and left the drug-scene were not easy to contact. I suspect that there were many in this group whom I failed to contact or observe.

Most of my field-work was centred upon specific places, public houses, cafes, and colleges and certainly missed groups of young people on housing estates and living in the suburbs, or in the countryside. A few people in all these categories were interviewed, but it is only possible to guess that the majority were not. Apart from those in the 'market situation' of the drug using groups, there are certainly young people who use drugs in isolation, unknown to their friends. Some of these use drugs which their parents have on prescription, others use glues, solvents, or other legally available substances. The end result of my field-work was the location of an interesting, but certainly biased, group of drugtakers in the Cheltenham area. I did not contact a random sample, and by the nature of the drug-using groups, random sampling may have been even more misleading.

The 'snowball' survey

Using the technique of 'snowballing', which has already been discussed, 200 drugtakers were interviewed during August, September, and October, 1972. Only eight people refused face-to-face to be interviewed, but I do not know how many refused indirectly when approached by other respondents.

The refusals

1) working-class male, unemployed
2) female non-manual worker

3) female college dropout, working in low-status manual job
4) male drug dealer, unemployed
5) male drug dealer, unemployed
6) male drug dealer, unemployed
   } all had poor employment records, of manual jobs and protracted voluntary unemployment
7) male graduate, temporarily unemployed
8) female student.

I do not suggest that those who were interviewed were representative of those who refused to co-operate. My observations suggest that the general lifestyles of all those who refused to be interviewed were similar to those of their friends who did co-operate. Five of the eight refusals provided me with a certain amount of biographical information during informal discussions which revealed that in their backgrounds and outlooks they appeared to resemble many of those included in the survey.

Table 1
Timetable of the research

1. *August 1970 – July 1972*
a) Establishment and maintenance of friendly relationships with a number of drugtakers in Cheltenham
b) Review of literature on drugtaking and deviance
c) Discussions with social workers and others in contact with drugtakers

2. *August – November, 1972*
a) Non-random selection and interviewing of 200 drugtakers in the Cheltenham area
b) Coding and tabulation of results

The Survey

In general, surveys are a convenient method of collecting a large amount of data in a short time. The main virtue attributed to surveys is that they permit quantification rather than simply casual observation. It is assumed that they provide 'facts' rather than 'impressions'. Surveys are intended to be *representative*. If limitations of time and resources preclude a study of a total population, informants are often selected so that they provide a basis for generalizing to the population at large. Surveys are used to provide a 'general view' of the group in which one is interested. It must be noted that while this approach may be useful for studying 'normal' social behaviour, it is generally less so for investigating illegal or deviant behaviour, which is likely to be concealed.

One important point is that exceptions, which may be overlooked during observation, are included. Also, a survey may expose discrepancies between belief and practice. Surveys may be used to test hypotheses about correlations between variables investigated and analysis of survey data may provide the basis for new hypotheses.

Sampling

Many of the problems of the survey method are problems of sampling or choosing a representative group within a population. It was decided at an early stage in the present research not to attempt a random sample. This means that there are no grounds to justify generalization beyond the data collected. The method chosen was a self-selected non-random group of drugtakers whom I located through a network of friends. This technique is called 'snowballing'. This probably produced a biased selection, missing some important groups of drugtakers altogether, and missing isolates.

Data collection

Information was collected through personal interviews, all of which I carried out myself using a standardized schedule. It is hoped that the schedule minimized bias, but it is possible that respondents reacted differently to my manner and appearance, especially since some knew me very well.

The interview

In order to minimize external influences and to achieve confidentiality, interviews were, as far as possible, carried out in private. Many were conducted in my flat or at the dwelling of the person being interviewed. Others, for practical reasons, were carried out in a parked car, or in the corners of parks, public houses, or cafes. No hostility whatever was evident from the respondents and, in general, a good rapport was established during the interviews, each of which usually took between half an hour and an hour to complete. All those interviewed answered all the questions put to them and many made additional comments and observations which were also recorded.

The schedule (see Appendix I)

The interview schedule was a lengthy document, containing more than 100 separate items. As far as possible, largely 'factual' questions were included, though several subjective or opinion questions were also asked. I had piloted each of the items, and some had been used in other surveys by myself or by Charles Reeves.

The main sections of the schedule were concerned with the following topics:

- i living conditions
- ii family background
- iii personal relationships
- iv geographical mobility
- v occupation and education
- vi self-image
- vii ideology
- viii delinquency
- ix drugtaking

The questions were arranged so that non-controversial, 'factual' items were introduced first, to enable the respondent to become used to the interview situation. 'Controversial' questions were asked later, when the interview was well under way. Nobody refused to complete the interview once it had started, so apparently this method worked. I made subjective comments on the physical appearance, and if possible, living conditions, of each respondent, and these were recorded upon completion of the interview.

Reassurance

At the end of each interview, a brief account of the aims of the study was given verbally, together with a reassurance about confidentiality. In only two cases did any of those interviewed indicate that they were at all nervous about the possible misuse of the schedules. Both were successfully placated.

Reliability and validity

The information in this study was collected in two ways, observation and interviewing. The result is a hybrid piece of work, midway between a self-reported deviance survey and an observation study. The salient point is that the information collected was information that drugtakers *allowed* to be collected, either by letting me watch their behaviour, or by answering direct questions. This raises the major criticism that if the drugtakers chose to lie, or to conceal information, the results would be a naïve total misinterpretation of the real situation. This problem has been examined elsewhere.[1]

Other research is interesting, but from the standpoint of the present study, purely academic. It indicates that under the right conditions, valid data can be collected from deviants. Becker maintains that deviants, and especially those engaged in illegal behaviour, are motivated to conceal or deny their proscribed behaviour. Nevertheless, much of Becker's own work is based on participant observation. Presumably he concedes that an observer may manage to penetrate the defences of a deviant group to collect useful information. Kinsey, in his famous studies of sexual behaviour, asserted that under appropriate conditions, people will be willing to describe their most private behaviour (Kinsey *et al.* 1948). This issue is clearly controversial.

The present study was not confined to a survey of strangers. Many of those interviewed were well known to me and virtually all were known to me indirectly, through information supplied by their friends. Some individuals gave me considerable autobiographical information during their informal discussions with me, and these encounters often provided second-hand and hearsay information about other drugtakers. A great deal of useful information was available 'through the grapevine' including rumours, tales of exploits avoiding the law, and other 'war stories'. News of who was buying and selling drugs and who had been raided or arrested was quickly passed around by word of mouth. I recorded some of this information and later checked it with interview data.

Care was taken to compare the answers of close friends, or of couples who were cohabiting or married. There was, in fact, considerable openness amongst friends within the drug using sub-

1. In Clark and Tifft (1966:516–23) and Ball (1967:650–54).

culture, and drugtaking experiences are discussed as avidly as a group of mountaineers might compare notes about the routes they have climbed. Much drugtaking is a social event and so it is often possible to start a group discussion '. . . about the time you all tried nutmeg and were sick . . .'.

In many cases I was able to learn a lot about people I was about to interview, even if I had not actually met them before. The 'snowball technique' which was used guaranteed that some information was available about the potential respondent through those who had already been interviewed. The use of snowballing rather than statistical random sampling ensured:

a) that the person to be interviewed was an 'accredited' drugtaker and
b) was known to at least one person previously known to me.

These points are important in assessing the validity of this study. First, it is a feature of the drugtaking sub-culture that there is a natural reluctance to divulge information to strangers who may pose a threat. For this reason an ill-planned survey, or a naïve approach, might cause the drugtaker to beat a hasty retreat, or to lie about his drug use. Snowballing allows the researcher to let his associates in the deviant group do his sampling for him. They know others who use drugs and have no reason whatever to select people who do not use drugs. This is very helpful to the researcher. During field-work in Cheltenham several individuals went to great lengths to guide me through their networks of drug using friends. It is a pity that a proper acknowledgement cannot be given! These guides not only provided the necessary introductions, they were sources of advance details about the people they recommended.

It would, theoretically, have been possible to check some details, such as criminal records, with 'official' sources, but I did not do so, since this may have threatened the confidentiality of the research. In cases where the respondent was well known to me diary notes were used to check recent activities and observed characteristics or behaviour. I also collected a great deal of hearsay information about people whom I subsequently interviewed. In all cases, observation corroborated answers given during interview.

'Reliability' and 'validity' are essentially experimental, or clinical concepts. I suggest that both are of only limited applicability to an observation study, which is valuable more for qualitative than quantitative findings. My experience in the field was unique and could not be precisely replicated elsewhere. I draw attention later to other studies of drugtakers which produced similar conclusions. Such agreement where it occurs is a useful reassurance but does not validate the present research since participant observation is not amenable to such rigorous appraisal. To some extent the survey was a check upon the observation, but both were subject to the influence of my presence as observer or interviewer – influences which cannot be assessed.

Shortcomings

My general impression is that I managed to know my subjects well enough to collect accurate information from them. Two 'controversial' topics did seem to be especially difficult to examine during interview: first, mental health. In many cases individuals readily supplied information about any psychiatric treatment they had received and went into great detail about this. I noted reluctance by a few, apparently disturbed, individuals to acknowledge that they were mentally ill. This applied only to a few 'extreme' individuals.

Second, it was easy to collect data about patterns of drug use. Yet in spite of this, there was a marked reluctance on the part of subjects to concede either psychological or physical dependence, even in cases when this was fairly apparent. These 'shortcomings' are important. As I shall indicate later, much of the research into drugtaking has been concerned with in-patients in hospitals and treatment centres. I believe there may be important (psychological) differences between drugtakers who refuse to acknowledge that they are drug dependent, and those who accept this label and see themselves in terms of the 'sick' dependent or 'junkie' image. There may be a final threshold of self-assessment in relation to mental illness and drug dependence which is hard to cross (Toll 1970:139–58). Future research could usefully examine this possibility. If there is such a psychological distinction, groups of drugtakers receiving treatment may indeed be of a different personality type to those remaining in the community. Few of those in the present study indicated that they accepted that they were 'sick' or in need of a 'cure'. This contrasts greatly with addicts in hospitals. A medical assessment of those encountered and interviewed was outside the competence of this study. Nevertheless, I feel this is an interesting conjecture.

The only other topic I felt dubious about was sexual behaviour. I am not wholly convinced that one can collect really accurate data about this subject. I have no proof of this, but knew several individuals who habitually lied about their exploits. I therefore feel one should treat the precise statistical details of sexual behaviour with reserve and caution. Nevertheless, I believe an interview in the context of an observation study is more likely than most other methods to elicit truthful answers about 'delicate' subjects.

Why should Drugtakers help Research?

An important consideration is what motivated the drugtakers who assisted this study to do so. Those encountered during field-work and those interviewed represented a varied group, ranging from an unemployed, homeless schizophrenic to a wealthy, highly qualified professional. Their only common characteristic was that all had used, or were currently using, cannabis. On a personal level, I formed friendly relationships with some. My interest in folk, 'progressive', and rock music enabled me to discuss matters of common interest with many who probably regarded me as a 'vicarious head' or semi-deviant – a person on the periphery of the drug scene. It is possible that a few were flattered, or at any rate, amused by being the subjects of research. Many of the students and non-manual workers were interested in social science and sociology had an academic appeal. The majority of drugtakers encountered volunteered that in their view much of the literature about drugtaking was written 'fifth hand' by people out of touch with the realities of drugtakers in the community. Most (objectively) denied that they were junkies and stated that they thought it was time that they had a chance to express the consumer's view about the drugs they had used. My experience totally contradicted the view that people have bad memories about their deviant or illegal behaviour. My diary notes and conversations with individuals substantially validated data provided during interview. In general, individuals have a good recollection of their clashes with the law and, if approached honestly and openly, are willing, even eager, to provide information about themselves. I believe it was an important finding that one can collect such information about illegal behaviour. It has widely been assumed that this is not the case, and research has tended to ignore the viewpoints of those best able to comment upon drugtaking, the users themselves.

There was little doubt that many of those interviewed believed that accurate information about drugtaking was preferable to myth and prejudice. To some the chance of confiding and talking to a neutral or sympathetic semi-outsider was welcomed as a quasi-therapeutic exercise. Several people told me that they appreciated being able to talk openly to a 'straight' (non-drugtaker). A few of those most deeply involved with the drug scene appeared to feel that their status was enhanced by having a tame sociologist in tow. Perhaps this accounted for the helpfulness of some towards the research.

It is probably a trait of minority groups that the absence of hostility is welcomed as tacit support. I was treated with the greatest courtesy throughout my field-work. Many of the drugtakers located put forward their own theories of why they and others, used drugs and, in general, great interest was expressed about the likely conclusions of the study. It must be stressed that most of those interviewed seemed intelligent and some were highly educated, cultured, and articulate.

A factor that certainly contributed to the willingness of people to co-operate with the research was the low level of police activity during the summer and autumn of 1972, when the interviewing was carried out. Most of those interviewed had never been searched or prosecuted in connection with drug offences, and there was little fear that the research would lead to trouble with the police.

2. Drugs, Drugtakers and the Law in Britain

Charles Reeves (1972) defines a drug as: 'any chemical substance or agent that affects the physiological and/or psychological and/or social functions and is taken "for comfort, stimulation or pleasure".'

Reeves suggests that a drug user is: 'any individual who takes these substances or agents for the above purposes or in some cases in order to re-live or create a "mystical experience".'

These are the definitions of 'drug' and 'drug user' or 'drugtaker' (these terms are used synonymously) that will be used in this book.

The following section is intended to provide an introduction to the basic terms and concepts of drugtaking and the main types of drugs covered by this research.

Non-Medical Drugtaking

The Interim Report of the Canadian Commission of Inquiry into the Non-Medical Use of Drugs (The Le Dain Commission) defines non-medical drug use as: 'all drug use which is not indicated on generally accepted medical grounds'. The Report goes on to point out: 'Clearly, non-medical use is not to be equated with illegal use. The use of alcohol by adults is generally non-medical but it is legal, whereas the use of marijuana is both non-medical and illegal' (1971: 16, section 5).

The area covered by this book is that of non-medical drugtaking, with particular reference to illegal drug use. Although some attention is paid to the non-medical yet legal use of tobacco and alcohol, the main emphasis is on the use of substances such as cannabis (marihuana), which are illegal.

The Classification of Drugs

Attempts have been made to classify drugs in terms of their effects upon the user. Some drugs are able to alter the psychological state of the individual. They change the perceptions, mood, thought, and the observable behaviour of the user. Drugs of this type are sometimes called 'psychotropic'. Alcohol is an example.

In fact there is no generally accepted classification of psychotropic drugs. Drugs may be grouped in terms of their chemical structure, legality, effects, medical purposes, or availability. The Canadian Government Commision of Inquiry used an eight-fold classification (1971: 33–4):

i sedatives and hypnotics
ii stimulants
iii psychedelics and hallucinogens
iv opiate narcotics
v volatile solvents
vi non-narcotic analgesics
vii clinical anti-depressants
viii major tranquillizers

This classification distinguishes between the main types of drugs in terms of their psychological and pharmacological effects and properties. It includes all the main groups of drugs that are used by young people. Some of these drugs have long histories of legal use in different societies, others have been produced recently, and some are controlled by law.

The extensive literature on drugtaking makes use of four crucial terms: (a) *tolerance* is said to develop when repeated doses of a drug produce a diminishing result, so that the amount used has to be increased to reproduce the initial effect.

The commonplace term 'addiction' has now been replaced by two more precise concepts. Addiction refers to a state in which a person uses a drug habitually to reduce depression, and cannot lead a 'normal' or bearable life without the aid of that drug. This phenomenon involves two components, physical dependence and psychological dependence.

(b) *physical dependence* entails the onset of a characteristic physical illness, known as (c) *withdrawal symptoms*, or the abstinence syndrome, when administration of the drug is suspended. Physical dependence usually follows the development of tolerance and can be very severe, sometimes causing death.

A vaguer notion is that of (d) *psychological dependence*. This involves the continued use of a drug to maintain an acceptable level of emotional contentment or satisfaction. In a practical situation it is very difficult to identify psychological dependence, and it is often alleged to exist solely because a person chooses to use a drug continuously, whether or not physical dependence is caused by this administration. In some cases an individual may exhibit an extreme emotional need to use a drug, and often psychological factors may be more important than physical ones in accounting for continued drug use.

It must, at this early stage, be pointed out that many of the popular ideas about drugs and 'addiction' are derived from the extreme case of the individual who is physically and psychologically dependent upon opiate narcotics. The following brief introduction attempts to distinguish between the psychological, pharmacological, and behavioural effects of the main types of drug covered by the research.

Cannabis

Extent of use

In 1951 the United Nations estimated that cannabis was used by 200,000,000 people. Its use as a drug has been known since 2,737 B.C. Historically use has been centred upon the Middle East and South East Asia. More recently the drug has been adopted by groups of people in industrialized centres. At first it was used mainly by low-status ethnic minorities and deviants. It is now used by many young whites as a social drug. Many surveys such as those by Blum *et al.* (1969) in America, Weiner (1971), and Young and Brooke-Crutchley (1972) in Britain, have shown that use is extensive amongst school, college, and university students. The Wootton Report (1968) estimated that between 30,000 – 300,000 people in Britain had used cannabis. Estimates such as these are speculative, but this may be a considerable underestimate.

Usage and supply

There is a considerable black market in cannabis, which is illegally imported into Britain. The quality of the drug varies greatly, and there is much evidence of 'cutting' with herbs and other substances to make it go further. It is generally smoked, but is often ingested either by swallowing, or by mixing it with beverages or cooking it in 'wacky cakes'. There is an important ritual involved in cannabis use in western countries. The drug, when smoked in a cigarette (joint), pipe, or chillum,[1] is passed around the group. It is a shared experience, a collective act, and people seldom smoke their personal joints. Howard Becker, in his celebrated essay 'Becoming a Marihuana User' (1953) asserted that one learns to appreciate the effects of cannabis as a part of group behaviour, rather than because of the pharmacological properties of the drug.

Effects

Cannabis is the generic name for Indian hemp, Cannabis Sativa. It exudes a resin containing Tetrahydrocannabinol (T.H.C.), a hallucinogen. The two forms are the resin (hashish) and dried leaves (grass).

> 'Smoking cannabis has the following effects: a hallucinogen, its effects, depending naturally upon quality and quantity, last between an hour and six hours. The "high" feeling is basically an increased sensory awareness which simultaneously intensifies the aspects of the world around and by so doing, distances the smoker from his surroundings as he concentrates, bit by minute bit, on all the phenomena that become apparent through smoking. Inhibitions are lessened, though paradoxically a strong dose can induce paranoia – everyone is staring at you, no one really likes you, etc. – which will be over as soon as the peak of the dose has passed by. The appetite, especially for more exotic foods, will be increased. Physically there is a dryness in the mouth, a certain lethargy and an ability to do nothing, to the external viewer's eyes, for long periods.' (Green 1972:12)

The drug is more similar in effect to alcohol than to the opiates with which it is often (wrongly) linked by the mass media. The results

1. A chillum is a hollow receptacle, resembling a gourd, in which cannabis is sometimes smoked.

are noted as a mild euphoria. It acts as a relaxant and is far more likely to induce passive introspection than extraverted behaviour. It is typically a social drug and, like alcohol, may reduce inhibitions. Like alcohol, too, cannabis slows measured reactions, and has broadly similar effects upon those driving cars. It does not cause physical dependence, in fact a reverse – tolerance occurs, since experienced users learn to get 'high' (become intoxicated) more quickly than novices.

The Wootton Report concluded:

> 'Having reviewed all the material available to us we find ourselves in agreement with the conclusion reached by the Indian Hemp Drugs Commission appointed by the Government of India (1893–94) and the New York Mayor's Committee on Marijuana (1944), that the long-term consumption of cannabis in moderate doses has no harmful effects.'

There remains considerable controversy about whether or not the long-term effects of cannabis are harmful, but while this debate continues, the drug is being used by a growing number of young people.

Alternative names for Cannabis

Dope, shit, charge, hash, grass, marijuana, bush, tea, ganja, smoke.

L.S.D. (d-Lysergic Acid Diethylamide 25)

Extent of use

Virtually restricted to industrialized societies.

Usage and supply

Invented in 1938, its psychotropic effects were accidentally discovered by Hoffman in 1943. It is associated with cannabis smoking and with mysticism. Some people have hailed it as the way to attaining spiritual enlightenment (e.g. Leary *et al.* 1964) and it has been adopted as a means of producing transcendental experiences (e.g. Wolfe 1971). The drug is illegal, and is distributed illegally. Because of its great potency, it is easy to smuggle, and to produce, given the use of a laboratory.

Effects

L.S.D. is an ergot derivative. It is a very powerful drug, a hallucinogen which acts directly on the central nervous system and alters the perceptions, often dramatically. Only tiny quantities (such as 250 micrograms) are needed to produce the desired effects. The usual L.S.D. 'trip' or experience lasts about seven hours. The drug disorganizes normal psychological functioning, distorting space and time perceptions, and intensifying colours. Users frequently report that they are able to derive profound insights during L.S.D. trips, but the effects of the drug are unpredictable and may be unpleasant or psychotic.

> 'Some L.S.D. users, but by no means all, may have "true" psychedelic experiences, that is transcendental "peak" experiences which have been compared to mystical states, and to religious ecstacy. As with all true mystical states, these experiences cannot be clearly communicated to others by means of verbal description, but remain at an intensely private, introspective level.' (Le Dain 1971: para 403)

Because L.S.D. has such a powerful effect upon the perceptions, it can accentuate the user's original mood, intensifying depression or fear to an unbearable extent. Cases of acute horror have been known, but are largely attributed to the user's antecedent mental state. The unpredictability of L.S.D. has led many users to insist upon the company of a friend who can provide comfort, reassurance, and 'guide' them through a trip.

Alternative names for L.S.D.

Usually known as 'acid'.

Other Hallucinogens

Mescalin is derived from the Peyote cactus and is rather milder in its effects than L.S.D. It is also harder to obtain.

Psilocybin is derived from the mushroom Teonanactl. Also rare in Britain.

D.M.T. (dimethylamine) is a milder hallucinogen, which provides what has been called the 'business man's trip' due to its short-lasting effects.

S.T.P., supposedly standing for Serenity – Tranquillity – Peace, is a dangerously powerful hallucinogen. Originally produced as part of the United States' chemical warfare programme, its effects may last two or three days. The protracted psychological disorientation involved leads users to maintain that the chances of a 'bad trip' exceed those of a good one.

M.D.A. (methylenedioxyamphetamine) is another amphetamine-based drug. It is not common.

Cther hallucinogenic drugs are contained in Nutmeg, Morning Glory seed, and several naturally occurring sources, such as the poisonous Belladonna, and mushrooms such as Aminita Muscarina. Devotees of psychedelic drugs eagerly experiment with a wide range of substances in hopes of discovering new ways of attaining Nirvana.

Amphetamines

Extent of use

Between 50,000 and 100,000 people regularly take prescribed amphetamines (Young 1971:26). In addition many people use them on the black market. Towards the end of the 1960s the medical profession undertook a voluntary restriction of prescribing amphetamines in order to curtail the quantities available to be stolen and sold illegally.

Usage and supply

Available cheaply on the black market in pill or powder form. Sometimes liquid or crystalline methamphetamine is available.

Effects

Amphetamines are artificial amines, similar in chemistry to natural adrenaline. Amphetamine itself was produced in 1887 and methamphetamine in 1919. They have been widely used in medical treatment since the 1930s to combat minor depression and obesity. Amphetamines are stimulants and induce a surge of energy and confidence. The consensus of medical opinion now is that their clinical value is low and that tolerance and dependence are easily produced by their euphoric effects. Reports of craving for amphetamines appeared from the 1940s onwards and it became increasingly evident that they were being used by young people to stay awake at dances (Friedenberg and Camden 1940:956).

Amphetamine misuse reached its peak in Japan, where it was estimated that 500,000 people were using them non-medically in 1954. Professor Masakai, in a report to the World Health Organisation Expert Commitee on Drugs Liable to Produce Addiction (1956) noted that in the city of Kurume in Japan, 1.1 per cent of the whole population, and about 5 per cent of the 16–25 year group, were dependent on amphetamines (Scott and Willcox 1965:9–27).

Amphetamines are generally swallowed, but are also sometimes injected. This latter practice produces a syndrome of undernourishment, insomnia and often infection. Some chronic users report that withdrawal from amphetamines can be more unpleasant than that from opiates (See Connell in Wilson 1968). The dangers of this practice are vividly described by William Burroughs jnr in his autobiographical novel *Speed* (1971).

Alternative names for Amphetamines

Generally 'speed'. A variety of tablets such as Dexedrine are available.

Barbiturates

Extent of use

Six to seven per cent of all prescriptions under the National Health Service are for barbiturates. In 1970 there were 15,000,000 separate prescriptions for barbiturates. Young estimated that in 1971 the number of people in Britain who were dependent upon barbiturates was between 75,000 and 125,000, and the number of regular users without dependence was between 400,000 – 600,000. Young points out that: 'Although the commonest addicts are women in the 45–64 age group, the mass media limits its attention to the tiny minority of young people who have taken to injecting barbiturates intravenously' (Young 1971:25).

Usage and supply

Barbiturates are freely available from the National Health Service, and their possession is legal. Barbiturates are often used recreationally by young people in industrialized societies.

Effects

Introduced into medicine in 1903, allegedly synthesized on St. Barbara's Day in 1899, and derived from barbituric acid, they are sleep inducers, tranquillizers, and sedatives. Over 2,000 separate types of barbiturate have been synthesized. Barbiturates produce drowsiness or intoxication and can cause all the symptoms of physical and psychological dependence. An overdose can be fatal. Barbiturate overdose is a common means of committing suicide.

Alternative names for Barbiturates

'Downers', 'goof-balls', 'sleepers'.

Other Hypnotics — Mandrax

Mandrax is another depressant drug very similar to barbiturate in its effects. One problem is that people suffering from an overdose of Mandrax exhibit the same symptoms as those having overdosed with barbiturates. The antidote for one may be fatal if used to treat the other. Mandrax tablets, like barbiturates, are used recreationally by young people, often in conjunction with alcohol.

The Opiates

Extent of use

The first clear description of opium was written in the third century B.C. though there were earlier possible references. The widespread use of opium did not develop until the British East India Company began to trade in it during the eighteenth century. Opium smoking was adopted in China after the introduction there of American tobacco. China's attempts to exclude the drug led to the Opium War (1839–42), when British naval strength forced the Chinese to accept the dubious trade. This led to the legalization of opium in China and to its production by the Chinese Government. At the same time the medical use of opium as a pain reliever grew rapidly and in Britain laudanum, a tincture of opium, became a standard drug. Opium is used illegally, as are its derivatives, morphine and heroin. Morphine was produced in 1803 and heroin in 1874. In 1959, 454 individuals in Britain were known to be dependent upon heroin and allied drugs. These were 'therapeutic addicts', that is, were mainly middle-aged people who had become dependent during medical treatment. Fifteen per cent were in medical, or associated professions. During the 1950s a new phenomenon emerged, that of the young, self-addicted junkie. Using heroin rather than morphine, this new younger type of drug dependent sought to encourage others to copy his behaviour. The Home Office figures recording the numbers of known addicts rose to a peak of 2,881 in 1969. In 1972, 1,619 narcotic drug addicts were recorded.[2] (In absolute terms these figures are low compared with the estimated 40,000–60,000 heroin dependents in New York, or the 400,000 chronic alcoholics in Britain.)

Usage and supply

Some doctors, through over-prescription, enabled more people to begin using heroin. Since 1968 general practitioners have not been allowed to prescribe heroin to addicts, and the drug has only been available at hospitals designated as special treatment centres. The restriction of legal supplies of heroin has been followed by an increase in illegal supplies of 'Chinese heroin' available on the black market.

Effects

The opiates are all derived from the opium poppy and are the classic drugs of dependence. Opium is generally smoked, morphine and heroin are more often injected. Opiates depress the central nervous system, though larger amounts may stimulate. Tolerance develops, followed

2. Information supplied by Drugs Branch, Home Office, December 1973.

by withdrawal symptoms if usage is discontinued. The literature indicates that heroin *per se* is lethal. In fact the circumstances in which it is used are likely to cause sickness or death. Many heroin users certainly manage to lead 'normal' lives, as evidenced by the therapeutic addicts, who, if regularly supplied with their drugs, function normally.

Alternative names for Heroin

H, horse, smack.

Other Narcotics

Codeine like morphine, is an alkaloid in raw opium.

Methadone (Dolophone or Physeptone) is a synthetic substitute for heroin which has become a drug of dependence in its own right. Theoretically methadone is taken orally and blocks the effects of heroin. It is widely used to 'maintain' people who were formerly dependent upon heroin. Other heroin substitutes are Diconal or Omnopon. These are all sometimes available on the black market.

Cocaine

Extent of use

Originally used by South American Indians as a stimulant, it is currently in vogue with rock musicians. Its use in western countries is associated with the opiates. It is expensive, currently at £350 per ounce.

Use and supply

Used in medicine, it is available on the black market.

Effects

Cocaine comes from the coca leaf which grows in the Andean foothills and in South East Asia, Africa, and the West Indies. A stimulant, prolonged use does not appear to create tolerance, yet withdrawal from excessive use may cause paranoia, depression, and even heart damage. Often sniffed, it is sometimes injected. When mixed with heroin in a 'speedball' it increases the euphoric effect of the opiate.

Other Drugs

A wide range of non-barbiturate tranquillizers are in medical use. Substances such as Librium and Valium are used to treat anxiety states. Some writers distinguish between 'minor' and 'major' tranquillizers. The so-called 'major' tranquillizers include chlorpromazine and reserpine and are used to control severe mental illness such as schizophrenia. Most tranquillizers are used both medically and non-medically to replace barbiturates. They resemble both alcohol and barbiturates in their effects. Tolerance may develop due to continued use of tranquillizers, though most of those dependent upon them are certainly middle-aged and receive them on prescription.

All manner of other psychoactive substances have been used non-medically. Solvents, glues, cough linctuses, inhalers, herbs, etc. Most of these ploys are unsatisfactory, some are very dangerous.

Drugs and The Law in Britain

For the purposes of the present study, we are only concerned with twentieth century measures to control forms of drugtaking officially viewed as harmful and problematic.

In 1916 the Commissioner of Police for the Metropolis of London reported the trafficking of cocaine, mainly by prostitutes and servicemen. Measures to counter this were introduced under the *Defence of the Realm Act* (1916). These were strengthened in 1917, and again in the *Dangerous Drugs Act* (1920) which widened control regulations to cover all drugs dealt with by the First International Opium Convention, 1912.

> 'Nevertheless, abuse of cocaine continued to be a problem in London for some years, as is shown by the fact that in 1921, the first year of operation of the Dangerous Drugs Act (1920), out of 67 prosecutions in respect of drugs other than opium, 58 related to cocaine, and in 1922 and 1923 the corresponding figures were 70 out of a total of 110 and 68 out of a total of 128 prosecutions.' (see Jeffery in Phillipson 1970:60)

Between the wars drug abuse apparently declined. The only steady trafficking involved opium.

In 1924 the Rolleston Committee was set up to examine the British approach to drugtaking. This body reported in 1926 and established the foundations of the so-called 'British System'. The Rolleston Committee interpreted the existing drugs legislation to mean that those dependent on drugs were sick and should be given controlled regular supplies of their drug if this meant that a relatively 'normal' life could be led. Doctors who abused this system were liable to have their freedom to prescribe curtailed. During the first twenty years or so of its operation, this system had to cope with a few hundred 'therapeutic' patients, mainly middle-aged people, who had come into contact with drugs through medical treatment or through their work. Between 1935 and 1955 the number of addicts known to the Home Office declined from 700 to less than 400.

After the Second World War, returning troops and immigrants introduced cannabis smoking to Britain. At the same time there was an increase in non-therapeutic heroin dependence. Initially confined to people who had become dependent through accident, drug dependence followed the American pattern. Doctors were confronted by proselytizing drug dependents, people who tried to recruit others to their habit.

In 1958 the Brain Committee was established to review the situation. They reported in 1961, just before a new set of Home Office figures were released showing a dramatic increase in heroin dependence. The Brain Report recommended no changes in the existing system. During the same year Britain ratified the Single Convention, an international treaty which covered a wide range of 'narcotics' and included cannabis in the list of proscribed drugs. Cannabis use was increasing fast during the early 1960s. It was at first used by jazz musicians, painters, and 'beatniks' but spread amongst other groups as well.

In 1964 the *Dangerous Drugs (Prevention of Misuse) Act* was passed to strengthen the hand of the Police. This Act covered amphetamines but was amended in 1966 to cover L.S.D., mescalin, and D.M.T. in addition. During 1965 the reconvened Brain Committee produced a second report. This concluded that since they had first reviewed the situation, drug misuse had increased alarmingly. In the same year the *Dangerous Drugs Act* (1965) became law. This extended the *Dangerous Drugs (No. 2) Regulations* (1964) and implemented the recommendations of the Single Convention. This legislation covered raw opium, coca leaves, poppy straw, and cannabis, as well as the derivatives of these raw substances. The police were given controversial powers to search premises if they had sworn evidence that an offence was being committed.

Some doctors abused their powers to prescribe, and many drug dependents passed on their surplus supplies of drugs to friends, who in turn became dependent too. Considerable publicity was given to the 'junkie doctors' who illegally 'sold' drugs to drug dependents. The Interdepartmental Committee on Drug Addiction recommended in 1965 that the supply of heroin be drastically restricted, and this proposal was implemented in 1967 by the *Dangerous Drugs Act.* This limited the number of doctors who could prescribe heroin to a few at special hospital clinics. General practitioners were no longer allowed to prescribe. Jock Young comments:

> 'The treatment centres instituted in 1968 a much more cautious and restrictive programme to heroin dispensing. To this extent they have eliminated the problems associated with over prescription; that is the development of a proselytizing grey market of surplus heroin. But when illicit supplies are available, and this at the moment is infrequent, a black market quickly springs up to replace it. Moreover the displacement of drug use to other more readily available drugs occurs repeatedly.' (Young 1971:208)

Under Section 6 of the *Dangerous Drugs Act*, 1967, the police were given power to stop and search without warrant any person 'reasonably suspected' of being in unlawful possession of drugs. This measure, though controversial, made the enforcement of the drug control laws much easier to implement.

The Wootton Report, published in 1968, recommended reducing the penalties for possession and sale of cannabis. Its recommendations were not fully implemented, though the penalties for possession of cannabis were reduced. This was done by the *Misuse of Drugs Act* (1971) which forms the basis of the drug control laws at the time of writing.

The Act divides proscribed drugs into three categories, A, B, and C.

A: Heroin, cocaine, morphine, methadone, L.S.D., mescalin, opium, psilocybin, T.H.C., and all derivatives of any of these.

B: Amphetamines (Methedrine, Benzedrine, Drinamyl, Dexedrine) Codeine, cannabis.

C: Amphetamines (Bezphetamine, Fencamfamin, Mepheteramine, and six others all of which are considered less dangerous or potent), Mandrax.

The 1971 Act does not cover barbiturates although these produce all the symptoms of dependence associated with the opiate narcotics.

The *Misuse of drugs Act* differentiates between different types of drug, and does separate cannabis from the opiates such as heroin and morphine. The maximum penalties for possession of a class B drug, such as cannabis are twelve months in prison, or a £400 fine, or both, for a summary conviction, and five years imprisonment, or a fine, or both, on indictment. Anybody convicted of supplying other people with cannabis could face a fourteen year prison sentence and a fine, on indictment. This carries the same potential sentences as armed robbery or murder.

Cannabis possession and trafficking are still treated as serious criminal offences in spite of the evidence by the Wootton Report that moderate use of cannabis appears to have no harmful effects. Even so, even the possession of less potent class C drugs carries a possible two year prison sentence, plus a fine, on indictment.

The great increase in the number of drug convictions is as much a result of the level of police vigilance as the spread of drugtaking. Many towns have formed specialized drug squads, and the police have wide powers to search without warrant people suspected of possessing illegal drugs.

In my own experience in the Cheltenham area, local prosecutions of drug offenders were widely publicized. Public opinion has been influenced by such publicity, and by the nature of those convicted, who are generally unemployed, or manual workers. It is clear that drugtaking is regarded, along with sexual perversions, as something 'respectable' people loathe, yet long to read about. The law reflects and fosters this view.

Table 2

Misuse of Drugs Act, 1971

	Schedule 4 Prosecution and Punishment of Offences				*Section 25*	
				Punishment		
Section creating offence	*General nature of offence*	*Mode of prosecution*	*Class A drug involved*	*Class B drug involved*	*Class C drug involved*	*General*
Section 4(2)	Production, or being concerned in the production of a controlled drug	(a) Summary . . . On (b) Indictment	12 months, or £400 or both. 14 years or a fine, or both	12 months, or £400 or both. 14 years or a fine, or both	6 months, or £200 or both. 5 years or a fine, or both	
Section 4(3)	Supplying or offering to supply a controlled drug or being concerned in the doing of either activity by another	(a) Summary . . . On (b) Indictment	12 months, or £400 or both. 14 years or a fine, or both	12 months, or £400 or both. 14 years or a fine, or both	6 months, or £200 or both. 5 years or a fine, or both	
Section 5(2)	Having possession of a controlled drug	(a) Summary . . . On (b) Indictment	12 months or £400 or both. 7 years or a fine, or both.	6 months or £400 or both. 5 years or a fine, or both	6 months or £200 or both. 2 years or a fine, or both	
Section 5(3)	Having possession of a controlled drug with intent to supply it to another	(a) Summary . . . On (b) Indictment	12 months or £400 or both. 14 years or a fine, or both	12 months or £400 or both. 14 years or a fine, or both	6 months or £200 or both. 5 years or a fine, or both	

Section 6(2)	Cultivation of cannabis plant	(a) Summary . . . On (b) Indictment	–	–	–	12 months or £400 or both. 14 years or a fine, or both
Section 8	Being the occupier, or concerned in the management of premises and permitting or suffering certain activities to take place there	(a) Summary . . . On (b) Indictment	12 months or £400 or both. 14 years or a fine, or both	12 months or £400 or both. 14 years or a fine, or both	6 months or £200 or both. 5 years or a fine, or both	
Section 9	Offences relating to opium	(a) Summary On (b) Indictment	–	–	–	12 months or £400 or both. 14 years or a fine, or both
Section 11(2)	Contravention of directions relating to safe custody of controlled drugs	(a) Summary On (b) Indictment	–	–	–	6 months or £400 or both. 2 years or a fine, or both
Section 12(6)	Contravention of direction prohibiting practitioner etc. from possessing, supplying etc. controlled drugs	(a) Summary On (b) Indictment	12 months or £400 or both. 14 years or a fine, or both	12 months or £400 or both. 14 years or a fine, or both	6 months or £200 or both. 5 years or a fine, or both	
Section 13(3)	Contravention of direction prohibiting practitioner etc. from prescribing, supplying etc. controlled drugs	(a) Summary On (b) Indictment	12 months or £400 or both. 14 years or a fine, or both	12 months or £400 or both. 14 years or a fine, or both	6 months or £200 or both. 5 years or a fine, or both	

Table 2

Misuse of Drugs Act, 1971

Schedule 4 Prosecution and Punishment of Offences — *Section 25*

Section creating offence	*General nature of offence*	*Mode of prosecution*	*Punishment* *Class A drug involved*	*Class B drug involved*	*Class C drug involved*	*General*
Section 17(3)	Failure to comply with notice requiring information relating to prescribing, supply etc. of drugs	Summary	–	–	–	£100
Section 17(4)	Giving false information in purported compliance with notice requiring information relating to prescribing, supply etc. of drugs	(a) Summary On (b) Indictment	–	–	–	6 months or £400 or both. 2 years or a fine, or both

Table 3

*Offences involving drugs covered by the Dangerous Drugs Act (1965)**

	Cannabis	*Opium*	*manufactured drugs*	*Drugs (Prevention of Misuse Act, 1964)*
1945	4	206	20	
1946	11	65	27	
1947	46	76	65	
1948	51	78	48	
1949	61	52	56	
1950	86	41	42	
1951	132	64	47	
1952	98	62	48	
1953	88	47	44	
1954	144	28	47	
1955	115	17	37	
1956	103	12	37	
1957	51	9	30	
1958	99	8	41	
1959	185	18	26	
1960	235	15	28	
1961	288	15	61	
1962	588	16	71	
1963	663	20	63	
1964	544	14	101	
1965	626	13	128	958†
1966	1,119	36	242	1,216
1967	2,393	58	573	2,486
1968	3,071	73	1,099	2,957
1969	4,683	53	1,359	3,762
1970	7,520	66	1,214	3,885
1971	9,219	55	1,570	5,516
1972	12,611	98	2,068	4,134

(From 1945–53 inclusive, the figures relate to prosecutions. From 1954 onwards the figures relate to convictions.)

*Information supplied by the Home Office Research unit, December 1973.

†This figure is in respect of the period 31 October, 1964 to 31 December, 1965.

3. Existing Research on Drugtaking

Information about drugtaking has been largely gathered in the following ways:

1) studies of individuals receiving medical or psychiatric treatment, or convicted of offences, because of their drugtaking;
2) surveys of the extent of drug use amongst groups such as schoolchildren and students;
3) a number of observation studies of drugtakers in their social environments have been undertaken and some information about case histories has been provided by social workers, probation officers, and others in contact with drug using groups.

In addition autobiographical accounts, such as those by Trocchi (1966) and Burroughs (1966) have provided rich first-hand data.

Clinical studies have been mainly concerned with individuals dependent upon opiate narcotics and in attendance at treatment centres.

> 'The conventional view of addiction is that it is an escape mechanism for defective persons, variously characterized as "inadequate", "inferior", "frustrated" or "psychopathic". It is assumed that persons become addicts for the "purpose" or "motive" of escaping from or alleviating their psychic troubles.' (Lindesmith 1968:17)

Psychological theories of addiction abound. Laskowitz describes the frequency in drugtaking New York adolescents of a combination of an absent or ineffective father figure and a pampering, over-compensating mother (in Harms 1965:67). However, the case histories of addicts suggest that any type of background may produce addiction. There is no specific formula.

A large number of addicts are either psychopathic or otherwise psychologically abnormal, yet as Lindesmith points out (1968:17), a high proportion of addicted persons appeared to be 'normal' until they become addicted, and some others became addicted accidentally as the result of medical treatment, and not by choice.

A stereotype of the opiate dependent, the junkie, has been developed. This is a typical description of the 'junkie syndrome': 'Usually people who become addicted are either hedonistic (pleasure seeking individuals), psychopaths or are psychoneurotics' (O'Callaghan 1970:18).

This view, that addicts are likely to have a specific type of personality, is supported by many medical studies, but does not answer the question of what the individuals concerned were like before they became addicted. It is possible that they became psychotic or psychoneurotic as the result of opiate use.

Some studies have suggested that 'normal' people find opiates nauseating, and that only aberrant personality types are attracted to them, or that certain psychoneurotic types are especially susceptible to narcotics.

> 'Thus a sensitive man, with certain neurotic ailments, may be tremendously impressed with the soothing qualities of the drug, and by contrast with his usual state of mind, may feel intense pleasure. On the other hand, a prosaic and stolid person, with no sense of strain or conflict, may be wholly unaffected.' (Lindesmith 1968:27)

Information about opiate dependents who receive hospital treatment is only applicable to such individuals. There is no evidence to support the view that they are representative of other drugtakers, and it is probable that they may, in some ways, differ from people who use drugs but do not seek medical help.

Similarly, Home Office figures showing the numbers of persons convicted of drug offences are not a reliable guide to the number or type of drug users in the community. Some areas have specialized drug squads while others do not, and the number of convictions in any given year may be an indication of police activity rather than the scale of drugtaking. It is also probable that individuals who are searched for possessing drugs are amongst the most conspicuous drugtakers, and not necessarily a representative cross-section of those in the community.

Several studies of drugtaking amongst young offenders have been carried out. These provide some useful background information about specific groups of young people.

Noble's study of delinquent boys showed that 19.1 per cent of those using non-narcotic drugs progressed to the use of narcotics during the three years of the research (Noble 1970:102–5). A follow-up study of girls in a London remand home by Noble and Barnes (1971:620–23) revealed that progression to narcotics was associated with peer group behaviour:

> 'The time each girl spent in the company of other drug users frequenting places where drugs were available, and in obtaining and taking drugs, was used to rate her involvement in a drug milieu on a three-point scale. There was a pronounced trend for the progressor and narcotic groups to be more involved in a drug milieu.'

This study found that amongst the delinquents examined, those who had used drugs were more likely than others to come from disturbed home backgrounds, with a high incidence of parental unemployment. Those who progressed to narcotics were especially likely to come from larger families, exhibited more psychiatric disorders, such as aggressiveness and anxiety states, and a high incidence of suicide attempts. A high proportion were sexually experienced and a majority had unstable work records.

These studies raise several points which are examined in this research. The main consideration is to what extent 'known' or institutionalized drugtakers differ from those who never come into contact with the law or with medical treatment. In the current study I examine peer group behaviour, family background, progression to other drugs, as well as sexual behaviour and attempted suicide.

Gordon, in a study of males attending a drug treatment centre (1971), found that 48.0 per cent of those studied had convictions before their drugtaking began, and 90.0 per cent before their attendance at the clinic. As Noble and Barnes point out, studies such as this, which link drugtaking and delinquency, do not impute a causal relationship between the two phenomena.

R. Cockett in two studies of drugtaking amongst young offenders

(1971), examined patterns of drug use, psychological factors, and social backgrounds. He concluded that there was no necessary 'escalation' to opiates and that some people voluntarily discontinued drug use altogether. Cockett's research was confined to delinquents but did indicate that length of delinquency and length of drug use were linked. This suggested that there was a tendency for the early onset of one to be associated with early onset of the other. There was no evidence that drugtaking was linked with the break-up of the parental relationship. Drug users were generally better educated and more intelligent, than non-users. These findings challenge the popularly held view that drugtaking is associated with family disruption and lack of education. Since the drugtakers concerned were all delinquents, they were scarcely a 'representative' group.

The studies of in-patients at hospitals or offenders in prisons, have been concerned with very limited groups of people. Almost certainly these are atypical of the drugtaking population in general, and it is not justifiable to assume that all drugtakers resemble those referred to in clinical studies. My review of research is a partial one. There have been a great number of medically-oriented or psychiatric studies of in-patients which investigate rather different issues to those covered by the present study. Much of this research has been epidemiological, concerned with medical biographical data rather than with social variables. Examples of such work are the studies of Easton (1965), Gilbert and Lombardi (1967), Hekimian and Gershon (1968), Ritson *et al.* (1973), and Woodside (1973).

One of the most thoroughgoing British studies of drug dependents receiving prescribed heroin was carried out by G. V. Stimson. This study involved interviewing 111 addicts in attendance at thirteen clinics. Dr. Stimson's investigation examined six key topics (1973:37)

1) extent of criminal activity
2) involvement and contact with other addicts
3) employment patterns
4) means of support and type of income
5) care taken with preparation and administration of injections
6) social and other activities engaged in.

Stimson identified four distinctly different groups of addicts: stables, junkies, loners, and two-worlders. He suggested that the addict population did not appear to be homogeneous, and that not all addicts necessarily suffer social or physical complications because of their drugtaking.

It is important to note that there are several distinctly different approaches to drugtaking. The 'medical' model treats drugtaking as a form of individual sickness. This model has been related to individuals receiving treatment for physical drug dependence, which is a pharmacological or biological condition. Psychological theories have also been put forward (McClelland *et al.* 1972). Both medical and psychological theories have been concerned with individual, rather than collective, characteristics.

Dr Richard De Alarcon suggested that a 'prone personality' type exists: 'Some people are apparently born with a penchant for getting into trouble, and that trouble is very likely to include taking drugs' (De Alarcon 1973). In the same statement Dr De Alarcon asserted that his research showed that personality factors were more important than the availability of drugs.

Psychiatric research has asked different questions from those posed in sociological studies. Their subject matter has been different (in-patients rather than drugtakers in general) and so there has been a divergence between the conclusions of medical and social research. In the present study I examine both education, delinquency, and family background in order to discover to what extent the drugtakers I located resembled those in clinical studies of what I assume to be atypical, 'captive' populations.

Surveys

Surveys have generally been used to establish the incidence of drugtaking. This approach is limited, since many drugtakers may refuse to co-operate, or may not be located during field-work. Most surveys have been confined to limited groups, such as young people at educational institutions.

The classic large-scale survey was carried out by Chein and his associates on New York heroin users between 1949 and 1958 (Chein *et al.* 1964). Chein's study investigated the social factors associated with high rates of drug dependence. This involved sampling school populations in three boroughs and comparing samples of delinquent addicts with non-delinquents. In addition, an analysis of drugtaking amongst street gangs was made. The main defect of such cross-sectional approaches is that in comparing drug dependents with non-dependents, it is not clear whether the differences are due to drug dependence, or were present before the onset of drugtaking behaviour and may have caused it.

Binnie and Murdock (1969), in a survey of drug use amongst students in higher education at Leicester, found that 9.4 per cent of their sample had used drugs. They described the 'ideal typical user' as 'a middle-class male from London or another large town, in his first or second year at university, atheist or agnostic with a tendency to hold left-wing political opinions and regarding himself as an average student academically.'

In the Leicester study the majority of students, both drugtakers and non-drugtakers, asserted that they believed the opiates to be a danger to health and favoured strengthening legal controls on such drugs. Walsh's investigation (1969) of student cannabis use found that students who had used the drug were more likely than others to have criminal convictions. As I have already pointed out, this does not impute a causal relationship between drugtaking and delinquency. Both may be responses to other factors.

Other surveys of limited British populations were carried out by Weiner, Hindmarch, and by Young and Brooke-Crutchley. Wiener's study (1970·37) revealed that 6.0 per cent of a sample British school pupils reported having used drugs. Hindmarch (1972) found that about 10.0 per cent of a sample of British schoolchildren had used drugs, and Whitehead (1970) established similar figures for schoolchildren in Halifax, Nova Scotia. A number of Canadian studies are reported in the Le Dain Report. These showed that in some samples of high school pupils, over a fifth reported having used drugs, and in certain universities, a third of the students had at some time used drugs. Information about American student surveys is given by Blum and associates.

Young and Brooke-Crutchley carried out a survey of drugtaking amongst students at a London polytechnic. This involved the completion of questionnaires by 1,000 students, of whom 10.0 per cent were also interviewed. Questionnaires were submitted at the first term of the academic year as well as the fifth term, during 1968, 1969, and 1970, so that it was possible to distinguish initial characteristics from the effects of college life. The study included engineering, business studies, and social science students, and found that the latter were especially likely to have used drugs (54.0 per cent of males and 48.0 per cent of the females). The differences between male and female rates of drug use were even closer amongst regular cannabis users.

> 'Typical (cannabis) smokers are more likely to enter stable sexual relationships, more likely to set themselves up in a flat independent of parents and play a part in the social life of the college. It is the social isolate who lives with parents (or surrogate parents in digs), has few friends at college and approaches his studies with a "nine to five" attitude who is most likely to be immune from marijuana use. Nor does smoking relate very closely to "intergenerational conflict", at least, on the family level. For the smoker is only a little more unlikely to have an unsatisfactory relationship with his parents than the non-smoker. We found no indication of a relationship between family breakdown and marijuana smoking.'

Young and Brooke-Crutchley found that drugtaking students were more likely than others to have parents with high educational qualifications. They suggest that the phenomenon of 'bohemianism' stems from better educated groups. They found that middle-class youth had adopted an alternative romantic value system: 'Our findings suggest that there is a link between student bohemianism and a class background of a non-commercial middle-class nature. Our hypothesis is that this class has always been critical of the pecuniary values and instrumentality of the managerial bourgeois class.'

Young and Brooke-Crutchley suggest that 'bohemian' or 'hippy' solutions arise to achieve ends which are frustrated. They maintain that emotional or social dissatisfaction is a factor behind cannabis use. Students who were active Anglicans had no such dissatisfaction and were less likely to be critical of their college courses. Again, drugtaking students were more likely than others to favour militant political action. This survey produced no evidence to support the view that cannabis users 'escalated' their drugtaking to become heroin users. All of the student cannabis users interviewed were hostile to heroin use· '. . . the junkie, it was alleged, was 'hung up'. He neither engaged in expressive pursuits nor particularly enjoyed himself.'

Young and Brooke-Crutchley concluded that escalation to deleterious drugs was unlikely in a college situation, but possible in areas such as Notting Hill. They comment· 'The solution lies in providing adequate and meaningful opportunities for such individuals – neither stricter legislation nor psychiatric attention in isolation can offer any palliative to this predicament.'

The surveys to which I have alluded have been confined to limited geographical areas, or to specific, limited populations. There are no grounds at present for assessing the numbers of drugtakers on a country-wide basis. Surveys have shown that drugtaking is widespread amongst groups of middle-class young people, such as students, who do not correspond to the stereotype of the 'junkie' and who do not necessarily use injected drugs. Surveys have shown that there may be differences between drugtakers and others, and several of these factors, for example sex, ideology, and class background are investigated in the present study.

Non-Random Studies

The third main method of obtaining information about drugtaking is non-random 'sampling'. In fact, it is not possible to obtain a representative sample of drugtakers since their total numbers are unknown. Several researchers have gathered information from drugtakers wherever they can be found. Such studies do not purport to be representative and are essentially descriptive.

The classic sociological study in this field is that of Alfred Lindesmith. Lindesmith, examining the possibilities of producing a general theory of addiction, collected information by field-work involving close personal contacts with opiate users. This entailed making close contacts with drugtakers which enabled the researcher to collect a wealth of detailed information which would not have been possible through a single-contact survey conducted with a 'random' sample.

The Social Psychology Department of the London School of Economics carried out a pilot study during which forty-three drugtakers were located by personal contacts and interviewed (Benisiglio *et al.* 1967). The sample was probably an over-representation of the middle-class, but was designed to examine the differences between drugtakers, as there was no control group.

One of the few small-scale studies of heroin users that was neither simply a survey nor in a clinical setting, was carried out by the Addiction Research Unit (Kosviner *et al.* 1968). This study involved interviewing all the known heroin users in a provincial town. The main limitation of this study is that the drugtakers in one locality need not be representative of those elsewhere.

Another study which examined a group of admitted drugtakers was carried out by Ian Hindmarch. This involved participant observers who contacted drugtakers wherever they could be found. The interview consisted of thirty verbal questions and a semantic differential scale. A control group of non-drugtaking students was selected, matched by age, sex, and course of study. This survey indicated that 90.0 per cent of the drugtakers were using cannabis without evident detriment to their careers or social lives, and that 'hard' drugtakers showed poor examination performance. By the personalities of its members, the latter group were more disposed to addiction than either 'soft' drugtakers or non-drugtakers.

Hindmarch suggests that the distinction between 'hard' and 'soft' drugs was evident at a social/psychological, as well as a pharmacological, level. Casual cannabis users seemed none-the-worse in their examination performances than non-drugtakers. The evidence suggested that, especially amongst males, the origins of drugtaking appeared to be in the interim period between school and university (Hindmarch 1970).

Drug users came from larger families than non-users, although there was no correlation between socio-economic status and drug use. In general, as Young and Brook-Crutchley found subsequently, most drugtaking students were negative in their attitudes to heroin. Hindmarch suggests that future research could usefully examine the personality variables of individual drugtakers, in the hope that a 'prone personality' theory of drugtaking might emerge.

Erich Goode (1970) used a snowballing technique to contact 204 cannabis users in New York. He collected information about the social characteristics and lifestyles of cannabis users. He concluded that, in general, they were urban, middle-class, sociable, and tended to be radical and without a religion. He found an association between cannabis use and sexual permissiveness, but stated: 'Some deviants differ from each other as much as they differ from conventional society' (1970:88).

Goode's study, like the present one, was not of a representative group of drugtakers. It is of value because it produced a good deal of rich, impressionistic material derived from personal encounters with drugtakers.

The anthropological approach to drugtaking has been greatly developed by Charles Reeves. Reeves, a sociologist with considerable experience of the North American drug scene, spent a great deal of time during the period 1969–72 making contact with drugtakers in Southern Hampshire. Using the technique of snowballing described by Ned Polsky in his book *Hustlers, Beats and Others,* he approached drug using groups and was introduced to a number of drugtakers by a drug dealer, a key figure who could vouch for his goodwill and establish his identity. In this way he was passed around the drugtaking community by drugtakers who accepted him and could vouch for him. The success of such a method depends entirely upon the rapport the individual researcher manages to establish with his initial contacts. It is not a method every researcher would choose, or be able to implement.

Reeves kept a diary noting the lifestyles and behaviour of the drugtakers with whom he associated. He was able to gain some remarkable insights into the different groups he observed. In addition, he interviewed a group of 122 individuals. His interview schedule was divided into two sections, (a) general sociological data, and (b) drug behaviour data. The variables examined were (1) family background, (2) geographical mobility, (3) history of individual drug use, (4) socio-economic status, (5) academic attainment, (6) employment history, (7) aspirations, and (8) sexual behaviour.

Over a period of eighteen months, 106 of the original 122 respondents were re-interviewed in order to trace any changes in their drugtaking behaviour over time. No control group was used and the aim of the study was to examine differences between individual drugtakers (Reeves 1973)

Implications

This selective review of research into drugtaking suggested a number of possibilities which are investigated in this study.

Research on drugtakers in prisons or hospitals has produced a great deal of useful information about such individuals. There is no way of knowing how these differ from, or resemble, drugtakers in the community, or what proportion of the overall drugtaking population these represent. It is possible that there may be important differences between drugtakers who present themselves for medical treatment, or are convicted of criminal offences, and those who never come into contact with medical or penal institutions. In addition, studies of in-patients receiving medical treatment necessarily examine their subjects in conditions that are artificially divorced from their usual surroundings. Such studies produce invaluable biographical data, but do not indicate the importance of drugtaking to the lifestyle or behaviour of individuals within the community.

Most research into drugtaking has been carried out on a small scale, and surveys have generally been confined to very limited populations, such as students or school pupils. The 'hit and run' survey, involving only brief contact between researcher and subject, does not permit a detailed scrutiny of lifestyles, and may fail to establish sufficient rapport to investigate illegal, or private, behaviour. In addition, such surveys do not permit the researcher to check the information provided. Most surveys have been primarily concerned with establishing the prevalence of drugtaking within the groups investigated. There has been little attempt to assess the long-term consequences or the subjective meaning of drugtaking to those indulging in it. Surveys of relatively homogeneous groups, such as studies of people in hospitals or prisons, do not permit a comparison of possible differences between groups of individuals in different social positions. It is not justified to assume that any narrow group is typical of drugtakers in general. The only existing detailed British observation study of drugtakers within the community is that of Charles Reeves in Southern Hampshire. This work, though limited to one geographical location, did include a wide range of individuals in differing social positions, and personal communication with Reeves indicates that important differences between drugtakers were evident.

My review of the literature indicates that one of the main desiderata is an investigation of drugtakers in different social positions within their everyday social settings. In the present study, two important considerations were acknowledged, (i) the need to locate as heterogeneous a group of subjects as possible, in relation to occupation and lifestyle, and (ii) the importance of gaining insights into the qualitative aspects of drug use, such as values and self-images. These objectives necessitated the adoption of participant observation relying upon my ability to form close contacts with a wide range of drugtakers in the community.

Virtually all of the social characteristics examined in this research have been investigated before in relation to drugtaking. Many studies have sought to link drugtaking with a wide range of sociological variables. I suggest that the primary contribution of the present study is the use of *participant observation* as the main method of data collection. This approach has rarely been used in this field. The notable exponents to date are Becker, Lindesmith, Polsky, and Reeves. The classic participant observation studies such as Whyte's *Street Corner Society*, have enabled the collection of fascinating, valid data which would otherwise be unobtainable. The problems and virtues of field research are thoroughly discussed by Polsky, to whose writing I have already referred: '. . . if we are to make a major advance in our scientific understanding of criminal lifestyles, criminal sub-cultures, and their relation to the larger society, we must undertake genuine field research on these people.' (Polsky 1969·115).

My review of the research into drugtaking is confined to that of a broadly sociological nature. 'Drugtaking' is the subject matter of many disciplines, and it is naïve to suppose that any one has all of the answers. There is a danger that research in a single discipline may ignore or discount the contributions to be made in other fields. Many partial theories have been advanced which do not consider the importance of other disciplines. Drugtaking involves so many variations of behaviour, personality, and social background, that the idea of a key factor seems unlikely. Many of the existing theoretical approaches have much to commend them. Sociology has a unique perspective and can usefully examine drugtaking with its own specialized tools of investigation. It must be emphasized that the sociological approach need not be definitive, and that if any key explanatory factor does exist, it may be a psychological, or even genetic predisposition, as yet undiscovered.

4. The Drugtakers

This was not a random sample. The snowballing procedure I adopted to locate respondents was not designed to produce a representative cross-section of drugtakers within the community and my selection was certainly biased. The following analysis is a description of some of the characteristics of the 200 people interviewed, hereafter referred to as the 'study group'.

All of those interviewed had used cannabis at least six times during the period 1 August, 1970 – 21 October, 1972. In the majority of cases respondents were, or had been, frequent cannabis users, though it was seldom possible to record the precise number of times an individual had used the drug.

For the purposes of this analysis, the following main categories of drugtakers are distinguished:

1) Users and multi-users

Users are individuals who had used cannabis, and not more than one other type of drug, for example, L.S.D., regardless of the number of times they had used these.

Multi-users are individuals who had used at least three different types of drug, for example, cannabis, L.S.D., and amphetamines, regardless of the number of times they had used these.

It was assumed that, in general, a person's commitment to drugtaking and the associated lifestyles and outlooks was related to the extent and intensity of drug use. It was not possible to distinguish between 'light' and 'heavy' drug use, since this would have involved an arbitrary line of demarcation. Such a distinction would have required far closer observation of each respondent than was generally possible. A distinction was accordingly made between individuals who had used only one or two types of drug, and those who had used three or more. While this does not accurately indicate the regularity of a person's drug use, it does indicate the extent of experimentation.

2) Students and non-students

Students are individuals who were in full-time attendance at an institution of higher or further education, such as a college of education, college of art, college of technology, polytechnic, or university.

Non-Students are all other respondents, including school pupils.

My field encounters indicated that in many ways students were a distinctive group of young people and should be treated separately.

3) Males and females

Similarly it is thought useful to distinguish between respondents in terms of their sex, since this attribute is associated with many aspects of life experience.

Table 4
The study group

	students		*non-students*		
	users	*multi-users*	*users*	*multi-users*	*total*
males	23	31	16	83	153
females	8	11	11	17	47
total	31	42	27	100	200

No claim is made that I gave 'fair' representation to the different categories of drugtaker. The purpose of this analysis is to examine a group of individuals, not to make generalizations about all drugtakers. This study is concerned with individuals who were members of a network of drugtakers. No solitary drugtakers were located, and if such exist, they are outside the scope of this study.

Age

The ages of those interviewed ranged from fifteen to forty. I encountered a few younger people who had used drugs, but their experience had been too limited to warrant their inclusion in the study group. This finding is consistent with Erich Goode's conclusion that cannabis users are more likely to be young than old. Most surveys of drugtaking have been confined to school and student populations, or juvenile offenders, and the age distribution of the study group is consistent with the general impression derived from the literature, that illegal drug use is primarily a youthful phenomenon. The age distribution of the study group is strikingly similar to that of the drugtakers located in Goode's New York study, which in turn is similar to that of a postal survey conducted by the East Village Other, a New York 'underground' paper. In the April 1967 edition of the East Village Other, there was a fill-out, mail-in questionnaire on its readers' drug use. This type of survey is noted for bias and distortion, but the resemblance between the age patterns of the American sample and that of the present study is remarkable:

Table 5
Age range in Goode and Cheltenham studies (per cent)

age	*Goode†* *N 204*	*Cheltenham* *N 200*
17 or under	5.0	9.0
18 or 19	16.0	14.5
20 or 21	25.0	31.0
22, 23, 24, 25	30.0	34.0
26, 27, 28, 29	18.0	7.0
30 or over	7.0	4.5
total	101.0	100.0

†Goode 1970:31, Table 2-1.

Goode quotes a third study, conducted by two sociologists at the New York Medical College in early 1969 (Gagnon and Simon 1970). This involved interviewing seventy-four New York user respondents by 'reputational' methods. The age distribution of this group was virtually identical to the present study to Goode's, and to that of the East Village Other. Twenty-two per cent of the respondents were in their teens, 70 per cent were in their twenties and 8 per cent in their thirties.

None of these studies collected their data through random sampling. The close correspondence between the three American drug surveys and the present one lends a measure of validity to the suggestion that drugtakers are likely to be distributed as the age data shows. My discussions with drugtakers in other areas, such as London and Bristol, support the view that, in all probability, the age distribution of respondents in the present study is a reasonably good indication of the ages of drugtakers in the community.

Sex

Three-quarters of those interviewed in the present study were males. The 1971 Cheltenham Youth Trust survey showed that the majority, forty-six out of sixty-two, of drugtakers located were males, but the present study was confined to more experienced drugtakers and excluded those who had only used drugs a few times. Erich Goode comments:

> 'The user is more likely to be male than female. Or to put it another way, men are more likely to smoke, or to have smoked, marijuana than women. The differences between men and women in their pot smoking participation are always fairly small, but distinct. For the addicting drugs, especially heroin, the differences are massive. Only about one fifth of all known addicts turn out to be women.' (Goode 1970:32).

In Goode's New York sample there was a slight skew, 53.0 per cent of his respondents were males, 47.0 per cent females. Goode found that men were markedly more likely than women to have tried drugs other than cannabis, and to be deeply involved in a drugtaking milieu or to have bought and sold drugs. Goode maintains that usually a woman is offered cannabis by a man, and if she ever buys it, she buys from a man (Goode 1970:315).

Goode's study, like the present one was not a random sample. He states that there is no way of obtaining a cross-section of cannabis users. He speculates that three-quarters of the cannabis users in America are males (1970:317). This speculation is strikingly similar both to the actual sex distribution of the respondents in the present study and to my own general impressions.

Ross Speck and his associates, during their research into drug-using communes in America, found that there was a ratio of one female to four males in the groups (containing 500 individuals) they examined (Speck *et al.* 1972:89–90). They also found that females were generally regarded not as full members, but as adjuncts. The drugtaking groups I encountered were also predominantly male, and the distribution of drugs was largely, although not exclusively, carried out by males. There were exceptions and some females had both used a wide range of drugs and had, at times, bought and sold them. I agree with Goode's assertion that females were usually offered cannabis and other drugs by the males with whom they associated. Most of the females I encountered had originally been 'turned on' by their boyfriends, and their drug use was largely a function of their liaisons with specific males. I knew of few groups of female drugtakers, though there were several exclusively male groups. Possibly this conclusion was due to the fact that I, a male, managed to gain easier access to male than to female drugtakers. It is a point worth noting that most of the participant observation studies of illegal behaviour have been undertaken by male researchers. This may well have biased the conclusions of such work. There is little doubt that females might encounter far greater problems than males in associating with certain deviant groups.

In general, I found that females who were active socially, and in frequent contact with males, were those most likely to use drugs. My impression was that social isolates were unlikely to use drugs. Clearly, this impression may have been a distortion, due to my method of research. I believe it is important to reflect upon this speculation in view of the extensive medical research which has traditionally treated drug dependence as a form of individual disease. My personal impression was that people needed to associate with others in order to obtain supplies of drugs, and in order to be encouraged to use drugs. One of the traditional views of the drugtaker is that he is a person unable to relate to or form social relationships with other people. My field experience did not generally support this conclusion.

The findings of the present study indicate that although females were far less likely than males to be drugtakers, the preponderance of males is not great enough to correspond to the widely accepted view that illegal behaviour in general is a male phenomenon. The evidence supports the view that a large minority of drugtakers are female.

Social Class

Sixty per cent of those interviewed came from families headed by a non-manual worker. Social class was determined by paternal occupation since most of those interviewed were young and could not be classified according to their own occupation. The class-distribution of the study group was far more 'middle-class' in bias than is true for the population as a whole.[1] While not suggesting that the study group was a representative cross-section of drugtakers, it is interesting to note that most came from non-manual backgrounds. This departs from the general consideration that crime is primarily a working-class phenomenon. Many of the surveys of drugtaking, both in North America and Britain, have indicated that groups such as students, not normally considered delinquent or 'deviant', use drugs.

Goode, writing about the American cannabis user, suggests that as a group, those who have used cannabis are from generally higher class backgrounds than the population as a whole: 'Probably the higher the income of one's family, the higher the education of one's parents, and the greater the prestige of one's father's occupation, the greater is the likelihood of smoking marijuana' (Goode 1970:35).

Goode quotes the evidence of a 1969 American Gallup Poll which verified the positive association between social class and the likelihood of cannabis smoking. Better educated respondents were much more likely than others to report that they had used the drug. Most British studies have been restricted to homogeneous groups, such as students or institutional populations, so there is little evidence of the overall class distribution of drugtakers in the community.

My field-work made it clear that many drugtakers were students and others with middle-class occupations. Some of the drugtakers I encountered came from professional backgrounds and did not conform at all to the stereotype of the drugtaker as low-status or economically under privileged.

Marital Status

Seventy point five per cent of those interviewed were single. Only 9.0 per cent were married and living together and 17.0 per cent were

[1] *Social Trends*, 1972, No. 3: 71, Table 16.

cohabiting. The low proportion of those who were married is probably largely a reflection of the youthfulness and general middle-class composition of the study group. It is one of the important characteristics of the drugtakers in this study that most were in the early, or transitional, stages of their careers. Most were free of family responsibilities and lived with others of their own age and sex. There was a considerable amount of non-sexual cohabitation. Several respondents shared dwellings with members of the opposite sex with whom they had no sexual relationships. Within several of the groups I observed cohabitation was widely accepted, and many individuals stated that they believed marriage was not necessarily the form of association they would choose. Attitudes to marriage were consistent with the generally radical or anti-establishment ethos of the groups I encountered.

The Sub-Groups

There were considerable differences between individual drugtakers. In order to distinguish these differences I identify three sub-groups with characteristic social positions, lifestyles, and values. It must be emphasized that there was considerable overlap between each of these categories, as well as considerable variation within them. Each category is used in order to elaborate the differences between the main distinctive groups of drugtakers observed during my field research.

a) *Students:* seventy-three of those interviewed, 36.5 per cent of the study group, were full-time students.
b) *Middle-class bohemians:* forty of those interviewed, 20.0 per cent of the study group, were non-manual workers, or were still attending school.
c) *Low-status unemployed or manual workers:* eighty-seven of those interviewed, 43.5 per cent of the study group, were either manual workers or were unemployed.

The students were a distinctive group with their own social position and lifestyle. They were a transitional group of young people, most of whom were from non-manual backgrounds. Contrasted with these were two other categories of non-students. An important sub-group of respondents was broadly similar to the students in class backgrounds, lifestyles, and values. These were 'middle-class bohemians' or non-manual workers. The third sub-group, which appeared to be different in many important respects from either the students or the middle-class bohemians, consisted of primarily working class or unemployed non-students. In terms of many of the factors examined in this study, this third sub-group was probably the most interesting from the social policy/social problems point of view. In the discussion that follows I shall attempt to elaborate the differences between these three sub-groups.

5. Becoming a Drugtaker

The subjects of this study had one characteristic in common: all had used illegal drugs. All had crossed the threshold from social acceptability to social deviance. The drugtaker using substances such as cannabis, which are proscribed, is in a completely different position from the person who obtains drugs legally from a doctor. The latter faces neither legal nor social stigma.

The stereotype of the opiate dependent or junkie has widely been applied to all drugtakers. The law supports the view that drugtaking should be discouraged or controlled and this has created, as well as reflected, public opinion. The mass media have given considerable publicity to the sensational, as well as factual, aspects of drugtaking. For example, the *Guardian* carried a report by Dr Christine Savill that: 'Children of 12 were being seduced to drugtaking with the invitation "Have a sweetie – it will give you sweet dreams".'

This article also contained a statement by Dr Peter Chapple that there were half a million schoolchildren in London who had used drugs. This statement was not substantiated by any evidence, and has subsequently been disputed.[1]

The attributes associated with heroin dependence have been generalized to apply to all other drugtakers, and this has been justified on the grounds that people using drugs may eventually 'progress' to heroin dependence.

Jock Young suggests that there are three major reasons for the social reaction against drugtaking (Young 1971:95–100):

[1] The Guardian, 31 January, 1973. This article was criticized in *Drugs and Society* 2 (6):36–7 (March), where it was pointed out that Dr Chapple's statements were invalid, since there were not as many as half a million pupils in London schools.

1) Conflict of interest. Young maintains that drugtakers are seen as affecting the interests of different groups. For example, drug use affects a person's attitudes to work, or his political values.
2) Moral indignation. Deviant activities, even if they do not harm others, may be condemned because they involve 'dodging the rules. . .'

   'Following on from this it is interesting to note how the social reaction against a particular form of drugtaking is, in general, proportional to the degree to which the group involved embraces values which are hedonistic and disdainful of work.'

3) Humanitarianism. Powerful social groups may wish to change the behaviour of others. A social problem is defined and action is taken to help, or to enforce conformity. Young asserts that there is an absolutist tendency in society which amounts to a moral or material conflict. He suggests that moral indignation is justified by the perceived consequences of disapproved behaviour; 'thus premarital intercourse is wrong because it leads to V.D., masturbation because it causes impotence, marihuana smoking because a few users will step unaware on the escalator which leads to heroin addiction.'

Erving Goffman expresses an additional view of the social response to deviance:

> 'The attitudes we normals have towards a person with a stigma, and the actions we take in regard to him, are well known, since these responses are what benevolent social action is designed to soften and ameliorate. By definition, of course, we believe the person with a stigma is not quite human. On this assumption we exercise varieties of discrimination, through which we effectively, if often unthinkingly, reduce his life chances. We construct a stigma theory, an ideology to explain his inferiority and account for the danger he represents, sometimes rationalizing an animosity based on other differences, such as those of social class. We use specific stigma terms such as cripple, bastard, moron in our daily discourse as a source of metaphor and imagery, typically without giving thought to the original meaning. We tend to impute a wide range of imperfections on the basis of the original one, and at the same time to impute some desirable but undesired attribute, often of a

supernatural cast such as a sixth sense, or "understanding".' (Goffman 1968:15–16)

Goffman's comments are broadly applicable to the social responses to drugtaking. Becoming a drugtaker involves entering a stigmatized category and being labelled in generally derogatory terms.

There are broadly three ways in which a person may become a drugtaker. The first is through accident. People have become inadvertently dependent upon drugs due to medical treatment. This does not involve any choice on their part. Second, a person may be psychologically unstable and use drugs for quasi-medical reasons. Such individuals conform to the 'sick' or junkie image. It must be noted that countless thousands of people receive legal supplies of drugs, such as tranquillizers, from their doctors. These are beyond the scope of the present study but are still drug dependents. The third possiblity is that an apparently sane, healthy person may choose to use drugs because they have an attractive or prestigious significance or for the perceived or imagined pleasure of their effects.

My field research revealed that a few individuals who used drugs had histories of medical treatment for psychiatric illnesses and thought that drugs could ameliorate their general psychological state. It is a further possibility that all forms of drugtaking are motivated by other psychological pressures, but such possibilities are outside the scope of this study. My main preoccupation is with the process involved when a person decides to become a drugtaker. My field work did not enable me to contact solitary drugtakers, if such exist, and only one respondent reported having begun using drugs because of medical treatment he had received.

If people make calculated decisions to adopt a deviant identity, particularly one characterized by illegal behaviour, such as theft or drugtaking, it seems logical that they will rationalize to minimize guilt and to justify their deviance. The evidence of many surveys suggests that large numbers of young adults have some experience of drugtaking and that many do not appear to be psychotic, or to have become drugtakers through accident. Howard Becker's examination of how a person becomes a marihuana user describes a fairly complicated learning process as the novice takes instruction in the techniques necessary to become 'high'.

The 'official' social view of drugtaking is that it is undesirable and pathological. The mass media, educational films, and the law actively aim at discouraging people from using drugs, and drugtaking is labelled a social problem. To become a drugtaker, therefore, necessitates that a person redefines drugtaking as positively rewarding, rather than as deleterious, behaviour. A person must be able or willing to 'neutralize' or suspend his acceptance of the conventional evaluation that drugtaking is a sign of weakness or moral folly.

David Matza suggests a departure from a rigidly determinist view of delinquency, or deviance:

> 'Some men are freer than others. Most men, including delinquents, are neither wholly free nor completely constrained, but fall somewhere between. The general conditions underlying various positions along a continuum from freedom to constraint may be described.' (Matza 1964:27)

Matza puts forward the concept of 'drift':

> 'Drift stands midway between freedom and control. Its basis is an area in the social structure in which contact has been lessened, coupled with the abortiveness of adolescent endeavour to organize an autonomous subculture, and thus independent source of control, around illegal action. The delinquent *transiently* exists in a limbo between convention and crime, responding in turn to the demands of each, flirting with one, now the other, but postponing commitment, evading decisions. Thus he drifts between criminal and conventional action.' (Matza 1964:28)

He suggests that a person will move into and out of a deviant role as complex social forces put pressure on him:

> 'Drift is a gradual process of movement, unperceived by the actor in which the first stage may be accidental or unpredictable from the point of view of any theoretic frame of reference, and deflection from the delinquent path may be similarly accidental or unpredictable.' (Matza 1964:29)

A similar view is expressed by Goffman:

> 'Given the ambivalence built into the individual's attachment to his stigmatized category, it is understandable that oscillations may occur in his support of, identification with, and participation among his own. There will be "affiliation cycles" through which he

comes to accept the special opportunities for in-group participation or comes to reject them after having accepted them before. There will be corresponding oscillations in belief about the nature of our group and the nature of normals.' (Goffman 1968:51–2)

'Deviance' is a process of departure from what is considered acceptable, or usual. The term implies that it is a temporary state. To deviate one has to conform in order to change one's behaviour. Most juvenile delinquents do not become adult criminals. Presumably they drift out of crime as they drifted in.

Young suggests drugtaking is a special case. He maintains that the activity itself changes the individual's frame of reference so that a return to society ceases to be viewed as desirable, or worthwhile. This process is in addition to the normal social reaction that labels and stigmatizes an individual enacting disapproved behaviour. Young develops this view to describe the ideological alienation of drugtakers from the values and norms of society. Goffman suggests that persons who have a mutual social stigma share specific learning processes regarding their situation. This involves similar changes in their self-images, which he describes as a 'moral career' (1968: 108, 114). This moral career, he suggests, is both a cause and a result of sharing a similar process of redefinition. Matza discusses drift in relation to the classical sociological concept of 'anomie' or unregulated choice. He uses the term 'drift' to emphasize the episodic release from moral restraints (1964:45). He suggests that in the absence of complete control the actor may become deviant if a suitable motive is present. The delinquent or deviant is aware of criticism from 'reputable' sources, such as policemen, and the mass media. Matza points out that most, if not all, norms arc conditional. Individuals make exceptions to them. People dissent by interpreting their situation as outside the law. Even so, Matza suggests, they tend to accept the general lines of the law. He maintains that even though deviants may break the law, there is an 'obscured similarity' between conventional and deviant view-points.

In relation to drugtaking, individuals often explained their behaviour by justifying themselves in conventional terms 'I knew drugtaking was illegal, but I thought that I was well-balanced, and would not move on to use harder drugs. You see, the law aims at stopping people who might become junkies; people like me are O.K.'

A common line of argument was to challenge the assumptions perceived as underlying the drug laws: 'We are a persecuted minority group. Straight society has its drugs. Ours are probably safer.'

The evidence of my personal experience is consistent with Matza's view that deviance is preceded by a process of redefinition of the behaviour concerned. I use my personal experience as an example.

Before I met any drugtakers I was aware of the dangers of heroin dependence and assumed, as did my parents and friends, that drugtaking must be a social problem, and would have been horrified at the suggestion that I should use drugs. I was very interested in the publicity given to the use of drugs by celebrities such as the Rolling Stones and Beatles and by the claims of Timothy Leary and others concerning the powers of L.S.D. The imputation that there was a positive side to illegal drug use challenged the traditional view about drugtaking. The fact that successful cult figures such as rock music stars were using drugs seemed inconsistent with the idea that drugtakers were either economically underprivileged or social misfits. My first encounters with people who had used drugs such as cannabis similarly undermined this view.

The first drugtaker I ever met was a university student whom I had known for some time in connection with our common interest in folk music. One evening he started a conversation about drugtaking and told me that he was a regular cannabis smoker. I knew him to be academically successful, a talented musician, and thought him likeable. I was accordingly influenced by his view that cannabis smoking was pleasant and had caused him no ill-effects. He clearly had a very positive opinion of the drug and talked about its effects with great enthusiasm:

> 'Being stoned is different from being pissed (drunk). It's more introspective, and you don't feel rough next day. Dope (cannabis) is O.K. I have no intention of ever using hard drugs. That's not my scene. Dope is nice. You ought to come over the next time I get hold of a deal, so you can try it too.'

My subsequent encounters with drugtakers have led me to believe such proselytizing to be commonplace. Since that initial discussion I have listened to many similar eulogies in defence or praise of cannabis and other drugs. The drugtaker, like the evangelist, is anxious to recruit others to share his experiences and to convert people to his own opinions. In general, deviants, or minority groups, seek support:

'I'd love to turn you on.' ('Lucy in the Sky with Diamonds' by Lennon and McCartney)

My first encounters with drugtakers were with people of my own age (early twenties) and whom I knew sufficiently to become involved in discussions on fairly intimate, or controversial, topics. They only mentioned drugs to me when sufficient rapport had been established to assure them they would receive a sympathetic hearing. Several 'sounded me out' by asking me about my personal views on drugtaking. When assured that I had no strongly hostile opinions on the matter, they told me of their own drugtaking practices and usually tried to persuade me to join them. Over a period of time my impression about drugtaking became confused, my face-to-face contacts with several drugtakers did not support the stereotypical 'junkie' image of drugtaking. Several were people I quite liked or respected and most seemed to be psychologically normal. All were of above average intelligence and educational accomplishments.

The first step in becoming a drugtaker is contact with people who have already used drugs. The second is forming a favourable impression of them and, by implication, of drugs. My initial reaction upon discovering that a friend of mine was a cannabis user was to assume that this otherwise 'normal' person had a hidden flaw, a secret vice. I was surprised and rather doubtful about his confidences.

The next step is reassurance:

> 'Well, just look at me. I smoke dope. I'm not a junkie, and never shall be. Neither are any of my friends who smoke. There is as much difference between smoking dope and being a junkie as there is between social drinking and alcoholism.'

The final step is acceptance of the idea that drugtaking may be pleasant. Just as Becker describes, first cannabis experiences involve being instructed how to inhale the smoke and hold it in the lungs before expelling it. This is certainly a process of tuition and is important to the appreciation of the effects of the drug.

The actual use of drugs is the final stage in a process of socialization or adapting one's behaviour to conform to the expectations and example of others.

Becker rejects the view that cannabis use is motivated by a need for fantasy and escape from problems. He bases this assertion on the fact that one learns to use the drug. While agreeing that this is so, I do not concur that people are generally unaware of what the effects of the drug are likely to be. Many respondents had a good idea of how it would affect them before they used it. Further, most of the types of drug covered by this study require no tuition in order that the individual may use them. One does not have to learn how to swallow a capsule or tablet. My observations do not support the view that Becker's contentions regarding cannabis are valid in relation to other drugs, nor, necessarily, in all cases, to cannabis.

Virtually all respondents attributed their first drug experiences to the direct influence and encouragement of friends and peers whom they knew well. It was clear that drugtaking developed as a group activity and was part of the leisure behaviour of those interviewed and observed. Furthermore, within the group drugtaking was a much discussed and conspicuous form of behaviour. Several individuals spoke of the tremendous peer group pressure to use drugs. One youth, who had taken L.S.D., reported that he had been afraid of the drug, believing it might make him become psychotic. Nevertheless, he was persuaded to use it by friends. These reports, together with my own field experience, confirmed the view that there was an emphatic process of socialization amongst certain groups of young people which instilled the image of drugtaking as a prestigious and beneficial activity.

The drugtakers I encountered appeared more influenced by their friends who had used drugs than by 'official' denunciations of drugs and drugtaking, In general statements by the police and other authorities intended to discourage drugtaking were rejected as ill-informed or politically dishonest. This finding has importance in relation to current approaches to drug education. Many of those interviewed and observed commented upon the failure of existing anti-drug propaganda to achieve its intended results. A number of the individuals I encountered stated that they believed that 'horror films' about the alleged dangers of drug use either increased interest in drugs, or were discredited by their lurid descriptions of 'junkies' which did not conform to the experience of most young people who had tried drugs, or whose friends were drugtakers. The whole field of drug education is a complicated one. In the light of the present findings, it may well be debatable whether the present policy of showing films or giving anti-drug lectures is effective, in view of the fact that many young people are more influenced by the advice and experiences of their friends and people they know well than by the pronouncements of strangers.

Many individuals described their first impressions of drugs in terms of their surprise that their friends enjoyed using them and seldom appeared to be harmed by their drugtaking. Several emphasized that they wished to emulate people whom they admired (including cult heroes and rock music stars) or because they wanted to affirm their positive identification with groups of people using drugs, or with the ideologies associated with illegal drug use: 'I wanted to be cool. I knew guys who smoked a lot of dope, and felt left out. They seemed like an elite, and I wanted to be part of the group. Smoking dope was a kind of declaration of intent.'

Half of those interviewed reported that they had first used drugs while visiting a friend's house or flat. Most of their first drug experiences had been in the company of friends, and only twenty-six of the 200 respondents reported having first used drugs in a semi-public setting such as a pop-festival, cafe, or public house. Most of the reported first drug experiences had involved the social, rather than solitary, smoking of cannabis, as is shown in the section on patterns of drugtaking. Only seven individuals, 3.5 per cent of the study group, reported that they had been alone when they first used drugs. These had either taken drugs from their parents who were receiving them on prescription, or had acquired them from other sources, and had taken them privately.

Only one individual interviewed reported having been introduced to drugtaking therapeutically, during medical treatment. Over 90.0 per cent of the study group had been introduced to drugs by friends or siblings, and only ten respondents, 5.0 per cent, reported having first obtained drugs from relative strangers.

Goode's evidence led him to conclude that proselytizing involves intimates rather than strangers: 'In no case did a peddler turn on the respondent unless he was a friend.'

Elaborating the importance of friendship in introducing people to cannabis use, Goode comments:

> 'More specifically, the relationship between the neophyte and his marijuana initiator is crucial. The lack of association in the naïf's

> mind with marijuana with a specifically unsavoury "scene" is, of course, important, but it lacks the immediacy and impact of his feelings for those who actually hand him a glowing joint. Although sexual parallels should not be pushed too far, something of the same significance is imputed to one's sex partner as to the person one has decided to be turned on by. With women, the conjunction is closer than for men, women are usually turned on by men, whereas men are more often turned on by other men.' (Goode 1970:125).

First-hand accounts of being 'turned on' repeatedly mentioned the role of close friends and people whom the neophyte held in high esteem: 'People I liked were smoking, and they offered me a joint. I turned on because I knew they were good people.'

The evidence of the present study suggested that most of the drugtakers encountered had become drugtakers as an affirmation of values held in common with others, or as the result of contact with others. The findings did not support the view that the 'pusher' or commercially motivated stranger, was an important factor in introducing people to drugtaking. In general, it seemed that close associates were much more likely to influence a person's behaviour in relation to drug use; either to avoid it, or to begin it.

Reasons for Using Drugs

90.0 per cent of those interviewed stated that they first used drugs because they were curious, or because friends encouraged them to do so. Several commented that the mass media have created a mystique about drugtaking which enhances the appeal of drugs as 'forbidden fruit': 'It's like getting layed. Drugs seemed dangerous but tempting.'

Some individuals reported that they have been influenced by the writings of Burroughs, Huxley, Leary or even Crowley. Current 'pop-culture' is very drug oriented, and many of the drugtakers I encountered commented upon the drug allusions in well-known songs. There can be little doubt that the use of drugs by cult figures and the inclusion of references to drugs in many songs assist in the process of socializing people into accepting the legitimacy of drugtaking:

> 'Everybody must get stoned'
> ('Rainy Day Women Numbers 12 and 35' by Bob Dylan)

Most of those interviewed described their first drugtaking experiences in terms of entry into a group of initiates. Several were emphatic that drugtaking was part of group experience. 'Smoking (cannabis) is just part of the whole scene. It's a way of life. . .an ethnic group. Yes, you should write about the drug scene as an ethnic group.'

I suggest that becoming a drugtaker is a process of socialization by contact with admired others. Some individuals reported having been influenced by considerable peer group pressure to use drugs. It is important to note that most of the drugtakers I encountered were living away from their parental homes, were generally in households of age peers, and therefore under considerable pressure to conform to the expectations, and standards of their friends. The data on first drug experiences reveals that in most cases drugtaking was precipitated by the encouragement of friends and peers. I suggest that social contact with other drugtakers was the primary factor in prompting people to use drugs. On several occasions I observed people being introduced to drugs, usually cannabis, and this always occurred in the company of people whom they knew fairly well and accepted as dependable advisors or exemplars. Contact with drugtakers is largely a function of general leisure behaviour. My field research suggests that people were most likely to become drugtakers as an affirmation of beliefs and values, or through contact with others. This view is consistent with Sutherland's theory that deviance is precipitated by the transmission of values through differential-association, contact with a deviant milieu (Sutherland and Cressey 1970). Since becoming a drugtaker entails a departure from 'conventional' behaviour, such persuasion is most likely to be effective when the individual is relatively free to establish his own lifestyle and values. Most of the drugtakers interviewed had concealed their first drug use from their parents and the evidence indicates that in general parents were perceived as hostile to drugtaking. Most of those interviewed reported that their first drug experiences had been in friends homes. Within the peer group young adults are freer to behave as they choose. In many ways drugtaking was similar to sexual behaviour. Both were clearly seen as marks of maturity and both were generally concealed from parents who would probably have disapproved.

The drugtakers observed were members of groups of age peers, most of whom had left their parental homes, with their own norms and styles of behaviour. Passage into the group entailed learning a number of behaviour patterns, only one of which was drugtaking. I observed several people who associated with drugtakers and lived in a similar way but who never used drugs. Conversely, some drugtakers were not deeply involved with the lifestyles of their peers and associated mainly with non drugtakers.

The evidence of my field-work suggests that there was considerable variation in individual drugtaking histories. Some people began to use drugs when they encountered a *rite de passage*, a change in their life situation; others began to use drugs for less apparent reasons. A few individuals I encountered had become drugtakers after specific events, such as the failure of their marriages, or upon entering a new group of friends, or an educational institution. Many first used drugs in company with people with whom they had grown up, without necessarily changing their patterns of friendship.

Virtually all respondents had first used drugs after, or about the same time as, puberty. There was little evidence from my field-work to support the view that pre-adolescents were active members of the groups I encountered. I believe this is a significant factor in identifying the groups I observed. Drugtaking, for most of those interviewed, had been part of a process of departure from the role of child, or school-pupil to a new status as adult, student, or worker. In general, the drugtakers I met during my field-work spoke about their drugtaking in terms of it being part of their personal development, a sign of maturity, and of establishing their own way of life and values in contrast to those of their parents.

Perceived Changes in Lifestyle Associated with Becoming a Drugtaker

Altogether 163 of the 200 respondents, 81.5 per cent, reported that they had undergone a change in behaviour or outlook since they had become drugtakers. Most of those interviewed believed that since taking drugs they had become more tolerant or perceptive in their approach to life. Significantly, five asserted that they had become less violent. All five had histories of violent behaviour and it seemed that they might have used drugs specifically to reduce the tensions precipitating this.

There was a wide range in variation between individual reports of personality changes associated with becoming a drugtaker (see *Table*

24). Some respondents spoke in terms of having retreated from the mainstream of society, rejecting conventional values, work, or even other people. Some individuals were very withdrawn and introspective. There was general agreement that becoming a drugtaker had involved a redefinition of both goals and values. Most of the respondents from middle-class backgrounds had continued with their education and careers, and so this redefinition had not been as drastic as in the case of those who had discontinued work, or become downwardly mobile.

Much of the language used to describe the changes associated with the adoption of drugtaking reflected the ethos of the 'flower power' phase of the 1960s. People frequently mentioned kindness, aesthetic perceptiveness, repudiation of violence, and distaste for material goods. Most of the drugtakers I observed paid at least lip service to these values, even though some appeared to fall short of embodying them.

In general, the students and middle-class bohemians reported that their outlooks rather than behaviour, had changed. They believed that in general, becoming a drugtaker had made them nicer and more perceptive. Some of the low-status unemployed and manual workers, those most deeply involved with drugtaking, attributed behaviour changes to their drug use. Some had given up work or left their former friends and it was evident that some had changed their lifestyles quite radically. Most stated that they believed these changes had been improvements. The evidence suggests that those individuals who had changed their lifestyles did not share the critical outsider's view that this metamorphosis had been an adverse one. Virtually all respondents reported that they enjoyed using drugs and that they valued drugtaking as part of their chosen way of life. An important finding was that very few respondents attributed their first drugtaking to 'pathological' reasons. One of the traditional assumptions about drugtaking is that it is usually an escape from, or reaction to, problems; a sign of psychological or social sickness or unhappiness. The evidence of this study does not support this view.

My own interpretation of the changes individuals underwent is broadly similar to that of the drugtakers themselves. Whereas some individuals claimed to have become more perceptive, an outsider might contend that they appeared more interested in trivia, more sensitive to things that were formerly taken for granted. Their general orientations changed, in varying degrees, from commitment to the conventional values of society to alternatives that were essentially introspective or spiritual. This appeared to be a rationalization of individual failure within, or hostility towards, the workaday value system. In general, it is reasonable to suppose that those whose psychological needs are already met will have less to gain than others by revising their lifestyles within the drug using group.

Drugtaking is part of a more general lifestyle. My field-work indicated that individuals continued to be drugtakers only as long as they defined their objectives within that milieu. I noted many individuals who drifted into drugtaking while associating with people who used drugs, but who later moved into different groups and ceased drugtaking. A student may spend three years at a college or university where there is considerable support for drug use and where it is easy to obtain supplies of drugs. The ethos of such an institution is dictated by age peers and in such a setting drugtaking may be approved of and commonplace. Upon entering a new phase of development, for example, by starting work, objectives and values may be determined by different criteria, and drugtaking may cease. I encountered many people who attributed their abandonment of drugtaking to new roles and responsibilities: 'Smoking dope does not fit in with being a teacher. It's not worth the risk and most of my colleagues wouldn't approve. I think dope smoking is part of being a student, but I doubt I shall ever use it again.'

Several individuals, most of whom had used a wide range of psychedelic drugs, discontinued their drug use upon marriage, or after becoming members of religious cults. They explained these changes in terms of having filled the emotional niche which drugs attempted to do. My impression was that many of the people I encountered became drugtakers in order to seek acceptance with a group and some emotional security. It is significant that most respondents were unmarried and had not yet established themselves in their careers. Drugtaking certainly seemed a response by some to ideological or emotional uncertainty. Some people reported that they hoped to find a sense of purpose and identity within the drugtaking group. Individuals with career or status objectives generally left the group or reduced these objectives. My impression was that those who were the most unhappy, confused, or guilt-ridden were the most vulnerable to conversion to a new way of life. While, in general, drugtaking seemed a corollary of sociability, membership of extreme or 'dramatic' cults appeared to result from an emotional need for a sense of community, friendship, and release from uncertainty. Several religious cults gained converts by stressing individual fears and uncertainties and offering a cure for this malaise.

The evidence of this study supports the view that personal involvement with drugtaking depended upon one's general social position. Those most deeply involved with drugtaking were either people with no conventional status aspirations, or the economically underprivileged, or alienated individuals who did not interpret their values and goals in terms of the conventional, workaday world. Some people became drugtakers to escape their sense of economic failure or privation. They chose drugtaking as a collective solution to antecedent social problems. The students and middle-class bohemians generally restricted their drugtaking so that it did not interfere with their education and careers. Some discontinued using drugs on the grounds that it was incompatible with their career roles. Those who continued to use drugs extensively were generally lacking in social status or aspirations. Some individuals had formerly been deeply involved with drugtaking, and had given up work for considerable periods of time, but had subsequently reduced their involvement with drugtaking and had taken regular jobs. One respondent reported his experience in these terms:

> 'When I was eighteen I wanted to be a hippy. I went on the road, smoked myself silly. I suppose that phase lasted a couple of years. I thought I was cool, but got nothing out of it. I have got a house and job together now, and I still smoke, but don't let it interfere with leading a normal life.'

This respondent suggested that it was important that, although he had tried to cut his ties off with the 'straight' world, he still had a chance to return.

> 'I was lucky. My family and boss were great. They let me have my fling and then made it easy for me to come back. I think their approach was more useful than ostracizing people who turn into freaks. Society needs to leave the door open, otherwise people get permanently cut off.'

Within several middle-class groups of 'bohemians' drugtaking was combined with leading relatively conventional lives. Several respondents were professional people. Invariably middle-class users controlled their drug use and generally restricted it to cannabis smoking and the occasional use of psychedelics.

> 'I smoke at weekends, but I only trip (take L.S.D.) when I've got ten days to spare. That way I know it won't interfere with my work. I believe acid is an important source of inspiration, and I don't appreciate it unless I have time to consider it and to concentrate on each trip.'

Those individuals who discontinued using drugs during my contact with them usually explained this by stating that they believed they had fully explored the potential of the 'safe' drugs, and had no intention of using other drugs which they regarded as dangerous. A few people were disenchanted with drugtaking and reported that they thought it was 'too trendy' or 'a bit of a fetish'. One student told me that he had smoked cannabis regularly for a year, but discontinued because he was bored with the 'stupid ritual' his friends insisted on every time the drug was used. Some people gave up drugtaking upon becoming enthusiastic about a hobby. One of my friends became a fanatical rock climber and explained his transition in these terms:

> 'When I used to smoke (cannabis) I wanted to extend my perceptions, and to deepen my sense of experience. Now I get the same intellectual stimulus from climbing, which I see as a mental, as much as a physical challenge. I suppose you could call me an adrenaline freak now.'

No single pattern of events was evident in becoming a drugtaker or in ceasing to be a drugtaker. As Lindesmith and Gagnon point out (in Clinard 1964:158–88), no single theory seems adequate to explain such complex evidence.

The processes of entering and leaving the drugtaking groups I observed seemed very similar and dependent upon a person's goals and values. In general a person became a drugtaker in order to realize valued aspirations. Ceasing to be a drugtaker often appeared to be the obverse of this process, when individuals values or aspirations changed. The evidence suggests that the groups concerned developed as a process of crystallizing values previously held by radical young people, or by those in a state of ideological uncertainty who wished to affirm their beliefs and attach themselves to the goals and solutions of respected others. Whether or not an individual chose to remain a drugtaker depended partly upon the permanence of his drugtaking peer group (students were generally only in college for three or four years) and upon the existence or availability of viable alternatives, such as career or educational prospects.

My general conclusion is that Matza's theory of drift between deviance and conformity, depending upon variable inducements to attach oneself to either, is a useful general assessment of the way people become drugtakers or cease to be drugtakers. 'Drift' should not be interpreted in this context as implying that the individual need be aimless or lack freedom of choice. This clearly was not the case with many of those whom I observed. Many individuals became, or ceased to be drugtakers in a very considered, purposive way. Their behaviour, to them, was meaningful and well thought out. An important aspect of the socialization process is that of the drug-taker's self-image at any given point of time. This related to the individual's general ideology and that of the groups with whom he associates or identifies himself. My field experience indicated that ideology was an important contributing factor to the growth of drugtaking groups.

THREE Values

6. Ideology

Several studies, such as those by Binnie and Murdock (1969), Young and Brook-Crutchley (1972), Goode (1970), have indicated that drugtakers were likely to be politically radical and to have no religion. This implies that as a group, drugtakers are less likely than other people to have a rigidly conservative world view or to accept society and the law as it stands. The fact that the subjects of this study were drugtakers meant that as a group they were not socially conformist solely due to their use of illegal drugs.

One of the stereotypes attached to drugtaking is that it is socially dangerous or subversive. It is illegal because it is viewed as a social problem. The subjects of this study had rejected this view and did not define themselves, generally, as social problems or as unhappy. As a group the drugtakers I encountered had a distinctive opinion of drugtaking and of the world in general. I suggest that their ideologies were an important characteristic of the groups I observed and that their drugtaking was associated with their general philosophies and chosen lifestyles. Ideology was an important factor in the process of becoming a drugtaker.

Political Beliefs

Of those interviewed 83.3 per cent reported that they were not interested in politics, or that their beliefs were left, or very left, wing. Only five individuals, 2.5 per cent, stated that they held right, or very right wing political beliefs.

Altogether, 41.0 per cent of those interviewed stated that they were not interested in politics. Some of these were apathetic to politics and made it apparent that they had no knowledge of political affairs. Others were very interested in political events but were hostile to consensus politics and to the conventional political system. Such individuals asserted that the conventional system was part of a materialistic society which they rejected: 'I'm not interested in the sort of politics you mean. Political parties are all the same. I believe in changing the whole system . . . in altering the whole structure of society.'

Comments of this sort were frequently made, and resemble the outlook of the beats observed by Ned Polsky:

> 'Far from being lumpen, beats are more keenly aware of the range of political alternatives than is the average voter. They are not apolitical but consciously and deliberately antipolitical, which is something else entirely and, as a common attitude, something new in American history. Beats suffer not from political apathy but from political antipathy. They totally "resign" from society insofar as this is possible, not least of all from its politics, and reject extreme political sects with no less vigour than they reject major parties.' (Polsky 1969:159)

Most of those interviewed expressed radical political views, at least on social issues. This is consistent with the findings of several surveys of drugtakers. Goode found a similar pattern in his New York study:

> 'One of the most empirically verified of all relationships with marijuana use is political ideology and activity. Marijuana users are far more likely to hold what are considered in America today as liberal or radical views.' (Goode 1970:43)

Many of the students and middle-class bohemians were very interested in politics, and some had extensive political libraries. Several were active in student politics and many had been, or were involved in, a variety of political campaigns or pressure groups.

Some of the low-status unemployed or manual workers were surprisingly well read and interested in politics, but most appeared politically apathetic (see *Tables 27* and *28*). Fifty-four of the eighty-three low-status sub-group stated they had no interest in politics; presumably this lack of interest was a function of social class.

It has been suggested that right wing or conservative political beliefs are incompatible with drugtaking, since the latter involves rejecting many traditional outlooks. Drugtakers are critical of society and many spoke in very idealistic terms about their political beliefs and objectives. Some young people regard drugtaking as an outward sign of political radicalism or liberalism. Obversely, critics of drugtaking have condemned it as anarchist and subversive. In fact some individuals, mainly low-status unemployed or manual workers, expressed views that were anarchist and claimed to have opted out of society as far as they could.

Three-quarters of those interviewed were working and some were academically very successful. These were more likely to be radical than anti-political. The latter outlook was more compatible with a thoroughgoing retreatist lifestyle.

The drugtakers I encountered were broadly in two groups politically. The overwhelming majority of students and middle-class bohemians had radical views and were above averagely interested in political and social issues. As Polsky stated of the beats, they were well aware of the range of political alternatives. Many told me that they regarded being a drugtaker as fully compatible with radical or liberal ideas:

> 'Have you ever met a head who is racist or fascist? Some of the Hell's Angels maybe, but they're different. Being a head means that you love people, and that you put human happiness before material possessions. That's what the scene's about.'

This type of comment was frequently and spontaneously corroborated both during informal encounters and during structured interviews. Many middle-class and some working-class drugtakers stated that they were highly politicized in their approach to life, and that drugtaking was a catalyst or activity compatible with their ideas.

The link between youth culture, drug use, and political radicalism has often been stressed by popular songs. The Rolling Stones' 'Street Fighting Man' and the protest songs of the 1960s expressed an ethos that was very closely allied to the growth of drug use amongst young people. The 'flower power' movement emphasized the philosophy of brotherhood and peace in conjunction with the use of psychedelic drugs. The folk heroes included Allan Ginsberg, Timothy Leary, Bob Dylan, Herbert Marcuse, and Angela Davis.

The content of much of the underground or hippy press is explicitly political, summarized by the cogent slogan:

'Turn on, tune in, drop out'

Many of the students or middle-class bohemians had read books by Bobby Seale, Norman Mailer, Regis Debray, Franz Fanon, Angela Davis and were interested in the drug-scene as an expression of their radical ideas and values. Contrasted against the liberal-intellectuals, many of the low-status unemployed and manual workers appeared indifferent to politics. Like many working-class groups, they evinced a fierce antipathy towards 'authority' or 'officialdom' but few were explicitly political. My encounters with manual workers who were not drug-takers indicated that apathy to politics was a general disposition of this group. In general, the working-class group was the least politically educated and concerned and generally did not express articulate or sophisticated political views, although there were a few notable exceptions to this rule.

Religious Beliefs

118 of the 200 respondents, 59.0 per cent, reported that they were either agnostic, humanist, atheist, or existentialist. Only twelve individuals, 6.0 per cent, identified themselves with the 'conventional' organized religions such as the Anglican or Roman Catholic churches. The remaining seventy respondents, 35.0 per cent, were interested in oriental mysticism, spiritualism, or cults such as the 'Jesus Movement' (see*Tables 25* and *26*).

Meditation and mysticism are currently part of the hippy way of life. Timothy Leary's *The Psychedelic Experience* is based upon the *Tibetan Book of the Dead* (Evans-Wentz 1951) and many of those who have used psychedelic drugs have linked these with a search for transcendental experience. 'I see acid as part of mysticism. I use the drug to expand my mind, and to reach higher psychic levels. Acid unlocks parts of the brain, in the same way Yoga or meditation do.'

Aldous Huxley suggested that psychedelic drugs can deepen the grasp of philosophical systems. In his book he states that mescalin aided his comprehension of other 'philosophic truths (Huxley 1972a).

The link between psychedelic drugs and mysticism is now firmly established. Many Eastern religions and philosophies emphasize spiritual and aesthetic, rather than material, goals. In addition, several offer a type of profound transcendental or ecstatic state which is broadly similar to that often sought through the use of psychedelic drugs. Philosophies such as these include a rejection of conventional Western outlooks and are attractive to people who are dissatisfied with industrial society.

Some drugtakers are highly critical of the present social order and state that they wish to find a new and morally superior, or more attractive, set of values. At the time I was carrying out my field-work, many drugtakers were attracted to the evangelical 'Jesus Movement' and to different forms of meditation and yoga. Several of these sects proselytized successfully amongst young drugtakers using the language of the drug-scene: 'Jesus really turns you on', or 'Meditation gets you higher than acid.'

Some individuals and groups stopped using drugs completely after joining such cults. This parallels the way in which black American narcotics addicts have given up drugs upon becoming members of the Black Muslims or Black Panthers.

Several people explained to me that they were searching for dramatic experiences or a sense of certainty when they used drugs. This contradicts Becker's assertion that this is not so. Drugs, they stated, were an attempt to escape reality by distorting their consciousness. Some said they were seeking some form of explanation of life through drug-induced experiences.

> 'I used drugs because I felt lost. I guess I wanted to find myself; to find the answer to the universe. I don't use drugs now. I don't need to. Acid took me up to the fourth astral plane. I can get there through meditation now so I don't want to use drugs any more. They're an escape, and are unnecessary when you can get there by yourself. I've got the knowledge (of meditation) now, and I know the answer to the universe.'

Some individuals appeared to seek a quasi-religious experience through drugs. It was significant that the sects that had the greatest appeal for drugtakers were generally those that placed the greatest demands on them and enforced a new lifestyle. Several theorists have argued that drugtaking is related to the demise of organized religion. My observations support this view. Many drugtakers had a deep religious feeling and freely discussed spiritual experiences. Such intense interest in religion was generally confined to the students and middle-class bohemians. The low-status manual workers were generally rather less interested in religion, but some of the most involved drugtakers were especially pre-occupied with mysticism and the occult. It must be noted that a bizarre association between drug use and religion was evident in the curious sect run by the American hippy, Charles Manson, who allegedly perpetrated the sadistic murder of the film actress Sharon Tate (Sanders 1973). Similar aberrations are illustrated by the various writings of the notorious Aleister Crowley, 'the great beast' (Crowley 1972).

The Le Dain Report suggests:

> 'Modern drug use would definitely seem to be related in some way to the collapse of religious values – the ability to find a religious way of life. The positive values that young people claim to find in the drug experience bear a striking similarity to traditional religious values, including the concern with the soul, or inner self. The spirit of renunciation, the emphasis on openness and the closely knit community, are part of it, but there is definitely the sense of identification with something larger, something to which one belongs as part of the human race.' (Le Dain 1971:224)

In many ways, the drug-scene is a simple, market place type of association. The ethos of the groups I observed was generally a very relaxed, friendly one, and the middle-class drugtakers often emphasized human, pastoral values and expressed an interest in nature and in spontaneity.

Erich Goode suggests that people with no religion are unconventional in many ways and politically far to the left of the ideological spectrum (Goode 1970:42–3). He found that 45.0 per cent of his study group were atheists and about 30.0 per cent had their own private versions of God, such as pantheism, 'God is love', etc. The recent literature on drug surveys now generally indicates that traditional religious beliefs are incompatible with drug use.

The intense interest in mysticism and the rejection of traditional organized religion was consistent with the generally radical or anti-conservative outlook of the great majority of respondents. Some of the more involved drugtakers appeared highly introspective. The term 'head' denotes a person who seeks psychological, rather than material, goals. The image of the head is that of the mystic, the seeker of hidden truths. Much of the literature, clothing, and behaviour of the middle-class bohemian and student drugtaking groups were influenced by the styles and traditions of the East. A large number of the more 'experienced' drugtakers had at some time taken the hippy trail to Kathmandu and were deeply interested in anything oriental. Preoccupation with mysticism is alien to the instrumentality of industrial society. Many of the drugtakers I encountered were discontented with the social order. Most were radical rather than revolutionary but some wished to change society altogether. The political and religious beliefs they expressed were consistent with this outlook.

Subterranean Values

Many of the drugtakers I encountered were emphatic that, in their view, 'being a drugtaker' was more important than simply using drugs. There was little doubt that many of the drugs used were taken explicitly for their pharmacological properties, but most of those I observed spent far more time discussing drugs than using them. The literature indicates that certain groups, such as students and ghetto Negroes, are particularly likely to use drugs. Jock Young suggests that in order to interpret this fact, one must learn the meaning of drugtaking in the context of group values and world view: 'For an item of behaviour cannot be understood in isolation from its social milieu: man is the only animal that gives meaning to his actions and it is his system of values which provides these meanings' (Young 1971:124).

Many drugtakers clearly saw themselves as part of a distinctive sub-culture, and stressed the differences between themselves and non-drugtakers:

> 'Heads refuse to play social games. We see through the pretence of capitalism, communism, or whatever names you give straight society. I want a human, natural kind of association. You see, heads care about the future and we are trying to create the kind of system that will really work.'

This statement, by a twenty-two year old female ex-Art student, exemplifies the sort of assertion that many of the more committed drugtakers made. Many of them appeared to have an almost romantic reaction against the perceived materialism of society. In general, those who put such views most ardently were those most deeply involved with drugtaking, but members of the three main sub-groups all expressed basic doubts about the validity of accepted social values. In general, the students and middle-class bohemians were less likely to express extreme hostility to society. Such opinions were mainly reported by low-status unemployed or manual workers:

> 'Being a drugtaker means that you are prepared to see society as it really is. Conventional people don't bother to question their environment. I think most drugtakers are basically people who care about the sort of world they live in. The drug-scene is idealistic.'

Comments like this are far removed from the critical appraisal of drugtakers as misfits or psychotics. Many drugtakers expressed a view that in fact they were a right-minded, yet generally misunderstood, minority. Erving Goffman, discussing social stigma, stresses the importance of deviants vocalizing their shared feelings:

> 'The names of well-known friends and enemies of the "group" are cited, along with information to confirm the goodness or the badness of these people. Success stories are printed, tales of heroes of assimilation who have penetrated new areas of normal acceptance. Atrocity tales are recorded, recent and historic, of extreme mistreatment by normals.' (Goffman 1968:37)

Becoming a drugtaker involves a process of social redefinition. If people regarded being a drugtaker as contemptible or pathetic they would not be attracted to this identity, if they had freedom of choice in the matter. In fact people become drugtakers because they have a positive evaluation of those who already use drugs and they wish to share in their collective identity. Matza and Sykes suggest that not all groups in society espouse middle-class values. In addition to the 'official' values of society, they suggest, there are 'subterranean' values:

> 'One of these, for example, is the search for excitement, for new "kicks". Society . . . tends to provide institutionalized periods in which these subterranean values are allowed to emerge and take precedence. Thus we have the world of leisure: of holidays, festivals and sport in which subterranean values are expressed rather than the rules of the workaday existence.' (Matza and Sykes 1961:716)

Jock Young (1971) applying A. K. Cohen's views on sub-cultural values to drugtaking, suggests there are two distinct value systems involved: formal work values and subterranean values:

	Formal work values	*Subterranean values*
1	deferred gratification	short-term hedonism
2	planned future action	spontaneity
3	conformity to bureaucratic rules	ego-expressivity
4	fatalism, high control over detail, little over direction	autonomy, control of behaviour in detail and direction
5	routine, predictability	new experience, excitement
6	instrumental attitudes to work	activities performed as an end-in-themselves.
7	hard productive work a virtue	disdain for work

The formal values, Young states, are not identical with the Protestant ethic. The latter interprets man's true nature through work and duty, the formal values regard work as purely instrumental. Young suggests that the Protestant ethic, outside the liberal professions, has declined.

> 'The high division of labour and rationalization of occupational roles have made them inadequate as vehicles of personal desires and expressivity. Work has come to be regarded instrumentally by nearly all sectors of society, middle class as much as working class.' (Young 1971:127)

Drugtaking was part of the social, leisure behaviour of the groups I observed. The students and middle-class groups were generally motivated to achieve their goals within the formal system of values and, indeed, several were embodiments of the Protestant ethic of intense interest in work for its own sake. The values of the drugtaking groups were essentially leisure values, though it must be emphasized that Young's two value systems are ideal types and most of those observed or interviewed had a divided allegiance. Most of the respondents compartmentalized their roles as drugtakers to their out-of-work hours. Some of the low-status unemployed or manual workers had adopted drugtaking as their primary identity, and stressed their attachment to the 'hippy ethic': 'I'm a head. I don't dig work, I doubt that I shall ever have a straight job again.'

There was a fairly explicit ideological commitment perceived by many of those who had become drugtakers. Several respondents reported that they regarded becoming a drugtaker as a process of choosing between contrasting value systems. One student expressed this separation from the mainstream of society by maintaining that 'freaks are people who can't get-it-together in straight society'. 'Getting-it-together' was a popular phrase amongst the low-status unemployed and manual workers. This was a flexible expression, but often referred to the ability to organize their lives or secure a job.

Many individuals talked to me at length about their ideal conceptions of society and how they intended to live in future. Several stated quite definitely that when they became drugtakers, they did so because they had made a thoroughgoing philosophical decision. The themes or values emphasized during such statements were generally consistent with the subterranean value system Young applies to drugtakers. Amongst the students and middle-class bohemians these values were acknowledged in an ambivalent way. Some respondents stated that they were aware of the danger of getting 'too involved' with the drug scene:

> 'Last year some students got into a "heavy scene", tripping all the time and smoking a lot of dope. Some of them got pretty messed up and were spaced out (under the influence of drugs) for weeks at a time. I don't want that to happen to me.'

While most of the students and middle-class bohemians appeared well able to control their drug use so that it did not interfere with their education or careers, some individuals did clearly have trouble in reconciling their routine commitments and being deeply involved with drugtaking. This relates to the numbers of respondents who had been downwardly mobile, or had dropped out of college, since becoming drugtakers. In general the students and middle-class bohemians were occupationally conformist and disapproved of what they regarded as excessive drug involvement. Such behaviour was discouraged within these two sub-groups and was more compatible with the ethos of the low-status unemployed or manual workers. As I shall indicate later, there was evidence that many respondents had 'fallen' from the conformist sub-groups and had become members of the low-status sub-group.

The general leisure behaviour of the different groups of drugtakers was related to the time they had available and their social positions. The students and middle-class bohemians spent less time in public houses and cafes than did the low-status unemployed or manual workers, who, like the youths Patrick observed in his study of a Glasgow gang (1973), seemed bored most of the time. Nevertheless, there was a certain classlessness about the overall leisure behaviour I noted. Fashions, music, and literature were relatively uniform, though my impression was that the manual workers were more 'extreme' in their activities. Great emphasis was placed upon spontaneity and excitement. Particularly amongst the low-status unemployed and manual workers there was an intense interest in seeking kicks, and a corresponding disregard, or professed disdain for conventional inhibitions against such hedonism. My observations corroborated Matza and Sykes' view that there is a continuum between 'acceptable' middle-class leisure pursuits, which are compatible with the work ethic, and undiluted pleasure-seeking, which replaces it. It is significant that one statement of hippy philosophy is called *Playpower* (Neville 1971).

The drug scene is a consequence of social forces and the ideological results of those forces – middle-class boredom, and working-class status-frustration. The aim of the drugtaker is to 'get high', to 'take a trip', to become 'spaced out'. The jargon of the drug scene emphasizes experience, sensation, and excitement. Many of those with the greatest involvement with the drug scene openly held work in contempt and eulogized their own 'freedom' by asserting that, as Marx claimed, work was alienating.

Some of the low-status unemployed and manual workers had little concern for long-term goals. Some talked vaguely about 'getting a cottage together', but, in view of the price of buying a cottage in Gloucestershire, and their lack of funds, few achieved this goal.

In general, materialism was disdained, though I sensed an ambivalence in the obvious admiration some of the low-status unemployed and manual workers exhibited for people who were wealthy. One individual commented about the affluence of a well-known singer whom he believed to be a junkie: 'All that bread. Man, he really fooled the system. He beat the straights at their own game. He's a junkie man, and just look at him. He's a millionaire.'

The theme of creativity was ubiquitous. A very high proportion of the study group wrote poetry, painted, or had some form of artistic interest or hobby. A few of the low-status unemployed or manual workers lived, or tried to live, by selling craftwork they made themselves. In fact most of those whom I encountered who tried to live in this way, were supported by Social Security payments, rather than by their own produce. I shall discuss the employment patterns of the sub-groups in the section on lifestyles later. It was apparent that some individuals claimed to have rejected 'the system' and 'straight' employment, yet were prepared to accept financial support from the society they rejected. Others made genuine attempts to become self-sufficient and a few were successful in earning a living through their artistic abilities.

Many respondents asserted that they expressed their individuality through their lifestyle, clothes, length or style of hair, and by their refusal to work. To an outsider, this may be interpreted as an assertion of membership of a group rather than literal individuality. There certainly seemed to be considerable uniformity in styles of dress – T-shirts, 'loon' pants, etc. One student observed that: 'even protest wears a uniform now'.

Using a 'middle-class' or 'conformist' definition of deviance, only the low-status unemployed or manual workers appeared to have rejected the 'formal values' of society at large. They were either economically underprivileged, and had no hope of gaining their objectives (society's rewards) through work, or had, like the college drop-outs, and those downwardly mobile, disdained, or failed to attain such rewards.

Young suggests that socialization into the work ethic is achieved by teaching people to want the material rewards obtainable, at least theoretically, through work. This socialization may fail in either of two ways:

1. If the means of obtaining these goals are unobtainable: if work suitable to realize the material aspirations of certain groups is not forthcoming.
2. If the material rewards or goals are not valued by the individuals, sections of the community which are beyond the work ethos.' (Young 1971:137)

I suggest that the low-status unemployed and manual workers correspond to the first of these alternatives, the students and middle-class bohemians only some extent to the second. Individual or group commitment to the subterranean values I have discussed was largely a reflection of social class and chances of achieving social rewards through the conventional career system.

The evidence indicated that the study group was generally radical, or uncommitted to conventional or traditional political and religious outlooks. There were clear differences between the ideological views of those interviewed. The students and middle-class bohemians were conformist in their career patterns and ideas and, as a whole, appeared highly motivated to achieve conventional middle-class status goals. Their outlook was radical, concerned with embellishing or amending society and its values rather than revolutionary or anarchist. The great majority of students and middle-class bohemians seemed content to accept the social structure and were intent upon gaining their objectives within its framework. As a group, they were idealistic, but not totally opposed to conventional society. Their commitment to the drug scene was strictly a partial one, limited by the constraints of conventional ambitions and other interests.

The most thoroughgoing drugtakers were the low-status unemployed and manual workers. These, for the reasons I have indicated, and which I shall discuss in greater detail, had least commitment to, or vested interest in, the conventional system. Their ideology was characterized by greater antipathy or indifference to conventional middle-class values (the work ethic, etc.) than was true of either students or middle-class bohemians. The low-status unemployed or manual workers emerge as the distinctive sub-group in relation to much of the ensuing discussion.

It was apparent that being a drugtaker involved more than a single type of act or single decision about morality and law. Drugtaking was a facet of the individual's chosen leisure behaviour, essentially perceived as pleasurable or beneficial. There is a rather amorphous 'youth culture' which covers the whole range of leisure activities of young adults. This has been widely discussed elsewhere (Musgrove 1964). The drugtakers I observed were members of social groups and were generally sociable people who were active participants in 'youth culture' with its characteristic styles of expressive behaviour. Music, clothing, and an emphasis on a range of activities which were regarded as 'mature' were all parts of the social behaviour of those in their teens and twenties. Several respondents suggested that drugs such as cannabis were 'social glue' symbols of their age group and reported that the debate about the legal status of cannabis was largely an intergenerational conflict.

The drugtakers in this study were distinctive in terms of political, religious, and philosophical views. They clearly regarded themselves as a distinctive section of society, although there were important differences between the main sub-groups. I shall move on to examine their patterns of association and self-images.

7. Friendship Patterns, Self-Images, and Reference Groups

I have suggested that the groups of drugtakers located during this study developed through a process of socialization amongst peers with similar values and aspirations. In this section I examine the network of drugtakers and the importance of that network to the individuals within it.

In my discussion of the processes of becoming a drugtaker I indicated that a person is attracted to a group of drugtakers by friendly contact culminating with the group becoming a reference point or embodiment of personal values. Many drugtakers stated that they regarded the use of cannabis and other illegal drugs as a mark of group solidarity and stressed their ideological alignment with those sharing their drugtaking behaviour. My observation enabled me to record some of the personal contacts between drugtakers and to establish a rudimentary idea of which individuals knew or were on friendly terms with which others. Inevitably my impressions were only partial since I could not hope to monitor the social behaviour of 200 people. I used my observations to construct a diagram illustrating the contacts I observed between respondents. Any group of people over time exhibits patterns of regular association. Some people will seek the company of certain individuals rather than others. Such regularities of association have been conceptualized in terms of sociometric structure. Sociometry is a movement founded by Moreno (1953). The literature on sociometry is an extensive one: 'Essentially, a sociometric test is a means of obtaining quantitative data on the preferences of group members for associating with other members' (Secord and Backman 1964:239).

A thoroughgoing sociometric assessment was not possible during this research. It must be emphasized that although participant observation is one recognized way of producing sociometric data, alone it is insufficient to quantify the interpersonal behaviour of the group being studied.

The Network

I collected information by being introduced by one drugtaker to another. In consequence the study group which was produced was selected for me by the drugtakers themselves, depending upon who they introduced me to and who was willing to co-operate. This method of obtaining contacts ensured that most of those interviewed were known by, and knew, other drugtakers. The only exceptions were a few individuals, usually visitors to Cheltenham, introduced to me by non-drugtakers.

Direct questions about friends would sometimes have aroused suspicion. I did, on occasion, ask such questions, but usually preferred to wait until I could observe friendly contacts as they occurred or until people volunteered the information I wanted. One of the golden rules of field research must be not to force the pace and not to ask pointed questions unnecessarily. My own experience suggests that one's subjects invariably tell you whatever you want to know eventually, without undue prompting. Often my subjects quizzed me about whom I knew and made their own comments about the usefulness of particular individuals to the research, or suggested potential respondents.

I rarely wrote notes in the field, believing this would have made my contact with my subjects appear too clinical. I recorded which drugtakers individuals were friendly with on a day-to-day basis. Some individuals were constant companions, while others were only seen to associate on single occasions. I make no attempt to depict the intensity or frequency of face-to-face contacts, except in the cases of two 'key' figures.

Initially my field-work began by contacting a few students from different colleges and two groups of non-students. Over time I was introduced to other subjects and it became evident that there was a certain amount of communication between groups I had previously regarded as separate. Some individuals were widely known and feature as key figures in the network. The two non-student groups eventually merged into a single, closely knit network and other groups blossomed, including one composed primarily of school pupils. I eventually traced the friendship patterns known to me of all 200 respondents, and produced a confusing maze of observed relationships.

The picture that emerges is that, while there were clear divisions amongst the respondents (students associating mainly with other students, and so on) each constellation of drugtakers had, at least, peripheral friendly contact with most of the others. In part, this may well be due to the fact that I traced a market situation. Cannabis was distributed mainly in two ways. First, there were sporadic supplies brought in by individuals who had been on holiday abroad or who had obtained drugs during a visit to another town or city. Much of the distribution of drugs was carried out on such a casual basis. Second, there were several regular dealers or suppliers who were known as reliable sources of supply. Some of these are included in the diagram, and appear as key figures (*Diagram II*). Respondent number 13, for example, had contacts with twenty-three respondents in several of the main groups I located because he regularly sold small amounts of cannabis and other drugs to them. Number 24 is another individual who engaged in dealing and who was a fairly well known source of supply. My observations suggested that such individuals were invariably well liked as well as well known, though there were notable exceptions. Drug dealing is a risky side-line and most dealers were careful to choose their customers in order to maintain their anonymity. I knew several drug dealers who were almost certainly unknown to the police because of their great care in restricting their activities to a closed group of friends.

I must emphasize that the diagrams only depict the patterns of association I noted between those drugtakers I interviewed. Most of the respondents had other friends who used drugs and my observation of the various groups was far from comprehensive. I could, beyond doubt, have interviewed many more individuals in each of the three main sub-groups than I did. At the end of my field-work I was in a particularly strong position to have continued interviewing the low-status unemployed and manual workers. This sub-group was in many ways the hardest to 'penetrate' successfully and as my interviewing progressed, I became generally better known and trusted. After a while I was accepted as part of the scene and was able to attach myself to various groups without apparently occasioning suspicion or resentment.

The Sub-Groups

I have suggested that important distinctions existed between three main sub-groups of respondents. From my informal encounters with individuals in the field I produced a list of those patterns of contact with other respondents (non-respondents are not included). The diagram shows how I was led by one drugtaker to his or her friends and acquaintances. There was a considerable overlap between the main sub-groups. As the diagram indicates, thirty-two of the forty middle-class bohemians knew of at least one individual in either the student or low-status unemployed and manual worker sub-groups, and there was a great deal of interaction between respondents. Nevertheless, my general distinction between the sub-groups is valid, since most of the interaction I observed was within each of these groups. As the diagram shows, most of the low-status unemployed and manual workers interacted more with others of their own sub-group than with either students or middle-class bohemians, and the other respondents similarly kept mainly within their own sub-groups. Ninety-eight individuals, 49.0 per cent of the study group, were observed to associate only with others of their own sub-group, and most of the other respondents appeared to spend more time within their sub-groups than with others. I must emphasize that my impressions of the patterns of interaction were probably distorted by the way I located my subjects. Many of the clusters which appear on the diagram represent groups of friends I encountered during field-work. I cannot accurately represent the frequency or intensity of contact between individuals, since I knew some better than others, and was able to observe some individuals more extensively than others. A good example of the nature of one of these clusters is centred around respondent number 12. My first contact was respondent 12, a middle-class bohemian. He introduced me to his brother, number 42, and to their friends, 1, 41, 43, 44, 45 and 47, all of whom belonged to the same sub-group, except numbers 44 and 45 who were university students. My informal encounters with these respondents indicated that they were close friends who spent considerable time in each other's company and that all had other friends, some of whom were

Diagram I

The Sub-groups

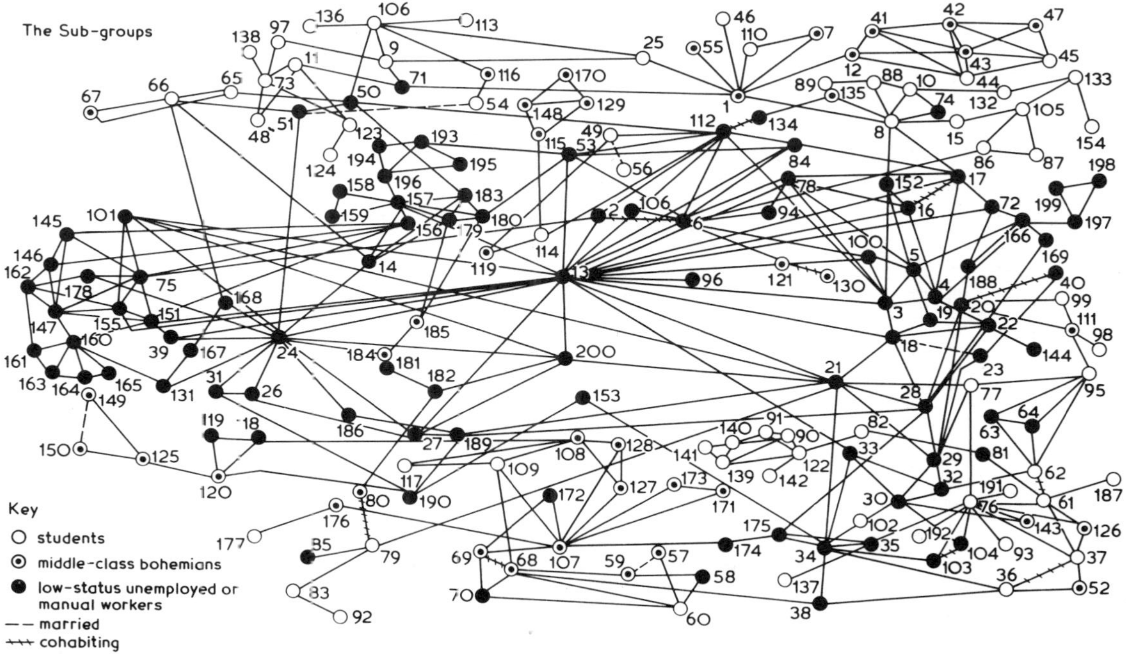

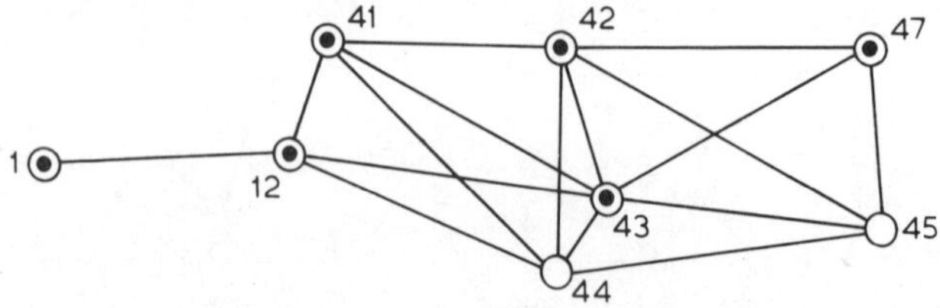

non-drugtakers. All came from middle-class families and five of the seven came from affluent professional backgrounds. Over the months I observed these individuals, who were all males, they all went out with girls who, for varying reasons, were not interviewed formally, though several had at different times used drugs. There can be little doubt that this 'cluster' represents a meaningful group of friends but depicts only one of the networks of which each individual was a member. For example, respondent 47 was a keen amateur musician and had a large group of primarily non-drugtaking friends in connection with that interest. Respondent 1 was a young professional whose friends included several students as well as other middle-class bohemians, who were interviewed. It would be possible to make a similar analysis of each of the configurations of individuals within the diagram. The point is that many had very close ties with some respondents and also with people who were not interviewed, some of whom were non-drugtakers.

My general impression was that the middle-class bohemians had more contact with the students than with the low-status unemployed or manual workers. Only two of the forty middle-class bohemians, respondents 184 and 185, were observed to spend more time associating with low-status unemployed or manual workers than with students. This supports my contention that there were great similarities between the two mainly conformist, middle-class sub-groups. Altogether, twenty-two of the middle-class bohemians had friends who were students, compared with only thirteen who had friends in the low-status sub-group. Nevertheless, it is clear that although respondents generally spent more time with others from the same sub-group, there was considerable interaction across sub-group boundaries and several individuals spent a great deal of time with people from all three sub-groups.

The nature and extent of the associations I observed was related to the social positions of those concerned. Twenty-nine individuals

Diagram II

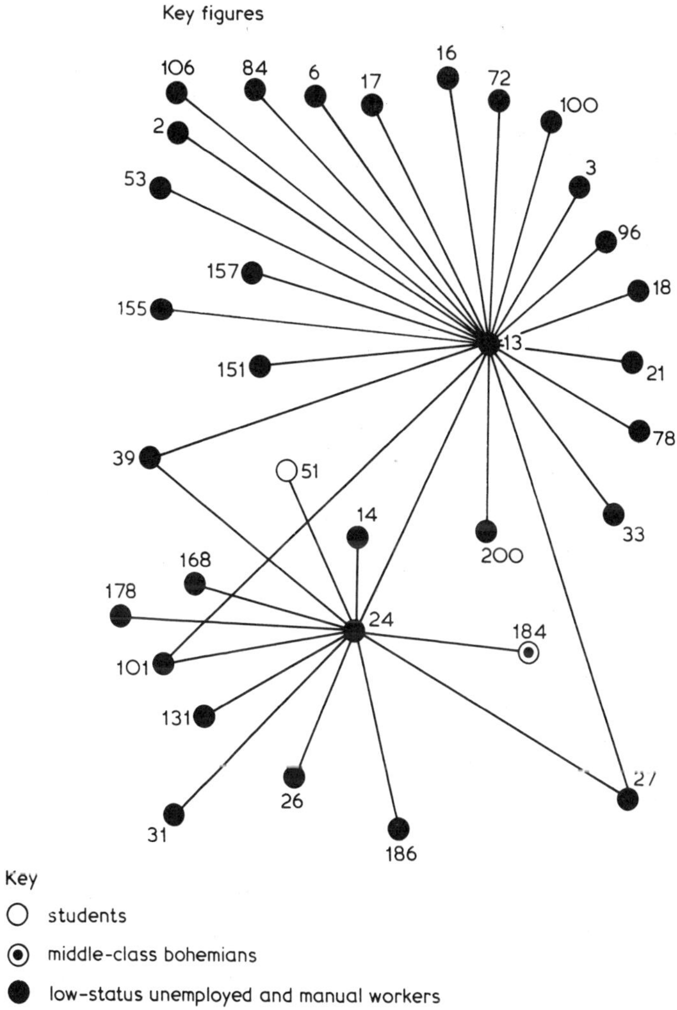
Key figures
106
84
6
17
16
72
100
2
3
53
96
157
18
155
13
151
21
78
39
51
14
33
200
168
178
24
184
101
131
26
27
31
186
Key
students
middle-class bohemians
low-status unemployed and manual workers

Diagram III

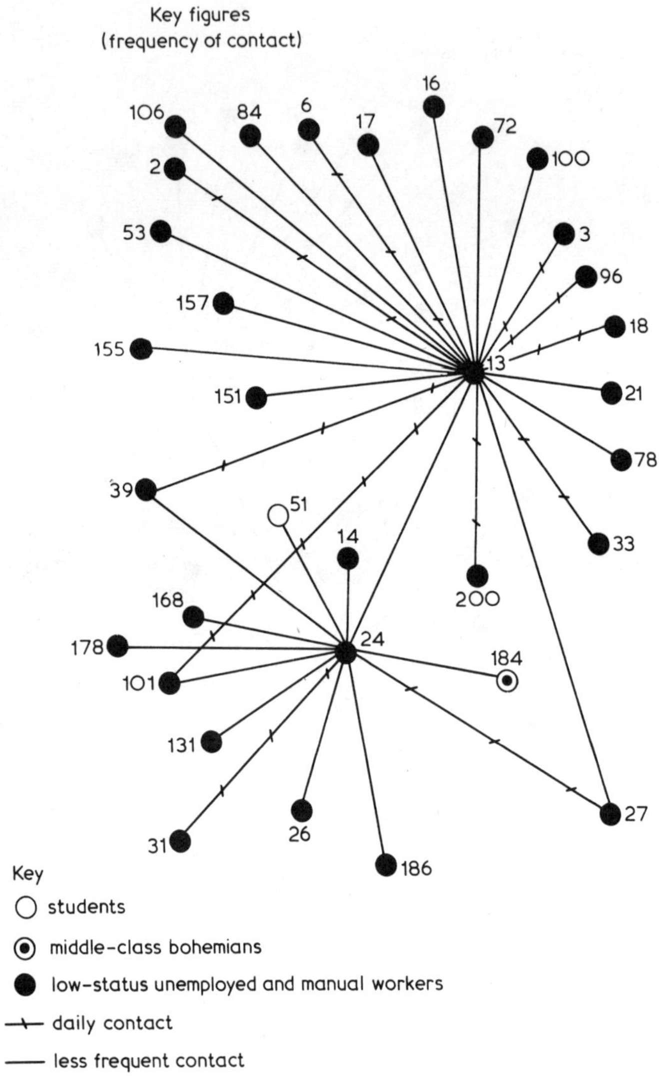
Key figures
(frequency of contact)
106
84
6
17
16
72
100
2
53
3
96
157
18
155
13
151
21
78
39
51
33
14
200
168
24
178
184
101
131
27
26
31
186
Key
students
middle-class bohemians
low-status unemployed and manual workers
daily contact
less frequent contact

Diagram IV

Unemployed through choice

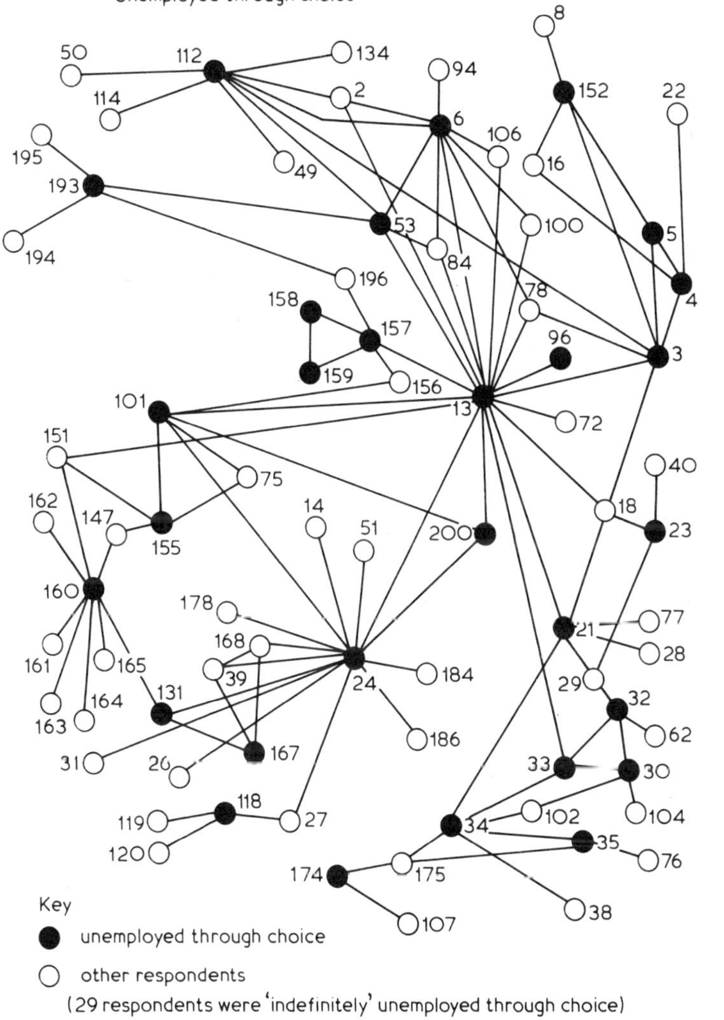

interviewed were unemployed through choice and reported that they regarded their unemployment as indefinite. In many ways these individuals were amongst those most deeply involved with drugtaking. As the third diagram shows, there was considerable face-to-face contact between these individuals (represented by the black dots) and other respondents. Altogether, the twenty-nine respondents unemployed indefinitely through choice were observed to associate with fifty-seven other respondents (see *Diagram IV*). Each individual knew an average of 5.7 other respondents. This emphasizes the great importance to the network of the low-status unemployed, who spent a great deal of time in each other's company and with other drugtakers.

The most gregarious of the sub-groups observed were the low-status unemployed and manual workers who spent a lot of time in public houses and cafes, or visiting other drugtakers. Those who were unemployed had little else to do but to meet others in a similar situation. Most of the unemployed through choice appeared to spend much of their time with other experienced drugtakers. In contrast, the students and middle-class bohemians appeared to spend most of their free time at home, or at friends' houses, rather than in public houses and cafes. I noted less social contact between these respondents, since their leisure time was much more restricted.

Most cannabis smoking occurred in private, and was usually amongst small groups of friends. I rarely observed more than a dozen people smoking cannabis on any single occasion; usually it was smoked by a group of half that size. The only exceptions to this were on well publicized occasions when drugs were conspicuously used at rock festivals or open-air concerts. In general, cannabis smoking in public places was regarded as risky or 'uncool' and was disapproved of.

My observations lead me to conclude that, in spite of the clear differences between individuals, there was a network of drugtakers known to each other by face-to-face contact. This conclusion was limited by my failure to note contacts with non-drugtakers. I knew that many individuals, especially middle-class respondents, had friends who did not use drugs and any appraisal of individual self-image or reference group must take into account the balance between contact with drugtakers and contact with non-drugtakers. The existence of a distinctive drugtaking milieu, with values and objectives of its own, presupposes that for at least some of those involved this is the primary reference point.

Source of Friends

Since I was unable to observe all of the friendly contacts between respondents and non-drugtakers, a question was included in the structured interview to examine with whom drugtakers mainly associated. My conversations with different individuals indicated that they often stressed that they saw themselves as primarily either drugtakers or non-drugtakers, depending on their general self-image. Some middle-class people stated that although they used drugs, they were not deeply involved with the associated way of life and did not let drugtaking interfere with their careers. Other individuals claimed to have cut themselves off from 'straight' society and that they mixed only with other 'heads'. While my observations suggested that friendships were generally consistent with reported self-images, it was not possible to evaluate the importance to each individual of contact with drugtakers or non-drugtakers without asking a direct question during interview. I believe that the question, 'What is your main source of friends?' elicited the respondent's self-image as much as an objective comment upon whom most of his friends were. It seemed logical and obvious that drugtakers will know other drugtakers, and that some of those who encounter drugtakers will, eventually, use drugs themselves. Altogether, 65.0 per cent of the study group stated that most of their friends had used drugs.

Multi-users were significantly more likely than users to report that most of their friends were drugtakers.[1] Altogether, 106 of the 142 multi-users, roughly two-thirds, reported that most of their friends were drugtakers, compared with only twenty-four of the fifty-six users, less than half.

These findings are consistent with my observations that many of the drugtakers I located had relatively little friendly contact with people who had not used drugs. As *Diagram IV* shows, most of the twenty-nine individuals who were indefinitely unemployed through choice were observed to be on friendly terms with each other and some were daily companions. Those individuals who were, for whatever reasons, unemployed, had a great deal of opportunity to visit, and spend time with, their friends. Most were living with or near other drugtakers and I noted that friendly interaction with drugtakers

[1] Throughout this book statements of 'statistical' or 'significant' association mean that a Chi-squared analysis revealed a probable difference of at least 95 per cent ($p < .05$).

Table 6
Main source of friends

	students				*non-students*				*Total*	
	users		*multi-users*		*users*		*multi-users*			
	male	*female*	*male*	*female*	*male*	*female*	*male*	*female*	*N*	%
non-drugtakers	9	2	4	3	2	1	7	1	29	14.5
evenly divided	7	3	5	2	9	1	13	1	41	20.5
drugtakers	7	3	22	6	5	9	63	15	130	65.0
total	23	8	31	11	16	11	83	17	200	100.0

was probably most frequent amongst those with the greatest drug-using experience, particularly those who had given up, or had a low commitment to, work.

Once a person becomes a drugtaker, he redefines his identity in such a way that he reduces his feeling of being an 'outsider'. As a drugtaker in a group of non-drugtakers he may be ill at ease and feel threatened. As one of a group of people with a common pattern of illegal behaviour, he is safer and a conformist within the frame of reference of the group.

Some individuals were on the fringe of the drug-scene and spent most of their time with non-drugtakers. Twenty-eight individuals, 14.0 per cent of the study group, had used only a single type of drug, cannabis. Only five of these reported that most of their friends had used drugs. Nine of these twenty-nine individuals had smoked cannabis for at least four years, yet appeared only partially involved with the drugtaking lifestyle. It is questionable to what extent, or in what way such individuals are labelled 'drugtakers'. By their own reports, and in terms of their drug histories, they had only a casual or minimal intermittent involvement with the drug scene.

It is important to bear in mind the fact that in addition to people who use drugs, there are others who tolerate the use of drugs or who share many of the attitudes and much of the lifestyle of the drug scene. I knew many individuals who lived and dressed like drugtakers and who were on friendly terms with drugtakers yet who, for various reasons, refrained from drug use themselves. It was clear that not all those included in the study group regarded the drug scene as their primary reference point, though they were prepared to identify themselves partially with it. There were many cannabis users who had tried the drug, out of curiosity, only a few times. I knew many people in this category and it is likely that thousands of young people in Britain have used cannabis experimentally. Most probably derived little, if any, significant effect from these few experiments. Some of those who use, or have used, drugs, do not regard themselves as drugtakers simply because they have not formed a commitment to the ethos of the drug scene. They may be sympathetic to the idea of other people using drugs more regularly but many of the casual experimenters I encountered stated that they had no intention of adopting drugtaking as their way of life. Most of the students, and those working at the time of interview, regarded drugtaking as a leisure activity and appeared well adjusted to their occupational or educational roles. Amongst some groups of young people a certain amount of recreational drugtaking was commonplace.

It is possible for many young people to mix with individuals who have used drugs without a drastic change in their lifestyles, as long as their own group is in a situation where there are strong attachments to clear and attainable goals. In a college or university most students are eager to finish their courses and to qualify academically. The norms therefore encourage academic effort and drugtaking is generally well regulated. Excessive drugtaking is regarded as foolish and dangerous to scholastic performance.

In groups with less attachment to 'cultural goals' (to use Merton's term) drugtaking may assume a higher priority. Intensive drug use is incompatible with meeting the demands of a normal job or education and most drugtakers realize this and, accordingly, restrict their own drug use. Most of the students who had used drugs drew a similar distinction between themselves and 'real heads' or 'junkies' to the one that is used to differentiate 'social drinkers' from alcoholics. The point they often made was that one may abuse virtually any chemical substance, be it cannabis, tobacco, alcohol, or heroin. A very large number of the drugtakers I encountered made this assertion, pointing to the fact that just as a high a proportion of alcohol users are not preoccupied with the drug, so many cannabis users and other drugtakers are neither physically dependent on, nor necessarily greatly influenced or perceptibly harmed by, the substances of their choice. This sort of comment indicated that many drugtakers regarded the stereotype of the junkie as the model that should be used to identify a 'problem drugtaker'. Clearly most of those I encountered did not regard themselves as junkies, whom they regarded as sick and unattractive figures.

The outsider's general definition of a drugtaker is clearly different from those of the drugtakers themselves, who tended to distinguish between the various categories of person covered by the general label 'drugtaker'. Many respondents stated that though they regularly used drugs, they did not accept that they were preoccupied with drugs in the sense implied by everyday use of the term 'drugtaker'.

Reference Groups

The influence of a group on the outlook of an individual is often discussed in terms of the concept of reference groups. A reference group is a group taken as a frame of reference for attitude formation and self-evaluation. Secord and Backman point out that such a group can have one or both of two functions:

> 'First it may set and enforce standards of conduct and belief: this has been called the normative function of a reference group. Second, it may serve as a standard or comparison point against which persons compare themselves and others: this has been called the comparison function.' (Second and Backman 1964:209)

It was clear from my field observations that some people were much more deeply involved with drugtaking than others. The majority of students and middle-class bohemians had 'conventional' career and status aspirations and were more peripheral to the drug using way of life than many of the low-status unemployed or manual workers. Some individuals stated unequivocally that they were 'heads', 'freaks', etc. and appeared to regard themselves primarily as drug-takers.

My conversations with several hundred individuals showed that there were great differences between self-images, values, and goals. In general these reference points were consistent with overall social position and with the balance between status opportunities at any one time. The processes of becoming, or ceasing to be, a drugtaker involved identification both with face-to-face contacts, peers and friends, and with more distant figures. Many individuals appeared to model themselves upon people they regarded as exemplars of their self-images. I knew several people deeply involved with the drug scene who were clearly influenced by cult figures such as pop musicians, political, or religious leaders. Many moulded their clothes and behaviour to imitate their idols and my impression was that the formation of self-images was significantly affected by distant, admired people selected as exemplars. Most of the study group were working or were in full-time education and appeared to take their primary orientations from mainstream society. These 'conformists' clearly saw themselves as guided by conventional status ambitions and modelled their lives to pursue these goals. Many students spent a good deal of time discussing academic matters and were as likely to quote the utterances of academics as of pop stars. On the other hand, many of the low-status unemployed or manual workers had 'unconventional' folk-heroes, such as Hell's Angels or rock musicians, who were regarded as models for imitation and admiration. Some of the unemployed appeared to regard themselves as potential musical stars even if they had no chance whatever of reaching this goal. Many young people are interested in rock music, wear long hair, and have pictures of their idols. Many referred to well-known individuals who advocated drug use, in order to justify their own behaviour.

Some groups of individuals became attracted to religious cults, which sometimes involved a rejection of drugtaking. Some dramatic and rapid 'conversions' occurred, involving a fairly drastic change of lifestyle and self-image. I knew one group of students who were all frequent users of hallucinogenic drugs and who claimed they derived profound mystical experiences through these drugs. They associated almost exclusively with other drugtakers and spent a considerable amount of time reading literature supporting drugtaking. Within a short period of time the group, who all lived in the same building, became members of a religious sect which disapproved of the use of drugs. Overnight, virtually, all drugtaking ceased and several of the males had their hair cut short as an outward sign of their metamorphosis. All drug-oriented literature was discarded and was replaced by religious pamphlets and books on mysticism and meditation. In addition, posters of musical stars were taken down and a shrine to the newly espoused religious leaders was erected. Several individuals denied that this was the replacement of one personality cult for another but this is a possible interpretation. One aspect of such transitions that I noted was that 'extreme' religious cults often provided a much more explicit and unequivocal lifestyle than those which people had before. Some cults were quite disciplined and claimed to provide absolute answers and values. These were especially attractive to individuals feeling lost or uncertain about their roles in society, including some who found it hard to make friends.

Many drugtakers were dissatisfied with society as it is. Some were radical or wanted to find 'real', dependable, or worthwhile values and goals. This outlook was held in common with many peers and was apparently consistent with the literature, lifestyle, and folk-heroes of those concerned. Amongst the well-known figures especially revered were those noted for their musical or artistic prowess or those seen as visionaries, critics of the existing social order, or advocates of a new one.

The differences in level of commitment to the drug using milieu are illustrated by these three hypothetical case histories illustrating each of the three main sub-groups:

case I: Jenny, a student-teacher smokes cannabis regularly at weekends when her boyfriend stays with her. She sometimes uses hallucinogenic drugs such as L.S.D. which she believes are spiritually inspiring. She is a conscientious student and ensures that her drug use does not impede her academic progress.

case II: Steven left school at fifteen and has been more out of work than in it. He has no career ambitions and leads a generally aimless existence. Boredom is interrupted only by his involvement with a group of working-class drugtakers. His use of legal and illegal drugs is considerable. He is delinquent, promiscuous, and estranged from his parents who live nearby.

case III: David is an office worker in his mid-twenties. He began smoking cannabis at parties with a group of friends who were students. He has used L.S.D., D.M.T., and mescalin and feels rather guilty about his drug use, which he believes would be disapproved of by his friends at work, most of whom are older than him. He keeps his drug use secret and regards himself as a Walter Mitty character.

Some individuals had less to lose by becoming deeply involved with drugtaking than others. Those most deeply committed to drugtaking regarded other drugtakers as their models and created a form of reference based upon the shared characteristics of drugtakers and epitomized by well-known cult fugures. Everyone has more than one reference group but it was apparent that those with the least commitment to career or status goals placed more importance upon being a drugtaker than those with greater commitment.

A person's primary reference group may or may not be the group to which he belongs. Most respondents had become drugtakers, or had ceased to be drugtakers, due to the influence of their peer groups.

Some individuals, such as the office worker described in the third case study, were aware of a conflict between their career roles and roles as drugtakers. Others were in situations that lent far greater support to drug use. Some of the respondents had little need to conceal their drugtaking since they spent most of their time with other drugtakers. They were members of their reference groups, while not having reference groups outside the drug scene. I knew several individuals who, because of career requirements, had to keep their drugtaking a well-guarded secret. Usually such people were only peripherally involved with drugtaking, or at least, accepted that their jobs or education were of primary importance.

8. Drugtakers as a Sub-Culture

Schur, commenting upon drug addiction in Britain during the early 1960s, asserted that there was no drug sub-culture like the one that had developed in the United States (Schur 1966). He based his discussion on the fact that in the United States addicts were forced to break the law to obtain drugs, whereas in Britain prescribing policies did not place such heavy financial pressures upon addicts. In this chapter, I shall evaluate the idea that the drugtakers I observed and interviewed were a sub-culture. It must be emphasized that Schur referred only to individuals who were drug dependent; users of opiates, The drugtakers in this study were not junkies attending treatment centres and few appeared to be physically drug dependent.

The drugtakers described in this study were part of a network of individuals with shared values and a characteristic form of behaviour, namely illegal drug use. The evidence of the survey corroborated my observations that there was a high degree of in-group solidarity and that most of those interviewed associated mainly with other drugtakers.

The evidence suggests that there was considerable variation between individual drugtakers but that many regarded their drugtaking as an important part of their lifestyles and preferred to associate with other drugtakers. Most of the students and non-manual workers did not appear to define themselves primarily as drugtakers, but had definite career and status objectives quite apart from their drug use. There appeared to be a continuum of commitment to drugtaking which was related to the general social position of the individual users. Taking into account this continuum, many of the drugtakers interviewed evidently regarded themselves as a distinctive social group:

> 'Being a head means that you're outside "straight" society. You can never be straight once you've started smoking (cannabis). You see through the system and want to get out of it.'

Some drugtakers were emphatic that they disliked associating with non-drugtakers. They described non-drugtakers as repressed and narrow, unable to be spontaneous and tending to authoritarianism.

> 'Man, like I can't talk to straights. They give me bad vibes. You're not really straight because your ideas are like mine. It's nothing to do with short hair. Straights are playing games all the time. I keep away from them.'

The idea that drugtakers are a deviant group within society was emphasized both by drugtakers and by non-drugtakers. Since Cohen's use of the term 'sub-culture' in his book *Delinquent Boys* (1955) this concept has been widely applied in relation to deviant behaviour. Cohen suggested there was a characteristic lifestyle amongst urban delinquents in America. The term sub-culture has been applied to many social groups. As David Downes comments: 'Sub-culture has evidently been used as an 'ad hoc' concept wherever the writer wished to stress the normative aspects of any behaviour that differed from some general standard.' (Downes 1966a:9).

The essential feature of a sub-culture is that it is a group within society that has characteristic counter-norms. Downes points out that:

> 'The concept of the 'subculture' embodies one . . . contradiction. What constitutes the 'culture' of a complex society: all its subcultures, their uniformities only, or the dominant subculture? Where, to put it crudely, does culture end and subculture begin? Does subculture refract or totally displace culture?' (Downes 1966a:4–5)

There is clearly a problem of definition. This must be confronted before attempting to use sub-cultural theories of deviant behaviour. Cohen suggested that sub-cultures arise in order to meet specific problems· 'What people do depends upon the problems they contend with' (Cohen 1955:51). This echoes C. S. Ford's view that culture is 'traditional ways of solving problems' or of 'learned problem solutions' (Ford 1942:546–557). On the one hand culture binds people together through common frames of reference and behaviour patterns, on the other, it involves choice. 'Culture' can only exist if the possibility of choice (or deviation) are present.

Downes suggest that good solutions create no new problems, and so a satisfactory solution will be reinforced or validated by the support of one's fellows. A sub-cultural solution, then, involves the support by other people of chosen ways of solving problems. Downes further points out that the 'migration' of an individual from one group to another need not involve the formation of a sub-culture:

> '. . . this can only emerge where there exist, in effective interaction with one another, a number of actors with similar problems of adjustment, for whom no effective solution as yet exists for a common, shared problem. Only on this basis is the joint elaboration of a new solution possible: and it emerges on a group basis, via the process of mutual conversion to a new point of view. That the group basis is a necessary catalyst is illustrated in extreme forms by the behaviour of 'crowds' or 'mobs'. These kinds of 'collective behaviour' embody quickly worked-out collective solutions to common problems: the moral frame of reference is not so much obliterated as rapidly transferred. This emergence of new 'group standards' is synonymous with that of a new subculture: it is simply that, in the area of 'collective behaviour' the subculture so hastily created is short-lived.' (Downes 1966a:7)

The theory of collective response to temporary problems has been expounded elsewhere (Smelser 1962). As Downes suggests, a sub-culture lasts as long as the initial problems remain unresolved, unless the sub-culture begins to perform additional functions. Cohen suggests: 'The crucial condition for the emergence of new cultural forms is the existence, in effective interaction with one another, of a number of actors with similar problems of adjustment' (Cohen 1955:59).'

The classic explanation of sub-cultures attributes their emergence to a corporate need for status. Cohen comments upon this situation in *Delinquent Boys:*

> 'If we lack the characteristics or capacities which give status in terms of these criteria, we are beset by one of the most typical and yet distressing of human problems of adjustment. One solution is

> for individuals who share such problems to gravitate towards one another and jointly to establish new norms, new criteria of status which define as meritorious the characteristics they do possess, the kinds of conduct of which they are capable. It is clearly necessary for each participant, if the innovation is to solve his status problem, that these new criteria be shared with others, that the solution be a group, and not a private solution. If he "goes it alone" he succeeds only in further estranging himself from his fellows. Such new status criteria would represent new subcultural values different from, or even antithetical to those of the larger social system.' (Cohen 1955:65–6)

David Downes in similar vein, comments:

> 'The more severely we are found lacking by these (criteria), the more we are faced by a "problem of adjustment". Those sharing such a problem could respond to it by gravitating towards one another and establishing new criteria of status, based on attributes they do possess: these new criteria may be different to those of the former group. The more the former group rejects the new, the more the new is strengthened in its emergent norms. The new group's value-system is further reinforced if its members devalue the esteem of the former group. The former group becomes the 'out-group', toward which hostility is felt, and whose members are repudiated as "outsiders".' (Downes 1966a:8)

Downes suggests that not all problems are met by sub-cultural solutions. He criticizes Cohen's theories on the grounds that he fails to distinguish between sub-cultures that lie beyond the 'dominant culture' of society and those that originate within it. Regional cultures exemplify the former and occupational cultures the latter. Beyond doubt, the term sub-culture has been used in a confusing variety of ways. On the one hand, it serves as a useful ideal type or hypothetical model, on the other, it is used descriptively to apply to empirical cases. Fishermen, farmers, the working-class, and beatniks have all been described as sub-cultures. The term has been used whenever writers wished to point to the distinctive features of a group within society. Several important problems arise from this ambiguity and lack of uniformity. First, if it is generally agreed that a sub-culture is part of a wider social structure, how and where does one draw the boundaries of the sub-culture in view of the likely similarities between all people in a single society? If we admit that drugtakers are different from non-drugtakers, are they necessarily a sub-culture if they generally resemble other people? Statements that a distinctive drugtaking sub-culture exists should be prefaced by a definition of what constitutes a sub-culture. It would be possible to describe virtually any aggregate of people and to identify similarities that separate them from other people. This need not imply that they are a sub-culture. I suggest that in the present study we are concerned with a group of people who, in addition to sharing a specific, illegal type of behaviour, namely cannabis use, had a generally distinctive ideology. In face of the great differences existing between the subjects of this study the term sub-culture can be applied only as an ideal type and not as a precise description of things as they really appeared to be.

Jock Young suggests that there is a drugtaking sub-culture which is a collective response to specific problems. The evidence of this study indicated that the drugtaking behaviour of those observed and interviewed was largely social rather than solitary, and that those individuals most deeply committed to drugtaking had indeed evolved a distinctive lifestyle and system of values. These were essentially an extreme form of the leisure values of the general youth culture. The notion of sub-culture is a stereotype in itself. As Simmons suggests, Yablonsky's concept of the 'near-group' as: 'a collectivity of people whose degree of cohesion and organisation falls somewhere between a mob and a true group' is a more useful description of the way deviants associate together.

Simmons takes issue with the idea that a deviant 'sub-culture' is necessarily monolithically cohesive, or paramount, as has sometimes been implied in the literature:

> 'There are shared understandings among the participants, but their interpersonal relations are also shot through with many misunderstandings and miscarried intentions. Any "organization" is usually informal, uncrystallized and unstable beyond a few weeks.' (Simmons 1969:89)

My own observations are consistent with Simmons' remarks:

> 'The ambivalence of the participants is the main thing that keeps deviant sub-cultures from becoming more solid. Most members are

of two minds about deviating and most of them still have conventional commitments. My observations suggest that the vast majority of deviants inhabit dual worlds of deviance/conventionality and when things aren't going well in the one they turn to the other. They vacillate between the two as situations and opportunities shift. This is essentially what David Matza found in his study of delinquent gangs.' (Simmons 1969:91)

Simmons' point is that, in reality, deviance is much more complex and varied than one would imagine from reading much of the literature. My own field research impressed me with the same realization. The closer I got to my subjects, the less any stereotype seemed to be a meaningful summary of their characteristics. In addition, it was obvious that many of those labelled 'drugtakers' were, generally, very similar to non-drugtakers. One would reach a similar conclusion from a study of virtually any social group. Deviants are generally only deviant in a few respects and for only some of the time. Most of my subjects led relatively 'normal' lives and had mundane daily routines. It would be a gross misrepresentation to suggest that, in all respects, they were a race apart from non-drugtakers. I could have located non-drugtakers with most of the attributes of the subjects of this study. There is a problem, then, of defining precisely what was distinctive about the individuals I observed and interviewed.

Drugtaking, as an illegal activity, is generally concealed from non-drugtakers. Drugtakers are a 'secret society', a group of initiates with a shared deviation. The illegality of cannabis use encourages secrecy in order to protect the drugtaker from social stigma and possible legal sanctions. Drugtakers are understandably wary of non-drugtakers who might be regarded as a threat, and who might endanger the drugtaker's self-image and belief in his mode of behaviour. The evidence of the present study indicates that drugtakers as a group shared and supported each other's values and goals. The primary constraint upon drugtakers was a need to preserve their anonymity and not to divulge their behaviour to outsiders. For this reason interaction with non-drugtakers was either minimized or kept separate from drugtaking behaviour.

Many drugtakers regarded their drugtaking as a statement of defiance or disapproval against officialdom and conventional opinions. There was little doubt that to many the drugtaking lifestyle was a response to generalized discontent with society as it stood. Drugtakers created a milieu that expressed their own latent values and goals. As Young suggests, they developed an immediate frame of reference, a collective response to shared outlooks and problems.

If the defining criterion of a sub-culture is a sense of group solidarity, this was evident amongst those most committed to drugtaking: 'I'm a freak, a druggy. I think I'm right and I'm proud of it.' There was no formal organization within the sub-culture, apart from gangs such as the Hell's Angels who are largely working class and quite different from any other drugtakers.

There was clearly a pecking-order, or prestige scale, amongst committed drugtakers. I heard many 'war stories' or anecdotes about individual exploits and certain individuals such as respondents 13 and 24 were well known and frequently mentioned in conversation. Some of the older drugtakers, those in their mid-twenties and thirties, were clearly highly respected and several drug dealers were also held in high regard. People who had used drugs extensively or for a long time were esteemed and cited as authorities to whom one should go for advice and guidance:

> 'Tripper has smoked for eight years now. He was one of the first heads in Cheltenham. He's very cool, and is into mysticism and self-hypnosis. If you want to find out about the scene you must talk to him. He grew up with it.'

Much of the conversation of the low-status unemployed and manual workers was concerned with events concerning conflict with the police. My impression was that the prospect of such conflict was a great source of interest and excitement. Many such discussions were self-justifying, portraying the police as malevolent and inept, and enhancing the prestige of the embattled drugtaker. Other popular themes were concerned with mocking 'straights' or non-drugtakers. On several occasions I was told about incidents when individuals had attempted to shock people whom they regarded as sedate or snobbish:

> 'Man, you should have been with us last Saturday. We all went into this cafe, see, and there were these old fools in there. They looked at us as if we were shit. I turned round to Gandalf and said out loud "Hey, man, I'm dying for a fix, have you got your needle with you?" Man, that really freaked those straights. The stupid cunts didn't know what to do. They were really freaked out man.'

A general characteristic of deviance is the wish to strengthen one's position vicariously by claiming that prestigious individuals share one's deviant behaviour. Thus, many drugtakers took great pleasure in proclaiming that well-known musicians, actors, or even politicians, were also drugtakers. I observed that in general those with the greatest interest in affirming their distinctiveness as drugtakers were those with the least social status in conventional terms, the unemployed and those with manual jobs. A more sophisticated approach was adopted by the students and middle-class bohemians who had some allegiance to conventional values and generally regarded themselves as a misunderstood minority group. Many middle-class drugtakers commented that they believed they were a sub-culture only in that they were drugtakers. Most were anxious to point out that they had conventional career ambitions and that they were not 'drop outs'.

As Downes found in his study of delinquents in East London, the working-class groups gave considerable support to delinquency and sexual exploits, but the groups did not depend solely upon one form of activity. As one respondent commented: 'Drugs are just part of the scene. They show where your head is at.'

David Matza, in his study of gangs, discovered that there was considerable ambiguity in the delinquent sub-culture:

> 'The subculture of delinquency consists of precepts and customs that are delicately balanced between convention and crime. The subculture points to objectives that may be attained through delinquency but also by other means. Its customs allow delinquency and even suggest it, but delinquency is neither demanded nor necessarily considered a preferred path. The norms and sentiments of the subculture are beliefs that function as the extenuating conditions under which delinquency is permissible.'
>
> 'The subculture of delinquency is one of many. It shares with other subcultures certain general characteristics. Foremost among these general characteristics is some degree of provisional utility or function. Subcultures are not the same as the parent culture, and they are not without social use. Beyond this, however, each subculture has special characteristics that reflect its constituency and its position in society.' (Downes 1966a:59–60)

Matza contends that there is a delinquent sub-culture. In other words, low-status urban adolescents are sympathetic to delinquency, but not all necessarily, permanently or primarily delinquent.

The concept of sub-culture was developed in relation to low-status, economically underprivileged, male delinquent gangs. It is a theoretical model, implying that individuals within a sub-culture are homogeneous, or cut off from the dominant culture of society. This need not be so. As Matza has pointed out, many deviants are ambivalent in their attitudes to their sub-cultures. Most of the drugtakers in the present study had dual commitments and only a partial or peripheral allegiance to drugtaking. Erich Goode suggests that the friendship network is the 'intervening' variable between one's background and one's pattern of drug use (Goode 1972a:39). Drugtaking stems from behaviour patterns expected within certain groups, and drug use is evident, in varying degrees, within different groups and reflects the social characteristics of the members of those groups.

The middle-class bohemians and students I encountered belonged to groups that gave considerable support to certain levels and types of drugtaking. They also regarded themselves as potential graduates, professionals, etc. and in most cases probably labelled themselves in non-drugtaking terms. Their drug-involvement was limited and relatively few placed great importance upon the role of drugtaker, which was simply one of several roles they had.

The low-status unemployed or working-class groups were in rather a different situation. Those who were unemployed through choice frequently spoke of themselves in primarily drugtaking terms. They saw themselves as drugtakers and had few, if any, career aspirations. Similarly many of those with unskilled or menial jobs were negatively oriented towards their work and were frequently explicit about their self images:

> 'I'm not "into" straight jobs. I'm working now, but only because I need bread (money). I don't mind having crap jobs because it gives me time to think. Heads are people who do a lot of thinking. That's why a lot don't keep straight jobs together.'

There were no rigid lines of demarcation within the groups of drugtakers observed. Many individuals had tangential or peripheral involvement. Others adopted the jargon of the 'hip' drug-user or junkie slang and were much more 'extreme' in their commitment. In spite of the heterogeneity of the individuals studied it was clear that many regarded themselves as a distinctive social group and that the majority conceded that, as drugtakers, they had a collective identity.

Confronted by considerable variations between individual drugtakers, it is difficult to pass from a statistical description of their attributes to a general theoretical explanation of how their drugtaking emerged and was sustained. Some of those interviewed had so little in common with other respondents that a sweeping generalization is likely to be misleading. All those interviewed had participated in illegal drug use. In addition all, to varying degrees, appeared to have some commitment to radical ideology. The primary token of group identity was the drug experience itself. This was the definitive criterion of the groups I encountered. The question: 'Do you smoke?' had a far-reaching significance, extending beyond the action of smoking a joint. My impressions indicated that drug use was seen as a conscious act of idealism, or at least, of stating one's wish to change reality, either actively through political or social means, or passively through the use of psychotropic drugs. Many non-drugtakers lived in similar housing, were unemployed, had permissive sexual attitudes, and were politically radical. I do not suggest that those attributes were peculiar to drugtakers. However, as a group, the individuals interviewed in this study were distinctive because they had made their drug use explicit to each other. They had all engaged in a common form of deviant behaviour, and by implication, either implicitly or explicitly, had all declared their renunciation of 'anti-permissive' morality. This is not to impute that all were generally deviant. Most were clearly conformist in terms of their careers and lifestyles. Nevertheless all were, to some extent, bound together by their illegal drug use and rejected the conventional assessment that drugtaking was generally regarded by the users themselves as indicative of a general attitude to life and to society. Some individuals used their identities as drugtakers to replace their 'conventional' identities. Other individuals adopted an intermediate posture. They compromised and remained conformist in relation to their work and education and used drugs as an embellishment of their leisure and an expression of their idealism, or doubts about society in its present form. Most drug experiences, whether profound or not, change one's emotions or perceptions. They are part of a wish to experiment, and to seek new experiences. Drugtaking involves at least a limited commitment to hedonism and is part of a search for new sensations. The groups I observed took this search for experiences as their central defining symbol. Those most esteemed were those with the greatest drug-experience and those whose experiences had been the most profound or unusual.

There were differences within the study group, but there was also an *esprit de corps*, a sense of general solidarity. Drugtakers acknowledged a common identity but often pointed to the differences amongst themselves. I noted many instances of great kindness and consideration being shown towards strangers who were also drugtakers. Many people often provided accommodation and food for visiting 'heads' they had met only briefly and there was an ethos supporting such hospitality and kindness to 'in-group' members.

There were some obvious differences between different groups of drugtakers. While cannabis and hallucinogenic drugs such as L.S.D. and mescalin were widely used and esteemed, the students and middle-class bohemians were overwhelmingly hostile to the use of injected drugs. In addition there were considerable differences between the middle-class drugtakers and the low-status unemployed or manual workers, to whom some students disparagingly referred as 'lumpenproletariat'.

Several groups of people who had used L.S.D. frequently had an elitist view of their relation to drugtakers who had not used psychedelics. This is a clear case of people deriving status within their own terms of reference. Similarly, individuals often broadcast the fact that they had used unusual or prestigious drugs:

> 'I was in London over the weekend, and we scored (obtained or bought) some cocaine. Man, what a buzz. It's just too much . . . I took peyote once. There was some growing in a greenhouse at Cannon Hill Park in Birmingham. We chewed it up but I didn't really trip. I just felt sick.'

Membership of the groups I observed was variable. Amongst the middle-class bohemians and students drugtaking was usually irregular and often at weekends or when friends came to visit. The low-status unemployed and working class had the least academic or career commitments and spent a great deal of time in each other's company, often in cafes or public houses. Some individuals were vagrants and often disappeared for several months, travelling to other towns to visit friends or seek pastures new. The low-status drugtaking group was very receptive to newcomers and information was passed around very quickly whenever a new 'head' appeared on the scene. I discovered that my own arrival as a researcher was rapidly advertised. This assisted my field-work, as word was circulated that I was trustworthy.

It would be specious to contend that most of those in this study were totally different from non-drugtakers. Most respondents appeared to be unremarkably different in many of their attributes from non-drugtakers. The study group and those observed were part of a continuum of overlapping sub-groups. There was considerable variation within the study group as well as clear similarities between certain groups of individuals. The three main sub-groups were not rigid entities. There were variations within each of them as well as similarities between them. The general differences between the sub-groups do permit an analytic distinction to be made between them. Much of the literature of the 'underground' press has been preoccupied with the idea of the drug scene as an alternative society. This conceptualizes the drugtaking fraternity not as an enclave within society but as an autonomous alternative beyond it. In relation to the very small number of individuals who were genuinely self-sufficient this claim is highly debatable.

Downes (1966a:9–11) discusses the suggestion made by Yinger (1960:625–35) that the term 'contra culture' should be used to describe any group whose values are inverse or in opposition to those of society at large. Downes indicates that the beats are an example of such a group, with values incompatible with those of their parent culture (Downes 1966a:10). The evidence of the present study suggests that some drugtakers, particularly the low-status unemployed or manual workers, had an ideological hostility to the values of society at large and that the drug scene had emerged as the crystallization of such antipathy. It is purely a semantic point, but it may be useful to apply Yinger's suggested label of 'contra culture' to that segment of the drugtaking population whose lifestyles and values were explicitly hostile to, and a rejection of, 'conventional' behaviour and beliefs. It was clear that, in terms of the factors examined during this study, most of the students and middle-class bohemians did not see themselves as separate from the rest of society but were conformist in most things. The term 'sub-culture' rather than 'contra culture' would seem to be more applicable to the two conformist sub-groups.

The concept of sub-culture is a useful paradigm for attempting to explain or describe the emergence of a shared form of behaviour that is in contrast to the dominant norms of society. I suggest that this concept is purely and simply a theoretical device. It has often been used to decribe a statistical configuration, or a group of people with a single common attribute, such as occupation or social class. In relation to the drugtakers in the present study, a sub-cultural explanation must be qualified by several statements. Most of those interviewed were working. Others were dependent upon Social Security. The study group was a varied group of people, many of whom had friends and interests outside the drugtaking milieu. There were important differences between individuals in different social positions, which reduced the applicability of many generalizations. Many of those interviewed stated that they believed they were members of a sub-culture that was quite distinctive from the rest of society. I suggest that such individuals tended to accentuate their distinctiveness and that most were not as far removed from society as they maintained they were. Most of those interviewed had not taken the step of relinquishing their educations or careers and had a strictly limited commitment to drugtaking. For many, 'deviance' was bounded by many conventional considerations. The majority were strictly 'weekend hippies'.

The evidence supports the view that some individuals, mainly low-status unemployed, associated almost exclusively with drugtakers, and that their general orientation to the values of society was distinctive and fairly uncompromising. To apply to these the label of a sub-culture (or contra culture) is meaningful only as a paradigm and does not describe a rigid boundary between groups of individuals or insinuate monolithic uniformity amongst them. My conclusion is that the groups I observed developed in response to shared ideologies and a wish to become part of a community, a believer amongst believers. Drugtaking was the overt affirmation of this wish.

There was great variation between individual drugtakers. This means that many of the generalizations about drugtakers which have been advanced in the literature did not seem applicable to a great proportion of the respondents. One of the great merits of participant observation as a method of examining relatively small groups is that the researcher can share some of the experiences of his subjects. In the following discussion of the living conditions and lifestyles of those I observed and interviewed, I draw upon my field research to elaborate upon, and illustrate the significance of the survey findings.

FOUR Behaviour

9. Patterns of Drugtaking

One of the main conclusions of this study is that drugtaking was part of a general lifestyle. By lifestyle I mean the behaviour of the study group. This is to be distinguished from the notion of sub-culture, which refers to values. Before proceeding to examine certain aspects of this lifestyle, and its associated problems, I shall discuss the drug use of the study group. This is crucial since the study group was selected by the criterion of using cannabis and allied drugs.

The Legal Drugs: Alcohol and Tobacco

The First Report of the United States National Commission on Marijuana and Drug Abuse concluded:

> 'Indeed, if any drug is associated with the use of other drugs, including marijuana, it is tobacco, followed closely by alcohol. Study after study . . . reported an association between the use of tobacco, and, to a lesser extent, of alcohol with the use of marijuana and other drugs.' (1972:87)

This study is concerned primarily with the lifestyles and characteristics associated with illegal, rather than legal, drugs, but an important relationship was evident between the two. While no information was collected about alcohol and tobacco use amongst non-drugtakers, the evidence did suggest that there was a high level of the use of these 'socially acceptable' drugs amongst the drugtakers observed.

Tobacco

Eighty-one per cent of the study group reported that they smoked cigarettes. This compared with under 60.0 per cent of the comparable age group in the population of England and Wales in 1968, when the trend was continuing towards a reduction in the incidence of cigarette smoking (Royal College of Physicians 1971). Virtually all of the study group had used tobacco while smoking cannabis. Sixty-five individuals, 32.5 per cent, reported that they smoked at least twenty cigarettes each day. Fifty-two of these were multi-users. Heavy cigarette smoking was significantly associated with multi-drug use. Cigarette smoking is a normal form of behaviour amongst young adults, although many individuals are hostile to this habit. I noted that some people began to smoke cigarettes after they had become cannabis smokers. A fifth of those interviewed reported that they did not smoke 'straight' cigarettes and several stated that they did not use tobacco even with cannabis, but preferred to take the drug in drinks such as coffee, or to eat it. Several respondents told me that they regarded cigarettes as dangerous to health and stressed their concern to avoid any drug they regarded as deleterious. It was frequently pointed out that weekend or occasional cannabis use was far less harmful than regular or daily tobacco smoking. In addition, several individuals contended that people use cigarettes as a psychological prop, whereas cannabis was a social or group ritual, and thereby different.

Alcohol

Ninety per cent of those interviewed reported that they used alcohol. Twenty-six individuals, 13.0 per cent of the study group, reported that they were heavy drinkers, of whom five stated that they had a drinking problem.

Many individuals, especially those who were unemployed, spent a great deal of their time in public houses, which were amongst their favourite haunts. The low-status unemployed and manual workers spent most evenings at a number of public houses, where many regularly drank to intoxication. Heavy drinking was an approved form of social behaviour amongst this sub-group and I often observed those from working-class backgrounds to be drunk. Several respondents had fathers who were also heavy drinkers. My field research indicated that, particularly amongst males, drinking was regarded as a sign of maturity and alcohol featured prominently in the social gatherings of the study group. The students and middle-class bohemians generally spent much less time in public houses and were usually far more restrained in their drinking habits than were the low-status unemployed or manual workers.

Many middle-class individuals stated that they regarded cannabis as an alcohol substitute and preferred not to use both simultaneously. The low-status sub-group often used other drugs in conjunction with alcohol. Barbiturates, Mandrax, amphetamine sulphate, cough linctuses, and inhalers were regularly taken with alcohol, and cannabis was smoked with conspicous regularity in some public houses. The majority of students and middle-class bohemians preferred to confine their drugtaking to the privacy, and relative safety, of their homes.

My general conclusion is that young people who use drugs such as cannabis are broadly the same as those who use alcohol and tobacco. Many drugtakers stated that they regarded legal and illegal drugs as basically alike and drew attention to the similarities between cannabis and both alcohol (which produces a comparable intoxication) and tobacco (which is also smoked). The objections to alcohol and tobacco use are broadly similar to those against cannabis use, that these drugs are harmful or imply a moral laxity. It was clear that drug use in general was encouraged by tremendous peer group pressure. People were entreated to smoke or drink in much the same way as they were introduced to cannabis, although illegal drug use had a great significance and mystique.

The low-status unemployed and manual workers were generally amenable to virtually any substances that were likely to provide pleasant sensations. Many people used a wide range of drugs simultaneously or as substitutes for one another. One construction worker described his alcohol-drug use in these terms:

> '. . . Yes, I get drunk quite often, mainly at weekends. I usually swallow a . . . (type of inhaler), or maybe two. They give a bit of a speedy buzz. I get drunk easily, but last weekend I had ten or twelve pints a night. My chick (girlfriend) drinks like a fish too. She can drink me under the table. Sometimes we take a couple of Mandrax, or some kind of barbiturates. We sometimes get newted on barbs, if we can't afford alcohol.'

A considerable amount of drug dealing was carried out at public houses, a fact that was clearly apparent. One reason for the importance of public houses to the social life of working-class drugtakers was the lack of alternative public or private gathering grounds. Some public houses were popular with young people and I knew of several where most of the clientele were drugtakers, or at any rate, had used drugs. There was considerable social support and toleration in such groups for drug use, and many individuals met their fellow drugtakers in the cigarette and alcohol-steeped atmosphere of the public house. Many individuals seemed indifferent to which agents they used to induce oblivion. One of the most experienced drugtakers I knew told me that during the late 1960s, when Treatment Centres replaced the general practitioner as the legitimate source of heroin, many of his previously addicted friends became heavy drinkers instead of opiate users. I knew several individuals who, when confronted by a shortage of heroin or morphine, would replace these by intravenous barbiturates, or simply alcohol.

It was distinctly possible that some individuals, due to psychological stresses and tensions, used drugs as sedatives. A few told me this was the case. I knew several individuals who were seldom without either a cigarette or a joint. One or two of my acquaintances in the study group appeared to be almost perpetually in a state of intoxication due to some drug or other. These were an exceptional minority of drugtakers, invariably unemployed, and mainly with histories of severe psychiatric illnesses.

Blum's study of multiple drug use amongst American students correlated figures for the use of each of the different types of drug. These correlations indicated that drinkers were more likely to use cannabis than non-drinkers. The Simon-Gagnon College Youth survey already cited revealed a similar link between cannabis and alcohol. There is no evidence to suggest any causal relationship between alcohol, tobacco, and other drugs, but it was possible that the use of legal, as well as illegal, drugs was likely to be regarded as acceptable or prestigious amongst the milieu observed. As Goode points out:

> 'The adolescent's first experiences with a psycho active drug are invariably with alcohol and not marijuana. And the alcohol-drinking adolescent is statistically more likely to "go on" to use marijuana, just as the marijuana smoker is statistically more

likely to go on to use heroin – or any other drug – than the adolescent who never drinks alcohol or smokes pot.' (Goode 1970:201)

In practice, the friendship networks that encourage the use of alcohol and tobacco may well also support the use of cannabis and other illegal drugs. In addition, individuals whose parents are frequent cigarette smokers or regular drinkers are likely to 'learn' that cigarettes and alcohol are normal and this may dispose them to adopt a sympathetic attitude to the use of other drugs. While this study did not examine in any systematic way the drugtaking habits of respondents' parents, it was apparent that many individuals were aware of their parents' use of alcohol, tobacco, and a great range of prescribed drugs such as barbiturates and tranquillizers. Several individuals told me: 'My mother's a junkie. She been living on Librium for years.'

Statements of this type appear to be attempts at 'neutralizing' their drugtaking. Rationalizations of this sort were commonplace and correspond to Matza's assertions that becoming deviant may involve a process of redefinition and considerable ambivalence about the adoption of drugtaking, or any other form of illegal behaviour.

The Illegal Drugs

Linken and Wilson maintained that little is known about the patterns of cannabis use amongst young people in Britain (in Wilson 1968:93–138), and so I shall examine the drug histories of the study group, in order to investigate which types of drugs they had used and in what sequence.

Drugs ever used

172 of the 200 respondents, 86.0 per cent, reported that they had used at least one other type of drug as well as cannabis. Only the remaining 14.0 per cent were solely cannabis smokers, mono-drugtakers. The study group had used a wide range of drugs and the results are broadly comparable with those of Goode's survey in New York. Sixty-eight per cent of those interviewed in the American survey had at some time used drugs other than cannabis (Goode

Table 7

Multiple drug use amongst cannabis smokers: two studies

	Cheltenham (N 200)	*Goode (N 204)*
L.S.D.	77.5	49.0
Amphetamines	54.0	43.0
DMT or DET	4.0	26.0
Barbiturate or tranquillizer	30.0	24.0
Opium	32.5	20.0
Cocaine	13.5	19.0
Peyote or mescalin	26.0	19.0
Heroin	12.0	13.0
Amyl nitrate	2.0	8.0
Codeine	1.0	5.0
Morning glory seeds	—	5.0
Psilocybin	3.0	4.0
Romilar	5.0	3.0

1970:184, Table 8–1). The mail-in survey carried out by the *East Village Other*, to which I have already referred, produced a very similar pattern of responses to those in Goode's survey and the present study. Some of the results of the E.V.O. survey were strikingly close to those of the Cheltenham study. For example, 77.5 per cent of the Cheltenham respondents reported they had used L.S.D., compared with 77.0 per cent of the E.V.O. respondents. In all three studies the use of drugs other than cannabis was the norm rather than the exception. In the present study, three-quarters of those interviewed were classified as multi-users, which means that they had used at least two other types of drug in addition to cannabis. It must be emphasized that this was not a representative sample, so it is not possible to tell from these findings the extent of multiple drug use amongst the general population of cannabis users in the community.

The National Commission on Marijuana and Drug Abuse (U.S.A.) carried out a study of 105 selected, young working adults in California who were cannabis users. This indicated that no other type of drug was used by more than 25.0 per cent of those studied (1972:45–6). This study has the disadvantage of being limited not only to a small number but of being confined to a narrow middle-class group of respondents. It did not cover a representative cross-section of the population. A number of American studies have indicated that the more frequently a person uses cannabis, the more likely he is to experiment with other drugs. One study, quoted by the National Commission showed that amongst mainly white middle-class students in San Diego, 80.0 per cent of those who used cannabis weekly or more often had used other drugs, compared with less than 33.0 per cent who had used cannabis less than weekly (1972:46).

Goode found that nearly all the daily cannabis smokers, 92.0 per cent, in his sample, had tried at least three drugs other than cannabis. This contrasted with the less frequent cannabis smokers, of whom only 9.0 per cent had used three or more drugs other than cannabis (1970:185). In the present study no record was made of how often respondents smoked or ingested cannabis, but my field-work certainly corroborated the view that there was a clear association between the frequency of a person's cannabis use and the number of other drugs he had tried. I knew only a few heavy cannabis smokers who had never used at least three other types of drug, while very few of the occasional cannabis users had used many other types of drug.

My observations, and the survey data, suggest that in the present study cannabis was overwhelmingly the most widely used drug, both in terms of frequency of use and number of users. My general impression was that cannabis was the mainstay of the groups I observed and was used, with varying degrees of regularity, by all of those interviewed. Many of the low-status unemployed and manual workers, and a few students and middle-class bohemians, smoked cannabis daily, but few people used other drugs as often, with the notable exceptions of those dependent upon opiate narcotics.

L.S.D. was the second most popular single type of drug, having been used at least once by 77.5 per cent of those interviewed. The majority of users had taken this drug only a few times. Half a dozen of the low-status unemployed or multi-users claimed to have taken 400 or 500 'trips', but these were exceptional and their estimates may have been exaggerations. There was little doubt that some of the most committed drugtakers had used L.S.D. and other psychedelics a great many times. The majority of students and middle-class bohemians generally regarded L.S.D. as a drug to be used sparingly and few had ever used it more often than once a week. Several stated that they regarded L.S.D. as such a powerful drug, with profound effects, that they did not gain anything from frequent usage. This view is

Table 8

Drugs used by the study group

	students				*non-students*					
	users		*multi-users*		*users*		*multi-users*		*Total*	
	male	*female*	*male*	*female*	*male*	*female*	*male*	*female*	*N*	*%*
Cannabis	23	8	31	11	16	11	83	17	200	100.0
L.S.D.	5	5	28	11	5	4	81	16	155	77.5
Amphetamines	2	—	15	7	2	1	70	11	108	54.0
Opium	—	—	12	3	—	—	43	7	65	32.5
Mescalin	—	—	7	3	1	—	42	5	58	29.0
Barbiturates	—	—	6	3	—	—	42	5	56	28.0
Mandrax	—	—	6	—	—	—	42	5	53	26.5
Cough linctus	—	—	6	2	—	1	35	4	48	24.0
Cocaine	—	—	4	1	—	—	22	4	31	15.5
Heroin	—	—	1	—	—	—	20	3	24	12.0
Inhalers	—	—	—	2	—	—	18	2	22	11.0
Methedrine	—	—	1	—	—	—	19	1	21	10.5
Morphine	—	—	—	—	—	—	14	1	15	7.5

Nutmeg	–	–	3	1	–	–	4	1	9	4.5
Tranquillizers	–	–	2	1	–	–	5	–	8	4.0
D.M.T.	–	–	–	–	–	–	7	1	8	4.0
Glues/solvents	–	–	1	–	–	–	6	–	7	3.5
Methadone	–	–	–	–	–	–	6	1	7	3.5
Psilocybin	–	–	1	–	–	–	5	–	6	3.0
S.T.P.	–	–	1	–	–	–	3	–	4	2.0
Banana skins	–	–	2	–	–	–	1	1	4	2.0
M.D.A.	–	–	2	–	–	–	1	–	3	1.5
Peyote	–	–	–	–	–	–	2	–	2	1.0
Datura	–	–	–	–	–	–	2	–	2	1.0
Belladonna	–	–	–	–	–	–	2	–	2	1.0
Diconal	–	–	–	–	–	–	2	–	2	1.0
Kava Kava	–	–	–	–	–	–	2	–	2	1.0
Codeine/Aspirin	–	–	1	–	–	–	1	–	2	1.0
Do-Do Pills	–	–	–	–	–	–	2	–	2	1.0
D.D.A.	–	–	–	–	–	–	1	–	1	0.5
Henbane	–	–	–	–	–	–	1	–	1	0.5
Aminita-Muscarina	–	–	1	–	–	–	–	–	1	0.5
Omnipon	–	–	–	–	–	–	1	–	1	0.5

supported by Erich Goode;

> 'Thus, L.S.D. typically is not a drug of frequent use. It is most often taken for curiosity, exploring unusual psychic states, affirming one's status in, and experiencing some of the bases for a distinctive sub-culture.' (Goode 1970:185).

Many respondents regarded an L.S.D. trip as an important event. Several planned each trip carefully arranging to be accompanied by friends and ensuring that they were in attractive, safe surroundings. The reasons given for L.S.D. use were complex and varied. In general the students and middle-class bohemians spoke about L.S.D. in terms of mental exploration or mystical experiences. Few indicated that they took it simply for pleasure. Some of the low-status unemployed and manual workers had a less intellectualized explanation of why they used this or any other drug. They wanted a 'good buzz', a pleasant sensation. Some individuals, invariably unemployed, used L.S.D. several times a week. This resulted in their appearing perpetually 'spaced out' or in a trance-like state. These individuals were all heavy cannabis smokers and gave a variety of explanations for their drug usage, often emphasizing their search for some meaning or sense of direction in life. These appeared to be amongst those most alienated from conventional society. They may have sought psychic gratification as an alternative for career or status rewards.

The majority of students and middle-class bohemians confined their drugtaking largely to cannabis and occasional psychedelics. By far the widest range of drugtaking was evident amongst the low-status unemployed and manual workers. Several individuals had tried more than thirty or forty different types of drug and, in general, this sub-group included those most willing to try a profusion of drugs.

The other drugs used by the study group, and these covered a wide range of substances, were generally things taken only occasionally. Mescalin, for example, was generally hard to acquire. Opium and cocaine were similarly regarded as occasional luxuries. Some of the low-status unemployed or manual workers were frequent users of amphetamine sulphate, Dexedrine, cough linctuses, and inhalers. These were often taken in conjunction with alcohol. Some of this sub-group smoked very large amounts of cannabis, often doing so conspicuously and emphasizing their defiance of conventional views on the subject of drug use. Many of the low-status unemployed and manual workers stated that they smoked cannabis in order to get 'smashed' or 'blocked out', rather than simply to become 'high', as most of the students and middle-class bohemians usually did. This difference is similar to that between being relaxed by alcohol and being thoroughly intoxicated. I suggest that the students and middle-class bohemians were generally 'conformist' in their values and lifestyles. They generally sought casual pleasant experiences rather than to achieve a total change in their lifestyles and perceptions. These two sub-groups were, in general, more restrained in their use of both legal and illegal drugs, since they were less totally committed to the identity of drugtaker than were the low-status unemployed and manual workers. My conclusion is that while the sub-groups were heterogeneous and individuals in one sub-group often behaved like those in other sub-groups, the extent of drugtaking was largely a function of social position, values, and self-image.

Whenever I observed cannabis being used it was very much a shared experience, sometimes a ritual of group solidarity. Usually the 'joint' or cigarette was passed from one person to the next. Many users told me that they believed cannabis smoking was a group activity, possibly largely psycho-somatic rather than pharmacological, in its effects. Becker (1953) suggested that marijuana (cannabis) use is primarily a social, rather than a chemical, experience. This study did not attempt to evaluate the pharmacological effects of cannabis and other drugs, though it was clear that, as Becker suggested, many cannabis users were probably influenced by the example and reactions of their companions during the cannabis smoking experience. Several reported that they had experienced a 'contact high', that is, that they had become intoxicated or felt euphoric because they perceived their friends were influenced by the drug. Some stated that they took their cue in getting high by copying their friends' behaviour.

In general 'excessive' cannabis use was disapproved of by the students and middle-class bohemians, since this might impair work performance. Many commented that they believed excessive preoccupation with drugs might lead to lethargy or indolence. Usually this view was qualified by the statement that such a reaction was due to the 'head' lifestyle rather than to the direct effects of the drug.

Amongst those involved with the drugtaking lifestyle, the low-status unemployed and manual workers, cannabis was almost accorded the status of a form of currency, a harbinger of prestige and pleasure. Much time was spent discussing the relative merits of 'Lebanese Red', 'Pakki Black', and different varieties of the drug which were currently available. In general, the drugtaking of the low-status sub-group was less discriminate than that of the students and middle-class bohemians. Some low-status unemployed and manual workers were extremely catholic in their choice of drugs and appeared willing to try virtually any substance likely to give them 'a good buzz'. They appeared to use drugs explicitly for their pleasurable sensations, although some reported using stimulants such as amphetamines for quasi practical reasons; to work, or to stay awake at dances or parties. It is hard to be precise, but I estimate that at least 90.0 per cent of the actual drugtaking activity of the study group was restricted to cannabis. The great majority of individuals, though technically multiple drug users, were essentially cannabis smokers who had, on a very limited number of occasions, also used other drugs. Nevertheless, my field-work suggested that the concept of the mono-drugtaker is, in general a confusing one, since it was evident that many drugtakers were prepared to use other types of drug if these became available and, on occasion, changed their normal drug of choice if for some reason their supplies were interrupted. This was not a random sample, and since the likely bias was in favour of those with greater drug experience, individuals who had only used a single type of drug such as cannabis were generally excluded from this study.

Drugs First Used

One hundred and fifty-eight of those interviewed, 79.0 per cent, reported that cannabis had been the first drug they ever used. Twenty-five individuals had first used amphetamines, five used L.S.D., and a further eight took either Mandrax, amyl nitrate, Librium, banana skins (smoked), or aspirins in Coca Cola (see *Table 30*). One respondent claimed heroin had been the first drug he ever used. These findings contrast with Hindmarch's conclusion that amphetamines were the usual first drugs used. Possibly this difference is due to the decrease in the availability of amphetamines since his study of adolescent drug use. Most of the respondents in the present study who had used amphetamines as their first drug were members of a rather older group, in their mid or late twenties, who began using amphetamines to keep awake at all night discotheques and rock concerts. My impression was that although amphetamines ('speed') were easy to obtain, often in raw powder form, they were not nearly as common as they had been a few years earlier. One reason for this is the reluctance of the medical profession to prescribe the drug, which has meant that smaller stocks were then kept in pharmacies and fewer available to be stolen and diverted onto the black market.

The majority of drugtakers interviewed reported that cannabis had been their first drug. There appeared to be a general consensus that it was the mildest of the psychotropic drugs, and that L.S.D., being a much more powerful drug, should generally be tried after one had become used to the effects of cannabis. I suggest that, in addition, the first drug a person uses is likely to be that most freely available and my observations certainly indicated that this was cannabis. There is no doubt that cannabis was available in relatively large quantities. A recent estimate suggested that transactions involving cannabis in Birmingham, only forty miles away from Cheltenham and easily accessible by motorway, amounted to £1,000,000 each year.[1]

A possible additional inducement to using cannabis was its relative cheapness in comparison with other drugs. In most cases people were 'turned on' free of charge by experienced smokers. Smoking cannabis was a visible proof of affiliation with the group, and almost always took place while others were present and could witness this 'initiation'. News of those who had been 'turned on' was quickly passed around the scene, just as early Christians must have proclaimed converts. Being 'turned on' was a relatively important event for many people and there was a prestige attached to whoever introduced the novice to the communal smoking experience. Several people told me who had 'turned them on' with a due deference indicating their gratitude to the instrument of their conversion. Some individuals suggested that in their view cannabis was *the* drug since it was essentially a symbol of brotherhood, of shared identity, and, therefore, especially suitable for one's initiation as a drugtaker. Many drugs are taken orally, and their use is a private affair. Cannabis is mainly smoked and is thereby conspicuous, a concrete expression to others that one is a drugtaker. I do not intend to suggest that cannabis is purely a symbol. People can and do become intoxicated by the drug and it is also sometimes smoked alone. Nevertheless, cannabis

[1] *Evening Mail* (Birmingham), February 26, 1973:10.

appeared to possess a mystique of its own, different from that attached either to L.S.D. or heroin.

Escalation to Other Drugs

> 'It cannot be too strongly emphasized that the smoking of the marijuana cigarette is a dangerous first step on the road which usually leads to enslavement by heroin.' (Quoted by Schofield 1971:100).

This statement comes from a pamphlet issued by the United States Bureau of Narcotics in 1965. Popular discussion of drugtaking has emphasized the possible relationship between different types of drugtaking behaviour. It has frequently been maintained that there is a process of 'escalation' or 'progression' from the use of one type of drug to another. This so-called 'stepping-stone' theory imputes a likely change from the use of cannabis and other drugs to more dangerous agents such as heroin or other injected and addictive substances. One of the main arguments levelled at cannabis is that it is a 'threshold' drug, that is, that is pre-disposes the user to experiment with other types of drug, especially heroin.

> 'Marihuana is especially dangerous because it comes in cigarette form. The great tobacco companies have prepared the way for the Devil's parade of death; they have popularized the use of cigarettes . . . until today in America, men, women, boys and girls think nothing of lighting up their choice tobacco . . . It is easy now, for a young man or woman planted by the peddlar, to pass out this new cigarette, and American youth, always looking for adventure, will fall easy prey. The step from Marihuana to . . . morphine is a short one.' (Rollings 1938, quoted in Goode 1970:181)

Statements of this type, emphasizing a supposed link between cannabis and heroin or other 'hard' drugs, were fairly common during the early post-war period and continue to be influential in creating public opinion about drugtaking. Such theories are founded on evidence that many heroin addicts examined in hospitals and prisons had used cannabis. This fact has been interpreted to imply a causal relationship. In other words, it has been inferred that unless people tried cannabis, they would not become aware of their latent predisposition for more deleterious drugs, or that the number of heroin addicts would be smaller if people did not smoke cannabis. Sometimes, it has been suggested that 'progression' from cannabis to heroin is very likely, if not inevitable. This view is subject to criticism on the grounds that it imputes too simple a process of causation.

> 'The most usual statement given in support of escalation is that most heroin addicts started on pot. The usual figure given is between 80 and 90 per cent and this is supported by retrospective investigations into the background of addicts, mostly from America. The same investigations show that the use of the word "started" is misleading, because cannabis was by no means always the first drug the addicts had taken; nearly all of them had taken alcohol and tobacco before cannabis, and many had also taken amphetamines. The implication of the statement is that cannabis leads to heroin, but it is a logical fallacy to state that pot smokers will go on to hard drugs because the majority of heroin addicts have taken cannabis. One might as well say that most whisky drinkers will go on to methylated spirits because most meths drinkers have drunk whisky.' (Schofield 1971:101)

The 'escalation' issue is controversial and important. As Schofield suggests, the fact that heroin addicts have often used cannabis is not sufficient evidence to establish a causal relationship. The evidence is conflicting. On the one hand, Home Office figures indicate that during the 1950s and '60s the increase in the numbers of 'known' heroin addicts accompanied the rise in prosecutions for the possession of cannabis. On the other hand, the likely numbers of heroin addicts, even assuming that Home Office figures are a gross under-representation, are far smaller than the likely number of people who smoke cannabis. In addition, more than three-quarters of known British heroin addicts live in London and cannabis is smoked elsewhere.

Information about individual drug dependents in clinical situations is valuable, but it must be emphasized that these are an 'extreme' and atypical group of drugtakers. While the present study involved a non-random selection procedure, I was able to contact and collect data from a considerable variety of individuals in the community with some drugtaking experience. This is valuable since the majority of those interviewed could not have been contacted through 'official' or 'clinical' agencies concerned with drugtaking.

As I have shown, most respondents had used drugs other than cannabis. Twenty-eight individuals, 14.0 per cent of the study group, had restricted their drugtaking to cannabis, even though all of these had smoked the drug for more than a year and nine for at least four years. Sixteen of these individuals stated categorically that they had no intention of using other types of drugs.

Thirty-one of those interviewed, 15.5 per cent of the study group, had experience of injecting drugs. Only three of these, or 1.5 per cent of the study group, were regularly injecting drugs at the time of the interview and may have been physically dependent upon heroin or morphine. The evidence does not support the view that cannabis users in general were likely to become heroin users, still less to become heroin dependents. In general, the students and middle-class bohemians were hostile to the use of injected drugs and these sub-groups gave little support to such practices. Most of those interviewed, although they had used drugs other than cannabis, were primarily cannabis users and made it clear, both in informal discussions and during interview, that they regarded heroin as a dangerous drug. This evidence is consistent with the student surveys of Binnie and Murdock and Young and Brooke-Crutchley, previously cited, which found that most cannabis users eschewed the injection of drugs. Many respondents suggested that the differences between cannabis and heroin use were similar to those between social drinking and alcoholism:

> 'People who smoke dope are usually well-balanced, sociable, and intelligent. Junkies are altogether different. They're either mentally ill or trying to escape from problems they can't overcome. Normal people aren't likely to become junkies. There would still be junkies even without cannabis.'

Many individuals were eager to display their drugtaking to others perceived as sympathetic or as admired and respected individuals. In general the patterns of drugtaking I observed reflected the ethos and self-image of the sub-group concerned. There appeared to be a continuum of involvement with the drugtaking sub-culture, depending upon one's position in conventional social terms. The students and middle-class bohemians restricted their drug use. Most appeared to regard the injection of drugs as a symptom of psychological or social disturbance. They did not, in general, regard the use of narcotics as potentially rewarding or prestigious. In fact, the 'junkie' was perceived as sick, pathetic, weak, and an object of pity, certainly not an image to be emulated or esteemed. Furthermore, most of those from middle-class homes and with definite career objectives regarded the use of narcotics as incompatible with the demands of their careers and a threat to their ambitions: 'Why should I want to fix (inject drugs)? I want to lead a happy, useful life. Junkies have a full time job just fixing and scoring (obtaining drugs). That's not really living.'

My impression was that there were two distinctly different images of the drugtaker. One was of the liberated, mystic, or seeker of insight and experience, the other was an altogether more 'deviant' or extreme figure: the junkie. While it was clear that most of the study group regarded the former image as at least partially acceptable, if not attractive, few, including some who had, or were still injecting drugs, were prepared to concede the virtues of the latter. The general view was that being a junkie involved relinquishing one's freedom of choice to the harsh biological constraints of physical dependence. This was the antithesis of the sort of intellectual progress many claimed to seek through the use of mind-expanding drugs.

Most of those I encountered who had injected drugs were low-status unemployed or manual workers. All had used a wide range of other drugs. Only one of the students interviewed had ever injected drugs and this had been while living with a group of unemployed drugtakers. I suggest that the injection of heroin, when it occurred, was in association with a milieu of people who had little or no stake in conventional social aspirations. It was an extreme stage in one's commitment to a very distinctive type of multi-drugtaking lifestyle. The evidence of the present study indicates that upon becoming a drugtaker many of those interviewed had used a range of different types of drugs in order to experiment and to emphasize commitment to the drug scene. There was a form of prestige accorded to those with the widest range of drug experience. Cannabis use was the commonest token of involvement, and the stronger hallucinogens such as L.S.D. indicated a greater concern with drugs and a more extensive range of experimentation and soul-searching. The injection of drugs, prompted as it may be by any biological or psychological factors, signifies a high level of commitment to drugtaking. This was not merely an acceptance of the stigma of being a drugtaker, which I suggest is incurred by smoking cannabis. It is a thoroughgoing rejection of conventional social beliefs and norms, most of which are, to some extent, still accepted by other drugtakers. I do not suggest that heroin dependence is purely a sociological phenomenon. All sorts of possible explanations may be equally valid or useful. It was evident, however, that the ultimate commitment to drugtaking it involved was unlikely to occur in the controlled milieu of the students and middle-class bohemians. This corresponds to Young and Brooke-Crutchley's observations about student drug-use in a London Polytechnic.

As Young comments, physical dependence upon drugs is incompatible with hippie values: '. . . it is anathema to the values of hedonism, expressivity and autonomy' (Young 1971:194).

My field research in Cheltenham and in other towns, suggested that far from generally encouraging heroin use, most drugtakers strongly discouraged it and disapproved of it. Individual opinions again related to personal social position and general lifestyle, and those who had experience of injecting drugs were amongst those with the greatest involvement with the drugtaking way of life. My general impression was that patterns of drugtaking were functions of whichever self-images the user had. In many respects those (very few) respondents who had experience of injecting drugs were the least entrenched in the conventional social system. Even those who had only used injected drugs experimentally were apparently highly involved with the drugtaking milieu and were on close personal terms with regular heroin users.

Continued Use of Drugs

The 'conventional' view is that when a person begins to use drugs he will continue to do so. This, like the 'escalation' theory, is an assumption based upon the case histories of individual drugtakers who have received medical treatment or who have otherwise come to the attention of 'official' agencies.

The information collected during the present study indicates that drugtaking need not be a permanent phenomenon. Altogether, thirty-one of those interviewed had experience of injected drugs, yet only three were still injecting regularly at the time of interview. In addition, I encountered many drugtakers, both in Cheltenham and in other British towns, who had stopped using drugs such as heroin of their own, unaided volition. During my two years' residence in

Cheltenham I noted several people giving up drugtaking altogether. The reasons for this varied considerably. There appeared to be a general pattern of experimenting with a range of drugs, depending upon their availability and the views of one's friends, after which most people used fewer types of drug. I suggest that a process of *de-escalation* occurred, usually involving the adoption of a single preferred type of drug, invariably cannabis (Plant 1974). This finding is consistent with that of Charles Reeves in his Southern Hampshire study.[2]

My field encounters with drugtakers, including some individuals with considerable drug experience, indicated that many people 'went through the scene', that is to say, they experimented sometimes extensively and at length with drugs and then reduced their drug use considerably. This experience was quite common-place. One respondent described his own drug history in these terms:

> 'When I was about seventeen I started using drugs, speed and dope mainly. I got "into" acid, and used a lot of other things too. Now I just smoke dope. It's the only drug I would really recommend. The others are all a bit much, or not worth bothering with . . . Yes, I fixed a few times, but I would never do that again. It's a kind of self-destruction and not a good scene. Most of my friends went through the scene too. We tried whatever we could get, but most of us just smoke dope now, and some don't even turn on any more.'

This type of comment was quite commonplace, especially amongst those in their twenties and thirties. Many intimated that they had derived a finite, limited, amount of pleasure from different drugs and that, beyond a certain stage, they thought they had exhausted the possibilities of most drugs. Several people stated that after a while they found hallucinogens repetitive and the other drugs disappointing. Cannabis, most agreed, was different, being a social drug, and generally a substitute for, or addition to, alcohol. Also, it was evident that many people regarded cannabis as a symbol of group membership, a badge of being 'cool'. It seemed to me that cannabis was *the* drug of group solidarity and that this had much to do with its lasting popularity. Several people told me that they regarded cannabis as 'our' drug, in contrast to 'their (i.e. non-drugtakers') alcohol and

[2] Personal communication with Charles Reeves.

tobacco. Several times during my field-work, I attended cocktail parties. I was struck by the way in which at such gatherings the use of certain wines and spirits was emphasized and regarded as prestigious. In 'straight' (non-drugtaking) circles the mixture, for example, of Campari and champagne, was regarded in much the same way as mescalin or 'good grass' amongst drugtakers. At both alcohol parties and cannabis smoking sessions, drugs, whether legal or illegal, serve as facilitators of sociability, reducing inhibitions, and causing extroversion (alcohol) or introspection (cannabis). Both in 'straight' circles and in the drug scene, psychotropic substances are an important topic of conversation and are taken as symbols of status, and marks of the 'in group'. In fact, most of the drugtakers I observed also used alcohol and tobacco, so cannabis was not simply an alternative drug. Usually it was an additional one.

Nineteen individuals, 9.5 per cent of the study group, reported that they intended to continue using several types of drug indefinitely. These were all either low-status unemployed or manual workers, or individuals associating with this sub-group. The low-status unemployed and manual workers were generally far more wide-ranging in their drugtaking tastes than either the students or middle-class bohemians. Sixty-eight per cent of the study group reported that they had no wish to try any additional types of drug. Most of those who named drugs they would like to use attributed this desire to curiosity. Thirty-seven named hallucinogens such as psilocybin, mescalin, and peyote. Seven respondents stated that they wanted to use heroin. All asserted that they believed heroin to be a potentially very dangerous drug, that they were wary of it, and only wanted to use it once or twice, experimentally. Only one individual attributed his wish to use an additional type of drug to a desire to reduce or combat depression.

The 'Fixers'

As I have suggested, there was a continuum of commitment to drugtaking, which ranged from experimentation with a single type of drug to frequent use of a wide range of psychotropic substances. In many ways the most extreme form of commitment to drugtaking was evinced by the injection of drugs. Much of the popular literature about drugtaking has emphasized the possibility that individuals will 'progress' or 'escalate' to the injection of heroin and other drugs. This view was not supported by the present findings, although thirty-one respondents, 15.5 per cent of the study group, reported that they had at some time injected drugs such as heroin, methedrine, or cocaine.

Information about the injection 'fixing' of drugs has largely been derived from in-patients receiving treatment for physical drug dependence. I located my respondents within the community and consequently obtained a rather different group of people. In fact only three of those with experience of injecting drugs were actually injecting regularly at the time of interview. The other twenty-eight had either discontinued the use of injected drugs or used them only occasionally, when available. There was no drug treatment centre in the Cheltenham area and illegal supplies of heroin and other injected drugs were fairly limited. It certainly seemed that the use of injected drugs in Cheltenham was rarer than in other areas, such as Southampton (Plant and Reeves 1973). This view was endorsed by many of the study group, who asserted that there was not such a 'heavy scene' in Cheltenham as in some other towns. This raises two points. First, supplies of injected drugs were restricted, and second, the demand for such drugs seemed limited. Presumably the demand limited the supply, although the converse could equally have been true, if these factors were directly related.

I have already discussed the stereotype of the junkie. This has been widely described in the literature:

> 'The world of the average junkie is a narrow one. He lives for his "fix", he has turned his back upon the ordinary world of work, sex and family relationships, for nothing outside his heroin obsession can attract his interest or make a claim upon his reduced energy.' (De Berker and De Berker 1973:142).

There is general agreement that dependence upon heroin is an extreme condition, and it has often been suggested that the use of injected drugs is a certain precursor to addiction and early death.

Patterns of use

Five of those who had injected drugs had done so fewer than ten times. Some of the others stated that they had, on occasion, had to overcome withdrawal symptoms but had managed to do this without

Diagram V

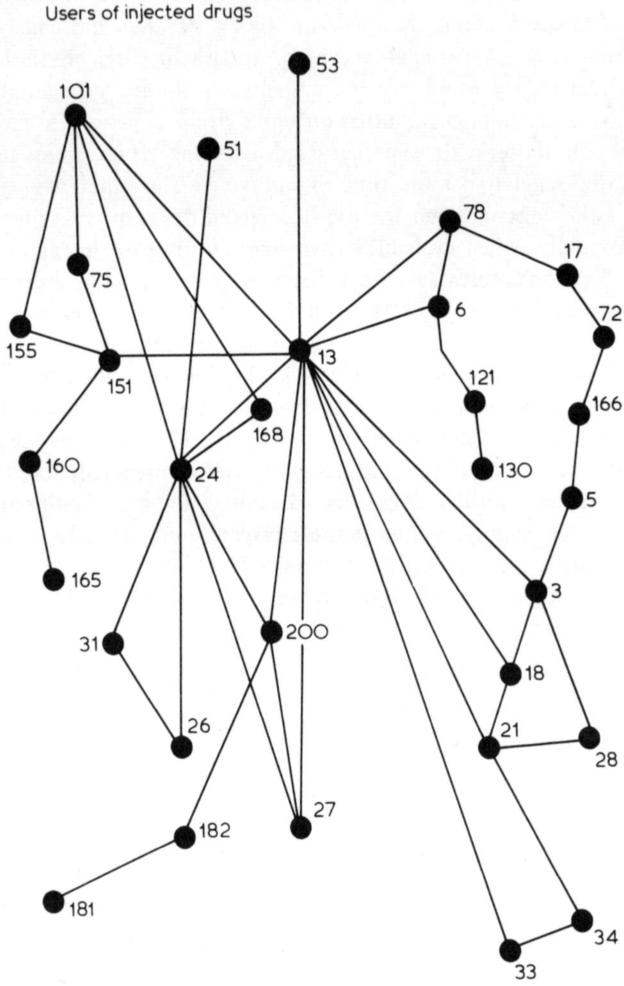
Users of injected drugs
53
101
51
78
17
75
6
72
155
13
151
121
166
168
160
24
130
5
165
3
31
200
18
26
21
28
27
182
181
34
33

medical aid. It was clear from the evidence that a certain amount of occasional or experimental injection had occurred, without the development of habitual use or physical dependence. There was a consensus that injection was dangerous, and several respondents stated that they had stopped using injected drugs for fear of the consequences if they continued:

> 'It was too nice. It (heroin) must be the ultimate drug. It gives total euphoria, total peace. Like it's too much. I stopped because I knew I could have got hooked on it. I know people who were junkies, and I had seen some bad scenes through fixing. I might use it again, but only very occasionally. It would be very easy to get carried away. . .'

Several individuals intimated that they used heroin if it was available. Most of the thirty-one who had used injected drugs had done so in other towns or cities, such as London, or Birmingham, at times when illegal supplies were readily available. There was general agreement that there was no extensive use of injected drugs in Cheltenham and it appeared possible that no more than half a dozen individuals in the town injected regularly. It was evident that people tended to use which drugs were obtainable and that some injected heroin at times, but used other drugs, such as cannabis or alcohol, when it was hard to get.

Characteristics of those with experience of injecting drugs

The thirty-one respondents who had experience of injecting drugs were different from the overall study group in several respects. Twenty-seven of the thirty-one were male, seventeen were from working-class families, and twenty-one had been in trouble with the police. Twenty-eight were low-status unemployed or manual workers and only one was a student. As a group, those with experience of injecting drugs were overwhelmingly those with the greatest involvement in the drugtaking lifestyle and milieu. All had used a wide range of other drugs and were observed to have a large number of contacts with other drugtakers. There was no significant association between the use of injected drugs and either unemployment, or crowded housing. Nevertheless, there was a statistical association between the use of injected drugs and delinquency, lack of educational qualifications, and low socio-economic status. Those who had experience of injected drugs were significantly more likely than other respondents to have been convicted of a drug offence, thirteen out of thirty-one, compared with only sixteen other respondents. I encountered many construction workers during my stay in Cheltenham who had used injected drugs. Due to the impermanence of this group, many were not interviewed, but my general impression was that the manual workers were especially likely to use whatever drugs they could get and were less likely than most middle-class drugtakers to be reluctant to inject. The great majority of students and middle-class bohemians disapproved of the use of injected drugs.

Medical treatment

Official figures are known to understate the numbers of people using heroin and other injected drugs. There have been many attempts to assess what proportion of the actual injecting population are represented by Home Office statistics. Any estimates to date have been little more than inspired guesses. It is unlikely that a precise enumeration will ever be achieved. The present study was restricted to the Cheltenham area and there are no grounds to suppose that the thirty-one individuals with experience of injected drugs were in any sense typical of the national pattern. Nevertheless, the evidence indicates that in all probability only a small number of those who inject drugs ever receive medical treatment or appear in official statistics as drug dependents.

Only three of the thirty-one individuals with experience of injected drugs had ever received medical treatment for drug dependence. Two had formerly received amphetamines on prescription and the third had once been given legal supplies of methadone. My observations suggested that several individuals used heroin without necessarily becoming dependent or requiring medical treatment. The majority of those who injected drugs (such as heroin, morphine, cocaine, methadone, barbiturates, methedrine, aspirins, distilled water, and cough linctus) obtained their supplies from friends who either received them on prescription or bought them on the black market. Most of those with experience of injection used such drugs only occasionally, when they were available. The regular users had contacts outside the Cheltenham area and spent a great deal of their time outside the town in connection with their drug requirements.

One individual, a male in his twenties, had been injecting drugs regularly for five years. He had at different times received medical treatment, including methadone maintenance. At the time of interview he and a small group of friends were injecting a mixture of heroin and morphine, supplies of which they obtained from a dealer outside the survey area. The individual concerned (let us call him Ian), stated that he was physically dependent upon opiates but that he was able, periodically, to cut right down on the amounts of drugs he injected and that he anticipated eventually ceasing injection.

> 'I suppose it is very negative really. Some of my friends have died injecting – in London and places like that. I have managed to curb my drug use and want to conform to society a bit more. I get very little out of being a junkie. A lot of "heads" don't like the fixing scene, my parents won't let me in the house, and I get hasselled (harassed) by the police. They have even made me roll my sleeve up in the middle of the High Street. It's not worth it. I shall get a job soon and try to lead a normal life. My mates have either gone straight, or finished up in a real mess. I want to go straight.'

My informal encounters with individuals in their twenties and thirties who had injected drugs, suggested that the general tendency was for them to discontinue this practice and to revert to drugs such as cannabis and alcohol. I came across no cases of serious illness due to drug effects during my field-work and the only drugtaker out of more than 400 individuals I encountered who died did so for reasons unconnected with drugtaking.

I must emphasize that the 'fixing scene' in Cheltenham appeared small in comparison to those in some other towns. In general, drugs were only injected by those most deeply involved with drugtaking and who were outside the influence of career-oriented, middle-class groups. This could be interpreted as a response to a feeling of status-frustration or a sense of estrangement from the values of the mainstream of society. All those I met who had injected drugs had done so in company with working-class or unemployed individuals and, I believe, at times when they wished not only to experiment but to stress their personal involvement with drugtaking. It was apparent that there was a scale of prestige within the low-status unemployed and manual worker sub-group which related to the range of drugs one had used. I contend that the social situation and the general lack of career opportunities of this sub-group encouraged heroin use, as well as any possible psychological traits that might have been influential.

There was no evidence to suggest that there was any association between the use of injected drugs and disturbed family background. Instead the heroin users were marginally less likely than other respondents to report that their parents were unhappy together. I encountered a few individuals, mainly temporary visitors to the town, who appeared to be severely psychologically disturbed. There was a significant association between experience of injecting drugs and parasuicide. I discuss this later, but this may well have indicated a high proportion of psycho-neurotics amongst those with experience of injection. One or two individuals stated that they had injected drugs to alleviate depression or psychological stress. Several writers have suggested that people may use injected drugs to ward off the onset of psychosis (Laurie 1967). This may have been true of those injecting regularly, but in most cases, injection had been prompted by curiosity, peer group pressure, or bravado.

Lifestyles

My contact with my subjects enabled me to observe their general lifestyles, or at least certain regularities, in their normal social settings. My field research suggested that the primary differences between individual lifestyles were associated with class background, employment patterns, and the ideology and self image of the sub-group to which one belonged. The main dichotomy that emerged was between the students and middle-class bohemians on the one hand, and the low-status unemployed and manual workers on the other.

There was certainly a sense of group solidarity amongst the subjects of this study, albeit there were acknowledged differences and aversions between individuals and sub-groups. The sub-groups I observed were distinctive, both compared to each other, and compared to many non-drugtakers in terms of their general ideologies and values, and, I conjecture, had developed as the crystallization of individuals sharing broadly similar life situations and beliefs. Within the drug scene or sub-culture of drugtakers in the Cheltenham area there were cliques of individuals from similar backgrounds and in similar social positions. The students mainly associated with other students, and so on. Most of those interviewed were young, unmarried people at early or transitional stages in their careers. A high proportion, three-quarters of the study group, had lived in Cheltenham for less than five years and half reported intending to leave the town within four years. Virtually all the students were purely temporary residents in Cheltenham and many stated that they would probably leave the area in order to advance their careers. I contend that the growth of drugtaking amongst the study group had been fostered by the fact that, as a group, they were in a transitional stage and were relatively free to establish their own values and way of life. All were sexually mature and most had some form of personal income or grant. Jock Young has described the differences between formal and subterranean values and suggested that being a drugtaker involves a commitment to the latter rather than the former. I shall attempt to elaborate this view in relation to the empirical evidence of this study. The survey data are crucial to this book, since some of the factors examined provide an important clue to the varying behaviours and social positions within the study group.

10. Employment Patterns

Fifty-two of those interviewed, 26.0 per cent of the total study group, were unemployed. These constituted 40.9 per cent of the 127 non-students interviewed. This is an extremely high incidence of unemployment, and further emphasizes that the study group was unusual in relation to the whole community. It must be remembered that snowballing is a non-random method of locating people and that the study group were largely judged to be experienced drugtakers. It cannot be assumed that the respondents were a representative group of drugtakers in the community. The methodology made it likely that having located one low-status, unemployed drugtaker, I would be thereby introduced to others. It must be emphasized that there certainly were other networks of drugtakers in the town which I did not locate or interview.

R. Cockett found in his study of drug use amongst juvenile offenders that there were proportionally more unemployed amongst the drugtakers than amongst the controls (Cockett 1971:93). Charles Reeves also found a high level of unemployment amongst those interviewed in his Southern Hampshire study.[1] Cockett found that the highest levels of unemployment were evident for the highest drug use groups.

Seventeen of the unemployed in the present study had been out of work for longer than six months. Sixteen of these were multi-users. Multi-users were heavily over-represented amongst those out of work. Altogether, forty-one of the eighty-three male non-student multi-users, and three of the seventeen female non-student multi-users, were out of work.

[1] Personal communication with Charles Reeves.

Thirty-two of the fifty-two unemployed stated that they were out of work through choice (see *Diagram IV*). My field encounters with many of those most deeply involved with drugtaking substantiated the fact that some were unemployed because they preferred to remain so. Some individuals were unemployed throughout the duration of my field-work, and some had not had a job for three or four years. A few may have been psychologically disturbed and unemployable, but such a judgement is beyond the competence of this study. Some individuals amongst the low-status unemployed lived a very precarious existence, moving around the country, beggins, stealing, and sometimes taking temporary jobs. One person I knew well had been 'on the road' for two years following a nervous breakdown and dismissal from his job. He slept rough for long periods of time and lived mainly by theft. He was seldom entitled to Social Security payments as he usually had no fixed address.

The unemployed group were mixed. Most were from working-class backgrounds, but a few were from middle-class homes. Several of those I encountered had been students, or in non-manual jobs, but had 'dropped out' for different reasons. Several complained of their difficulties in obtaining jobs suited to what they saw as their intellectual capacities. Others simply chose to be unemployed as part of a rejection of the 'straight' system. These adopted the identity of the unemployed 'head' or 'freak'. There was little doubt that a few of those I encountered, including three of the study group, were physically dependent upon drugs. Such individuals may well have

Table 9
Reasons for unemployment

reason	*no*
choice	32
dismissed from previous job	8
just finished college/university/school	4
unable to find work	2
temporarily between jobs	2
to have a baby	1
new arrival in Cheltenham	2
temporary job finished	1
total	52

been rendered incapable of normal work by their dependence. Others were clearly incessant drug users and may also have been limited in their working abilities by the effects of drugs. An appraisal of this type is beyond the scope of the present study.

Student drop-outs

Twenty individuals, 10.0 per cent of the study group, had failed to complete courses at institutions of higher or further education. These were either unemployed or had menial, low-status jobs. Some stated that they had failed their course exams and had been forced to leave college or university. Others had had nervous disorders or had decided that they wanted to leave. The general evidence suggests that the drugtakers, as a group, were not drop-outs but it was apparent that an important minority were in this category.

Antipathy to work

Several individuals stated that they rejected the work system:

> 'I doubt I shall ever get a straight job again. When I was at college I was faking it. Now I want to cut adrift from society. I hate the pace, the tension, I want to get some "sounds" (records) together, and a good stereo. I think maybe I'll work for a while for these . . . Then I'll move somewhere into the country and then I'll get a smallholding and work for myself . . . '

> 'They said at the Dole (employment exchange) that I'm avoiding work. What jobs do they give me? Labouring! They can stuff that sideways. I want to paint and I'm not digging ditches to please some stupid little turds like those. They won't pay me any more money now. I can hardly get enough by dealing to keep alive. They're fascist man, that's what they are, they fascist.'

The phenomenon of young men who remain out of work through choice has been commented upon elsewhere. Lord Justice Lawson remarked during his Newson Memorial Lecture at the Police College, Bromshill on 12th September, 1971:

> 'Time and time again I have to pass sentence on youths and young men who are said to be unemployed . . . When I ask what such

offenders have been living on I am usually told 'social security' payments. I can see no reason why criminal layabouts should live at the taxpayer's expense. I would give the courts jurisdiction to stop them doing so.' (*Report of the Committee on Abuse of Social Security Benefits* 1973:93)

Many of those in the present study who were unemployed through choice were living on supplementary benefits rather than unemployment benefit. I encountered several individuals who had at some time had their Social Security payments stopped for some abuse. (In 1971 Supplementary Benefits were withheld from 15,000 cases in England and Wales on the grounds that applicants were making little or no effort to find work (op. cit:90).)

As Polsky commented about the beats he observed, several people were vehemently hostile to 'the system'. These included highly articulate and well-informed individuals as well as those with no educational qualifications or from low-status backgrounds. Some of those most critical of the present social order had revolutionary political ideas, others simply wanted to get away from society, ideally to a pastoral setting where they could be self-sufficient. This was an extreme form of the radical ideology that characterized the drugtakers observed. One or two individuals did achieve their plans of obtaining country cottages, others joined communes. Most of the idealism of this group was non-productive and few of those with counter-philosophies of life did more than expound them.

The unemployed group was quite distinct from those who were at college or were working. Those who chose to be unemployed were regarded with disapproval by most of the students and middle-class bohemians. Several students appeared very interested to know about the 'full-time freaks' as one respondent called them. In general those respondents who were students or working had rather ambivalent views about the unemployed and low-status manual workers. Several people indicated that they regarded them as amusing eccentrics. Others were hostile to them.

This ambivalence was returned. Some of the unemployed drugtakers had been, or aspired to be, students. I discussed their views with several who conceded that while they thought that students were generally acceptable, they were basically career-oriented materialists and part of 'the system'. There was some mutual resentment between those who were academically successful and working, and those who were unemployed or who had menial jobs. One afternoon I was in a cafe where several of the 'full-time freaks' were gathered. A fierce argument developed over two students who had been convicted of possessing cannabis. Most of those present were very hostile to students whom they described as 'a bunch of idiots'. This view was justified by assertions that students were snobs and were bourgeois. There was a note of evident jealousy at the perceived privileges of students who were viewed as an opulent and effete group of people.

The unemployed were of two types: the first category were primarily locally born and from low-status backgrounds, the 'traditional' working-class unemployed. The others were disenchanted middle-class individuals. The latter group generally vocalized their alienation in political terms. The former sometimes used similar language but generally appeared politically apathetic. Some unemployed individuals were active drug dealers and appeared to make a living in this manner. Several augmented their income by criminal means. One respondent, a drug dealer not normally resident in Cheltenham, was married to a prostitute. It must be emphasized that the criminal group was almost exclusively from local working-class families and was regarded with general suspicion by most of the students and middle-class bohemians.

Employment Patterns Since Becoming Drugtakers

Popular discussion about drugtaking has stressed the possible deleterious effects of drugs on education or career. The case histories of opiate dependents indicate that being a junkie is a full-time preoccupation: 'This is the life of the junky, seven days a week, 365 days a year. Living by his wits, preying on the community, and caught up in a sickness from which there is no escape' (Seymour 1972:14).

The employment patterns of the non-students since becoming drugtakers revealed that only a minority, fifty-seven out of 127, had continued their careers 'normally'. Altogether, forty individuals, thirty-seven of whom were multi-users, had either given up regular employment, or had been downwardly mobile, while an additional thirty individuals had continued their already poor employment records. Virtually all those whose employment histories had

takes over life + career

Table 10
Employment histories of non-students since first drug use

	users		*multi-users*		*Total*	
	males	*females*	*males*	*females*	*N*	*%*
continued with career	13	10	21	13	57	44.9
downwardly mobile	1	–	17	–	18	14.2
ceased regular employment	2	–	19	1	22	17.3
poor record – menial jobs and unemployment	–	1	26	3	30	23.6
total	16	11	83	17	127	100.0

undergone adverse changes since first using drugs were multi-user males. It must be emphasized that this does not impute a causal relationship between employment patterns and drug use. Both could be influenced by other factors.

Altogether forty individuals, 20.0 per cent of the study group, had changed their employment patterns since they had become drugtakers. Three of these were judged to be physically dependent upon heroin and a further five had histories of previous psychiatric disorder. Altogether, nine of the forty had at some time made parasuicidal acts. As a group it appears that a high proportion of those whose employment patterns had changed were psycho-neurotics, in addition to those five with histories of psychiatric disorder. Possibly these were abnormal personality types before they became drugtakers.

Perceived Changes in Lifestyle

Fourteen of the forty whose employment patterns had changed since they had become drugtakers reported that they had completely altered their previous attitudes to work and to society. They stated that they had become less materialistic (2), more inactive and lethargic (2), less interested in their environment (2), and spent more time with other drugtakers (1). Six people stated that they rejected not only work but society in general, and one simply commented: 'I gave up work.'

In conversation many drugtakers spoke about their changed life styles as a rebirth which they regarded as an improvement: 'When I was straight I wanted material things, like houses and cars. Now I want to get my head together. I want spiritual things.'

Several individuals used the language of alienation to describe their rejection of the aims and values of the mainstream of society. Some of these reports gave support to the two value systems described by Young. Several maintained that drug use, especially L.S.D. use, had opened up new areas of their minds so that they began to have a fuller comprehension of the true nature of society: 'Once you've tripped with acid the world will never seem the same. You look right through things you used to accept. You see things for what they really are.'

Many individuals had worked out a coherent explanation of their change of orientation since becoming drugtakers. Several spoke of the redefinition of their objectives and most stated that they perceived the changes as beneficial. They rejected a materialistic interpretation of their situation as inappropriate and alien. In conversation they were bitterly critical of such standards being used to judge them, maintaining that it was because they disdained material objectives and conventional social status that they had elected to become drugtakers, or had given up work. It is clearly debatable whether all had made a dispassionate decision as they claimed or were simply rationalizing for their failure in conventional terms. One or two appreciated that from a conventional viewpoint they had declined in status and acknowledged that: 'heads are people who don't get it together in straight society.'

Middle-class standards of status evaluation are irrelevant when applied to people with entirely different criteria. Nevertheless the findings are consistent with R. Cockett's conclusions: 'As one would expect, the more an individual becomes involved in drug-taking, the greater is the likelihood that his work performance and general record will deteriorate' (Cockett 1971:95).

Against this conclusion, two points must be added. First, the majority of non-students had continued with their antecedent career patterns, either working regularly or continuing with their already poor employment records and, in addition, all the students interviewed had continued with their academic careers. Many respondents seemed to reconcile their drugtaking with the constraints of their employment.

Second, most of the very experienced drugtakers had used a wide range of different drugs, but in general, had lost interest in most of these and were primarily cannabis smokers. This is important, since few of the multi-users interviewed were using a wide range of drugs at the time of interview. The general tendency was for initial experimentation with a wide range of drugs to be followed by a reversion to one or a few preferred types of drug. Very few individuals seemed to be physically incapacitated by drug use. There was little to suggest that most or even many of the forty downwardly mobile individuals were made less able to work because of the drugs they were using. A few were often 'stoned' or under the effects of drugs but, even amongst the low-status unemployed and manual workers, this was sometimes disapproved of.

The main influence on those who had been downwardly mobile since becoming drugtakers was that of their overall way of life. Some of those whose careers had undergone what in conventional terms were adverse changes were clearly intelligent and articulate. Several were very introspective and the drugs they preferred, notably cannabis and the hallucinogens, were compatible with their preoccupation with contemplation and self-evaluation. This lifestyle was an explicit and considered rejection of the formal values I have already discussed.

The low-status manual workers without educational qualifications correspond to the former category. The middle-class 'drop-outs' to the second. Those from economically underprivileged backgrounds lacked the means of attaining 'conventional' goals through education or career. Some individuals, for example, the college students who had failed to complete their courses, had either been unable to meet course requirements and pressure or had decided that they were not committed to formal work values and had opted out of 'the system'.

The students and middle-class bohemians were apparently well-integrated within the economic system. Many had high academic attainments and were plainly quite status conscious in conventional terms. In contrast, the low-status unemployed and manual workers had little stake in the conventional economic and social system. They had no chance of obtaining prestige and status in the 'straight' system either because they lacked educational qualifications, or because they rejected the values of the work ethic. I conclude that the low-status unemployed and manual workers were distinctive from the other two sub-groups, both in terms of their general commitment to the workaday world, their self-images as drugtakers, and in other aspects of their life experience and behaviour.

11. Living Conditions

The overall living conditions of the study group reflected its position in a generally early stage of economic development and this established the context of the lifestyles I observed.

Housing is an important aspect of a person's social experience and is often regarded as an indication of social status or economic well-being. In this study I investigated housing in three ways:

1) statistical information about tenure and density of occupation;
2) reported satisfaction or dissatisfaction of respondents with their accommodation;
3) my subjective evaluation of the general condition of a dwelling.

Type of Housing

129, 64.5 per cent of the study group, were living in flats or bedsitters. Two thirds of the multi-users and half of the users used this type of accommodation. More than four fifths had left their parental homes and few were in digs or institutional accommodation (see *Table 32*). Most of the study group were relatively free to live more or less as they chose and shared their dwellings with other single people of their own age. As I have indicated, becoming a drugtaker involved entry into a network of peers. The majority of those interviewed reported that their first drug use had been in friends' flats (see *Table 31*), and the general leisure behaviour of many of those I observed was influenced by the possession of some type of accommodation. Certain areas of Cheltenham were predominantly multi-occupied. Some of the large Regency terraced houses had been divided into flats and bed-sitters of varying quality and, as the

Cheltenham Youth Trust Survey showed, large numbers of young people lived in these dwellings. The Lansdown area in particular contained many large Regency buildings, some of which were in a poor state of repair.

Certain roads had assumed the characterictics of zones of transition (see Rex and Moore 1967), though these were often under preservation orders, where newcomers to the town were most likely to find rented accommodation. These areas were viewed with distaste by some of the town's older residents. On arrival in Cheltenham I walked around some of the central streets in order to decide where I would look for a flat or bedsitter. While in the Lansdown area I was approached by an elderly couple who counselled me not to live on one particular road because it was 'infested', they maintained, with 'drug addicts and other riff-raff'. My subsequent field research corroborated the view that many drugtakers did, in fact, occupy the area and that young people were heavily over-represented in certain blocks which had been converted into flats. The multi-occupied areas of Cheltenham were rather like a small-scale version of parts of Notting Hill described by Jock Young (1971:169–70). Both areas were characterized by a high proportion of young people living in overcrowded and poor dwellings, and had a shifting, heterogeneous population. Young suggests that in areas such as these the usual processes of informal social contact are unable to curb the actions of their residents:

> 'They appear tolerant and permissive to the extent that there is not – unlike in many areas of the city – a monolithic homogeneous population which can dictate patterns of behaviour. It is in such a disunited community that one would expect bohemianism to be able to grow and flourish, and where social control is largely in the hands of formal agencies, chief amongst which is the police.' (Young 1971:170)

It is debatable whether in fact social control in such areas is entirely in the hands of formal agencies. My observations suggested that peer pressures were important. Some of the dwellings occupied by the study group were certainly occupied by a heterogeneous group of people. Several religious cults had formed communes next door to motorcycle gangs and some prostitutes were operating from flats in the area. Students, young workers, and the indigenous working-class groups shared the locality and gave it a volatile, and, as Young suggests, generally permissive character. Arrival in such an area must involve departure from one's previous self-image for young people from middle-class homes. Several respondents reported that as far as they were concerned, living in a shabby flat was all part of their temporary status as students or young workers. As several people pointed out, deviance is a relative label: is it meaningful to call a person deviant if most of his neighbours and friends live in the same way? Many of those interviewed lived in areas that were dominated by young people, and where they had established their own lifestyles. As I have already suggested, peer group pressure appeared an important factor in encouraging and sustaining drugtaking behaviour. People living in buildings or neighbourhoods occupied by a high proportion of young people had a generally free and easy attitude to life and drugtaking was not only evident but widely tolerated, even by individuals who did not use drugs themselves. I knew many students who, though not drugtakers, were well aware of the drugtaking behaviour of many of their friends. Such people correspond to the 'wise', the category of non-deviants who tolerate homosexuality. These are 'normal' people who are privy to the secret life of the stigmatized group.

One hundred and fifty-seven, 78.5 per cent of the study group, were living in privately rented accommodation. Only 4.0 per cent of the 200 individuals interviewed in the 'snowballing' study were in municipal housing, compared with a third of the total population of the Borough of Cheltenham. The study group was highly concentrated in the privately-rented housing sector. My field-work, and the 'snowballing' survey, indicated that flats and bedsitters were highly prized and in short supply in Cheltenham. The individuals interviewed were 'marginal' in terms of their accommodation. Few were eligible for municipal housing, since most were unmarried and many were recent arrivals in the town. Hardly any could afford to buy their own housing and many wanted only temporary accommodation in Cheltenham.

The students were mainly temporary residents in the area and, in general, accepted and even esteemed their flats. Many of the respondents were living independently for the first time and the flat was regarded as the hallmark of independence and freedom. Several individuals commented that they valued their ability to live as they chose, to come and go as they pleased, and, in particular, to entertain,

Table 11

The tenure of the study group

	students		*non-students*		*total*	
	users	*multi-users*	*users*	*multi-users*	*N*	*%*
council-rented	–	1	5	2	8	4.0
unfurnished, privately rented	3	1	5	21	30	15.0
furnished, privately rented	23	32	9	63	127	63.5
owner-occupied	3	8	8	11	30	15.0
occupied through employment	1	–	–	3	4	2.0
temporary	1	–	–	–	1	0.5
total	31	42	27	100	200	100.0

or sleep with, members of the opposite sex. It was evident that many of those interviewed had a very positive evaluation of their housing and the lifestyles they had established around it. It is incorrect to assume that most, or even many, of those in privately-rented accommodation were necessarily failed or thwarted owner-occupiers or potential council tenants. Informal discussions revealed that there was a general ethos centred around flat-dwelling. Social visiting was frequent and many people clearly enjoyed being able to entertain friends in their own homes without being in conflict with the routine of their parents. Many of those I observed regularly stayed up late at night and several commented that they could not have done this if they were still living in their parental homes. Some individuals had set themselves up in a flat in spite of the fact that their parents lived in Cheltenham. This was by no means always indicative of hostility towards their parents; simply a recognition that they had a different lifestyle and were less likely to conflict if living separately.

These findings are consistent with Young and Brooke-Crutchley's conclusion that cannabis smoking students were more likely than others to live in flats of their own, and with American evidence (Presidential Commission) correlating cannabis use with living apart from parents.

Densities of Occupation

Fifty-one individuals, 25.5 per cent of the study group, were living at densities of at least 1.5 persons per habitable room. This is a very high proportion in relation to the total community. The 1966 Sample Census of England and Wales showed that nationally only 2.5 per cent of the population were living at such high densities.

Table 12
Densities of occupation

	students		*non-students*		*Total*	
persons per habitable room	*users*	*multi-users*	*users*	*multi-users*	*N*	*%*
1.5 and above	5	9	3	34	51	25.5
less than 1.5	26	33	24	66	149	74.5
total	31	42	27	100	200	100.0

As the preceding table shows, the highest proportion of those living at high densities was amongst the non-student multi-users, of whom a third were living at densities of at least 1.5 persons per habitable room. In fact the sub-group most likely to be living at high densities was the low-status unemployed and manual workers. 'Overcrowding' is a very subjective, arbitrary concept. Many definitions have been suggested. The Census uses 1.5 persons per habitable room, while local authorities give 'weightings' according to the age and sex of those concerned. It is possible that the official definition of overcrowding differs from that of people living in such conditions. Nevertheless, the survey findings indicated that the housing conditions of the study group are highly atypical in relation to that of the general community. Some of the low-status unemployed and manual workers encountered great difficulty in finding places to live. Those who were unemployed needed permanent addresses in order to qualify for Social Security payments and were under some pressure to find a place to live. Many individuals moved around a great deal and managed to share temporary accommodation with friends. Many of those I interviewed were frequent hosts to such temporary guests who often stayed as long as they were allowed to. Some of those with especially bizarre appearances, such as the Hell's Angels and some of the low-status unemployed and manual workers, found few landlords willing to accept them as tenants. Some males sent their girl friends to negotiate the lease of a flat and moved in hoping that the landlord would accept such a *fait accompli* without argument. Communal living was quite commonplace and many flats were occupied by volatile groups of inhabitants of both sexes. Not all cohabitation involved sexual relationships and several flats were mixed without sexual involvement between those concerned.

Many of those most deeply involved with drugtaking put a great premium on the ideal of the commune or the 'family' of fellow-drugtakers and valued close contact with other drugtakers. Some individuals appeared grateful for the friendship and support they derived from other drugtakers and gravitated towards others sharing their social position. I observed that some communal households were very tolerant of eccentricity and were much more willing to accept individuals with strange personalities than most people would have been. The drug-scene was remarkably open to, and tolerant of, deviants and provided several psychologically disturbed individuals with a network of friends they would otherwise have lacked.

Some of the low-status unemployed and manual workers stated that they had always lived in crowded accommodation. One individual I knew well had previously shared a two-bedroomed house with his parents, ten siblings and four large dogs! This was a density, excluding the dogs, of 3.7 persons per habitable room.

Some of those with labouring jobs were in the habit of periodically sleeping in derelict buildings and I observed several who spent an entire winter in a cellar, sleeping under a few blankets on dirty mattresses. Nine of the low-status unemployed or manual workers were still living with their parents, but several seemed indifferent to where they slept, or with whom, and this indifference certainly accounted for some of the overcrowding that was evident. Thirty-six of the low-status unemployed or manual workers reported that they had lived in at least ten places during the preceding five years, and half a dozen respondents stated that they had been vagrants at different times and had stayed at 'countless' places. High levels of address-changing were significantly associated both with multi-drug use and low socio-economic status.

Another contributory factor to the high densities of occupation was the high incidence of cohabitation outside marriage. Several couples were living together unknown to their landlords. Many of these liaisons were long-lasting but would have been disapproved of by some elderly landlords. Several of the low-status unemployed and manual workers were unable to say exactly how many people were currently staying with them since they often accommodated friends and strangers for indefinite, and unknown, periods. One or two large houses were virtually communes and the numbers of people staying therein at any one time varied considerably. Some of the students shared in this free-and-easy approach to their housing, but many of the non-student bohemians adopted a more 'orthodox' pattern of housing. I must emphasize that the study group came from a wide range of housing types, and included some young professionals with very attractive, spacious accommodation.

Dissatisfaction with High Densities of Occupation

Half of those living at densities of at least 1.5 persons per habitable room reported that they were satisfied with their accommodation. A fifth of these were students who stated that they intended to leave their current addresses within a year or so and accordingly did not mind their crowded conditions.

Twelve of the nineteen non-students who stated they were satisfied with their accommodation also reported that they wanted to move elsewhere if they could do so. Nevertheless, it is notable that as many as half those living at the highest densities did not complain about their living conditions. Some individuals, all deeply involved with the drug-scene, were in conditions which struck me as appalling. One cohabiting couple with young children occupied a condemned damp basement throughout the two and a half years I lived in Cheltenham. They made no serious attempt to move from these conditions in spite of the fact that they had several opportunities to do so. Both parents were working and could easily have afforded, and obtained, a hygienic flat. They seemed indifferent to the most basic elements of hygienic housekeeping. Foetid scraps littered the floors and their children were invariably poorly clothed, ill-used, and physically dirty. Both parents had experience of injecting drugs, and virtually restricted their social contacts to other experienced drugtakers. They often allowed other drugtakers to sleep on the floor of their lounge (a pretentious word for a dirty, littered room) and their lives were dominated by the drug-taking milieu to which they belonged. Neither individual came from particularly impoverished families, but both expressed contempt for 'bourgeois conventions' and spoke in very hostile terms of neighbours whom they perceived as materialistic or 'straight'. An example of their attitudes to their dwelling occurred when I was talking to them. The male brought in mugs of coffee on a tray and, upon noting that the table was filthy and covered with litter, went outside and re-entered with the yard broom with which he proceeded to 'clean' the table.

Some of those most deeply involved in drugtaking, invariably the low-status unemployed and manual workers, were very introverted and withdrawn in their general demeanour. These individuals appeared totally indifferent to their physical surroundings and several slept on dirty mattresses laid on bare boards. These were extreme cases, but it must be noted that the local confidential counselling service, Contact, due to demand, began in 1971 to run a service to provide mattresses for young people with nowhere to sleep.

Several students and middle-class bohemians volunteered that in their opinions 'heads' ' flats were generally in a poor state of repair. I knew many of the low-status group who lived in very dirty accommodation. I illustrate this by describing one particular flat.

Three of those interviewed, all males in their mid-twenties, shared a bedsitter in a large Regency house which was drab and decaying. The lavatory seldom flushed and the communal kitchen, shared with four other bedsitters, was infested with mice and was very dirty. A pile of soiled clothes lay in the corner, amid a tangle of old newspapers and discarded cans and food containers. The shelves were grimy and the oven was so encrusted in grease that it threatened to ignite whenever it was used. The bedsitter itself was a large room, approximately 30 feet x 40 feet, with a high ceiling covered with a crumbling, ornate plaster design. Bedding consisted of three mattresses which had been 'liberated' from a nearby piece of waste land and the only furniture was two old chairs, exuding their stuffing, and a card table. The floor was bare except for two small strips of linoleum and a sheet of cardboard.

The room served as a base for half a dozen other casual visitors as well as the three regular occupants who frequently brought their girl-friends in for the night. The room's shabby walls were decorated by large posters of Jimi Hendrix, Jane Fonda, and Peter Fonda. These posters had been stolen from a nearby shop. In addition several large fold-outs from 'girlie' magazines were pinned to the wall, as well as a motif proclaiming death to the police in particular and to 'straights' in general.

Apart from a tangle of dirty clothing, the only other contents of the flat were a guitar (which had been stolen), several copies of Scandinavian pornographic magazines, and some children's comics. The occupants of this bedsitter were usually out of work but sometimes worked as labourers if they wanted money for any specific purpose. It must be noted that since an indeterminate number of the low-status unemployed and manual workers had no accommodation of their own, those who did possessed a certain cachet within their milieu. Possession of a 'pad' or flat was regarded as a prestige symbol, paradoxical in view of the professed disdain for material possessions evinced by many of the more committed drugtakers. Several individuals with very shabby, even condemned, accommodation asserted that they were 'really getting things together' since they had acquired somewhere to live. By no means all of these were from economically underprivileged homes themselves. One respondent, living himself in crowded, shabby conditions stated that he was aware that I must be taken aback at his surroundings: 'I can't really get things together just now. I know this is a pigsty, but I can't get round to sorting it out.'

As these quotations indicate, many of the low-status unemployed and manual workers were insistent in their use of 'hippy slang' expressions, even to the point of grating repetition. Many constantly re-affirmed their preoccupation with organizing their lives, with re-establishing some form of meaningful pattern or purpose. A great number appeared to encounter severe difficulties in overcoming fairly mundane problems, such as cleaning their floors. There was certainly a cult of being 'hung up' or confused and dissatisfied. Many of those most deeply preoccupied with drugtaking spoke often and at length about their 'hang-ups'. The ethos of this group lent support to interest in emotional problems and it would not be an exaggeration to state that a vicarious prestige was derived from being 'hung up'. This assertion seems ludicrous, and did not generally apply to the students and middle-class bohemians, but was valid in relation to many of those unemployed through choice. Some stated that they did not care about their physical surroundings because they were only concerned with their 'karma' or peace of mind. It is beyond my competence to attempt a psychological or medical assessment of these individuals. I can only state that many seemed neurotic and without a sense of purpose. In relation to their living conditions, it was evident that many did not judge their housing by middle-class standards even if they had been brought up by middle-class parents.

Those in the very worst conditions were invariably multi-drugtakers and usually either unemployed or in menial jobs. These conditions were often associated with low socio-economic status, but sometimes it appeared that a conscious attempt was being made to reject 'conventional' standards and values.

Amongst the students and middle-class bohemians there was an evident ambivalence towards their dwellings. There was no rigid distinction between the housing of these two sub-groups and that of the low-status unemployed and manual workers, except that I noted a more casual observance of standards of hygiene amongst the latter. Certainly the most 'conventional' dwellings and décor were associated with the students and middle-class bohemians, rather than with low-status individuals.

Many students and middle-class bohemians were circumspect and conventional but most decorated their flats with bright posters and paintings. Oriental drapes and psychedelic or mystical designs were popular. Posters by Salvador Dali were in vogue. There was a great interest in colour and form and many of those observed and interviewed had creative, artistic, tastes in décor, which contrasted sharply with the drabness of some of their flats. I noticed that many individuals had selections of books on drugs, politics, the 'alternative society', ecology, mysticism, and allied topics. *Lord of the Rings* was an especially popular book into which may people evidently read mystical or psychedelic significance.

Drugtaking, to some people at least, was linked with a desire to experience changes. Some spoke of their wish to transcend reality. I suggest that the neglect of material possessions that was evident was a function, possibly a rationalization, of their lack of such things and a preoccupation with aesthetic or psychological matters.

Subjective Realities

Many drugtakers stated that they had their own personal values and their own 'alternative' interpretation of life. One of the great problems of social research is that of attaining objectivity or of determining the extent of subjectivity. Social policy decisions and laws are based on arbitrary assumptions about the nature of reality. There is an absolute scale of norms delineated by law and acknowledged by common usage. Deviant behaviour involves a rejection of such absolute conceptions. Berger and Luckman (1966) have pointed out that sociologists attempt to step outside their own realities and to make 'objective' statements about a subject matter of which they are a part. Several individuals made similar comments and asserted that their chosen world view was as valid as anybody else's. Some went further and claimed that drugtakers have a specially penetrating appreciation of the nature of reality, which was why their values were different from those of 'straight' society. Most drugtakers I encountered maintained that cannabis and other drugs had enhanced their perceptions of reality. A minority, primarily those who had given up work or become very deeply involved with drugtaking, contended that since they had become drugtakers they interpreted reality in a totally new and different manner and utterly repudiated materialism and conventional criteria of evaluation.

My conclusions are that most of the students and middle-class bohemians accepted that they were en route to definite careers and accepted their temporary situations in privately rented lodgings. Other drugtakers, particularly those in low-status manual jobs, or those without jobs, were generally in poorer living conditions but often appeared to accept these either because they were from economically underprivileged backgrounds, and were used to such conditions, or because they had rejected conventional notions about housing, or were denied access to it.

Subjective Classification of Housing

I subjectively classified the accommodation of those 173 respondents whose dwellings I was able to visit and inspect. No formal points system was used, but overall condition of a dwelling was generally assessed. I exercised great restraint in making a derogatory assessment.

One hundred and thirty-nine of the 173 whose accommodation was noted were deemed to be in 'acceptable' living conditions. Four individuals, all low-status unemployed or manual workers, were in premises officially designated as unfit for human habitation, and a further nine were living in 'very dirty' conditions.

The evidence suggests that the general living conditions of the students and middle-class bohemians were those to be expected of any young people of this age-group and in broadly similar social positions. The high level of overcrowded and unsatisfactory accommodation was perhaps due to the disregard of many of the low-status unemployed and manual workers for conventional standards of evaluating their living conditions, and partly to the youthfulness of most of those interviewed.

'The Hippy Circuit' and Homelessness

Cheltenham attracted large numbers of young people who were only temporary residents. In addition to those with jobs, or in colleges in

and were seemingly willing to accept housing conditions which would be less satisfactory for longer-term residents or those with young children. The most worrying aspect was the fact that some low-status unemployed and manual workers were bringing up their children in poor conditions. Some of these parents were themselves psychologically disturbed and I noted in one case that children were being brought up in appalling living conditions, which seemed to be accepted by both parents. In such cases, the housing seemed to correspond to the general deficiencies of the parents concerned.

There was certainly a way of life amongst the low-status unemployed and manual workers characterized by their living conditions. Many of those observed during the research refrained from trying to improve their living conditions. A few individuals seemed too unstable to obtain rented accommodation. One schizophrenic nearly attacked a sympathetic estate agent who merely asked him to fill in a routine application form for a bedsitter. Needless to say, the drugtaker concerned encountered great difficulty in finding a suitable dwelling.

It was clear that some individuals were prepared to accept crowded or insanitary housing because it was cheap. The low-status unemployed and manual workers were especially likely to be found in poor accommodation. Some people were limited in their choice by the shortage of flats and by the high rent levels. Others, notably the low-status unemployed and manual workers, chose to spend their money on other things. Some were observed to be heavy cigarette smokers and spent a lot on alcohol.

12. Sexual Behaviour

The popular image of drugtaking in relation to sexual behaviour is ambivalent. On the one hand, drugtakers are often depicted as debauched hedonists, and on the other, as impotent due to the effects of narcotics. One methodological problem is that both drugtaking and sexual behaviour are notoriously difficult subjects to investigate. Both are emotively laden and there is very limited data on either. The only notable British study of sexual behaviour is Schofield's survey which was carried out during the mid 1960s. Schofield found no evidence of a link between sexual behaviour and drugtaking:

> 'No one gave drugs as a reason and indeed the drugs usually associated with teenagers (cannabis and amphetamines) have no aphrodisiac effect and are more likely to decrease sexual performance.' (Schofield 1968:66)

Sexual behaviour is a delicate area to investigate, and for this reason, questions about sex were introduced at the later stages of the interview (questions 78–81). It was hoped that by the time these questions were asked respondents would be relaxed and sufficient rapport established that truthful answers would be elicited. At this stage in the interview so many personal topics had been investigated respondents apparently felt that they might as well 'tell all'. No reluctance was evident in answering questions about sex but the answers obtained were amongst the hardest to validate. My informal contacts with many individuals, their casual statements and behaviour, validated many of their replies. My impression is that a confidential, standardized interview was probably the best method of collecting information about this singularly difficult subject.

Sexual Experience

A very high proportion of those interviewed, 96.0 per cent, reported that they had experienced sexual intercourse at least once. While there is little British evidence with which to compare these findings, they are consistent with Young and Brooke-Crutchley's conclusion that among the students they interviewed, drugtakers were more likely to enter stable sexual relationships than non-drugtakers. Erich Goode makes a similar general comment about American cannabis users:

> 'Pot smokers are more liberal and unconventional in a variety of ways, not merely in political orientation. Sexually, they are more permissive. Or, expressed differently, sexually permissive people are more likely to try to use marijuana than those who are more restrictive, conservative or conventional. The more liberal in sexual matters the individual is, the greater is his chance of using marijuana once, a dozen times, or regularly. The two are part of the same basic thrust – freedom from some of the more restraining mores of American society.' (Goode 1970:45).

These conclusions were supported by the results of a study of American students carried out by Simon and Gagnon. Far more of the sexually liberal students had used cannabis, 24.0 per cent of males and 14.0 per cent of females, than those whose sexual attitudes were rated as conservative, 7.0 per cent of males and 5.0 per cent of females (Gagnon and Simon: 1970).

Goode suggests that the sexual liberalism or permissiveness of cannabis users is a reflection of the predominantly middle-class composition of the drugtaking group: middle-class sexual relationships, he maintains, are more equalitarian, the female expresses more satisfaction and reports a higher frequency of orgasm. He contrasts this with the more 'exploitive' behaviour of working-class males with their sexual partners:

> 'All these attitudes and forms of behaviour have parallels in marijuana use. The more sexually permissive the person is, the greater the likelihood that the person will smoke marijuana, or try it at least once. The more equalitarian he envisions and acts out his sexual relationship, the greater the chances of pot smoking. The

more he rejects many of society's sexual restrictions and prohibitions, the more acceptable marijuana will seem.' (Goode 1970:46).

Goode hypothesizes that cannabis use and sexual liberalism are both dependent upon the same factor, rather than one being dependent on the other. All those interviewed were sexually mature and many, if not married or cohabiting, had regular friends of the opposite sex with whom they often or occasionally had sexual intercourse. Few of those interviewed ever indicated that they disapproved of pre-marital sexual relationships and, in general, such relationships were approved or taken for granted. Several individuals stated that they believed that as a group, drugtakers were 'liberated' people and contrasted themselves with repressed or 'uptight' individuals. These views are consistent with Goode's assertion that the more a person rejects society's conventions, the more likely he is to use drugs and to be sexually permissive. Returning to the suggested dichotomy between formal and subterranean value systems, the pursuit of sexual pleasure is fully compatible with the expressivity and short-term hedonism associated with the latter values. Many individuals spoke quite openly about the fact that they were having sexual intercourse with their current 'steady', and this was widely regarded as a prestigious situation.

The students and middle-class bohemians were generally monogamous in their behaviour and most sexual relationships were clearly stable and affectionate. Some of the low-status unemployed and manual workers were chaotic in their relationships and a few individuals, mainly those from poorer working-class backgrounds, were notably promiscuous. Those who were vagrants or who were usually unemployed appeared particularly prone to be exploitive in their relationships with females. Several had regular sexual relationships with much younger girls, invariably females from local working-class homes, and I was told several instances of such girls having sexual intercourse with several males in succession. The phenomenon of 'gang sex' has been discussed by Hunter-Thompson in relation to the American Hell's Angels, and by James Patrick in relation to Scottish delinquent gangs. Patrick notes that the delinquent males with whom he associated were generally disdainful of females and that, apart from any regular girlfriends they had, several had specifically sexual relationships with notoriously promiscuous females. Patrick reports that there were three females, known as 'cows' who associated with the gang he observed. He encountered one and comments: 'In all she was a pathetic little girl in need of care and protection' (Patrick 1973:107). There were several similar females on the fringe of the low-status unemployed and manual working group I observed. One or two were reputed to have been easy prey sexually. One drug dealer I noted, not normally resident in Cheltenham, invariably had a small harem of very young girls (aged probably about fifteen). These seemed very pathetic and in need of some sort of father figure. I suggest that this constitutes a peculiar form of working-class female deviance.

The promiscuity of some of the low-status unemployed workers was in marked contrast to the behaviour of most of the students and middle-class bohemians, though several of the latter were rather amused by it. One group of students I knew fairly well lived in the same building as a known prostitute. They regarded her as both bizarre and entertaining, but clearly wished to keep at a distance from her. One student commented:

> 'I'm broadminded, but I do feel a bit shocked at it (prostitution) sometimes. I think it's mainly a working-class thing. Most of the blokes who visit the girl downstairs seem to be navvies, or a bit messed-up psychologically. I don't think she uses drugs. She seems to be more "into" a rough cider scene at the moment.'

Amongst the working-class drugtakers there was a considerable emphasis placed upon sexual exploits. A large amount of time was spent bragging about alleged conquests and I noted a similar emphasis on aggressive masculinity and exploitive sex to that recorded by Patrick. One unemployed vagrant told me that he did sometimes form 'decent relationships with a chick', but that more often he 'picked up scrubbers' and had purely casual sexual intercourse with them. On occasion, he reported, he had shared such females with his flat-mates. One or two low-status females were reported to be very promiscuous. I knew of some who had certainly slept around fairly extensively, and one or two of the male respondents alleged that they had caught gonorrhea as the result of their fleeting encounters with these (possibly psychologically disturbed) females.

The high proportion of couples cohabiting reflects the generally unconventional, liberal attitudes of the study group to sexual matters.

I noted that, in general, these couples had very democratic, warm relationships with each other. Several stated that they preferred to cohabit rather than to marry, since their relationships were based upon love and not legal contract. This sort of attitude was quite widespread amongst the middle-class groups, as well as the low-status unemployed or manual workers. Some respondents who were cohabiting stated that they planned to marry eventually, if they had children, in order to safeguard their offspring. 'Marriage is for children' was quite a common contention. Speck and his associates similarly noted that many of their subjects married upon pregnancy (Speck 1972:107). One cohabiting couple who were students reported that they would have preferred to marry but that their joint grants would be reduced if they did, and so they had decided to postpone marriage until they left college.

In comparison with the young people interviewed during Schofield's study, the study group was highly sexually experienced. Thirty-eight of the males, roughly a quarter, and six of the females, about an eighth, reported that they first had sexual experience before they were sixteen. In Schofield's study only 3.0 per cent of males and 1.0 per cent of females reported that they had had sexual intercourse at this age.

Altogether, a third of the males and a fifth of the females stated that their first sexual intercourse had preceded their sixteenth birthday. The disparity between the levels of sexual experience in the present study and Schofield's findings may be attributable to two factors. First, it is distinctly possible that sexual behaviour amongst young people had changed since Schofield's survey. My personal view is that this has been the case and that the advent of the pill has reduced the risk of unwanted pregnancies. In addition, the sexual attitudes of young people appear to have become more liberal. The second point is that this study is not concerned with a representative group of young people in the community. Their high level of sexual experience is quite likely to be atypical. This is suggested by the American findings that drugtakers were generally more sexually permissive than non-drugtakers.

Early Sexual Experience

The low-status unemployed and manual workers were more likely than either the students or middle-class bohemians to report that they

Table 13
Age of first sexual intercourse

	students				*non-students*				*total*	
	users		*multi-users*		*users*		*multi-users*			
	males	*females*	*males*	*females*	*males*	*females*	*males*	*females*	*N*	*%*
14 or earlier	–	–	4	3	2	–	32	3	44	22.0
15	2	1	4	1	1	2	13	2	26	13.0
16	4	1	5	2	3	1	13	3	32	16.0
17	7	1	1	4	4	2	9	5	33	16.5
18	3	4	9	–	1	2	8	–	27	13.5
19	3	1	2	–	1	–	7	3	17	8.5
20 or later	3	–	5	–	2	1	1	1	13	6.5
Still virgin	1	–	1	1	2	3	–	–	8	4.0
total	23	8	31	11	16	11	83	17	200	100.0

had had early sexual intercourse. The survey revealed that males, multi-users, and those from low-status backgrounds were significantly more likely than others to report this.

Social Class

Schofield found that although drugtaking did not seem a relevant factor, girls from higher status backgrounds were more likely than others to be sexually experienced (Schofield 1968:117). In the present study, the reverse was evident. Respondents from working-class backgrounds were significantly more likely than others to report that they had experienced sexual intercourse before they were sixteen. Many studies have linked deviant behaviour with low social status and the evidence of the present study substantiates the view that precocious sexual intercourse was most likely amongst the low-status unemployed and manual workers.

Delinquency

Amongst males there was a significant association between having had sexual intercourse under the age of fifteen, and being delinquent. Twenty-six of the thirty-eight males reporting early sexual experience had also been in trouble with the police, compared with only forty-three of the remaining 115 males interviewed.

The students and middle-class respondents were generally more restrained by their later school-leaving ages and commitment to 'normal' careers or educational goals, than were the low-status unemployed and working-class. The latter had more free time to do as they pleased, and my observations suggested that, in general, the working-class groups were more overtly sexual and aggressive than either the student or non-manual workers. Those who were manual workers or who were unemployed were generally those most deeply involved with the subterranean values of the drug-scene and the least committed to conventional middle-class standards. Their sexual behaviour and their delinquency reflects this detachment from 'conventional' norms.

The values and socialization patterns of the middle-class are often alleged to instil greater 'moral restraint' than those of the working-class who are consequently likely to act more impulsively in pursuit of immediate gratification (Grey 1969). Sexual opportunities for many middle-class young people are limited until they leave home. Thirty-three of the seventy-three students reported that they had first experienced sexual intercourse after their eighteenth birthday when they were either at college or university.

The findings are generally consistent with the evidence of several studies which show that low-status delinquent males were especially likely to have sexual experiences that did not involve emotional commitments. Thrasher, in his study of the gang observed:

> 'There is a common practice among young men in Chicago, and this is by no means confined to boys of the groups of the underprivileged classes, of picking up girls, utter strangers, on the street and taking them for a ride in an automobile. During the course of this ride it is customary to indulge in passionate petting, and often the affair culminates in the sex act. If the girl refuses, it is commonly supposed that she is put out of the car some place in the country and asked to walk back.' (Thrasher 1927:238)

Patrick noted a similar pattern of behaviour amongst Glasgow gangs: One of his approved school boys wrote this:

> 'Nowadays the gangs only fight for kicks and mostly show off to daft girls who like a lot of attention and that's where the rape comes in. They take a girl round the back close, kiss her a few times and then expect her to drop her knickers. If she doesn't she gets raped and there's nothing the poor cow can do about it.' (Patrick 1973:107)

Some of the low-status respondents, generally those with labouring jobs, often picked up girls whom they scarcely knew for explicitly sexual purposes. One of two cases of rape were reputed to have occurred but it is doubtful if much serious resistance was encountered. Some of the students reported that they often picked up girls at college dances in a similar manner and there was no evidence to indicate that the only students who did this were drugtakers. Both sexual experience and drugtaking were related to general sociability, as well as to liberal ideology. Many of the girls I interviewed had originally been 'turned on' by males with whom they had sexual relationships, and so at least for females, drugtaking and sexual experience were closely linked.

Sex

Males were twice as likely as females to report having first had sexual intercourse before they were fifteen, a quarter, compared with an eighth. The numbers involved were too small to permit a test of statistical association, but these findings are consistent with Schofield's conclusion that males were more likely than females to report early sexual experience. In the present study the difference in this respect between the two sexes was no longer apparent by the time the age of sixteen had been attained. Most research shows that females are less likely than males to be deviant, with the exception of specifically sexual forms of deviant behaviour. The evidence of the present study indicates that the females were as sexually experienced as the males, at least after the age of sixteen.

Students

Students were generally less likely than the rest of the study group to report that they had had sexual intercourse before they were fifteen, seven out of 73 compared with thirty-seven out of 127.

Most of the students were from non-manual backgrounds, and I suggest that their generally later ages of first having sexual intercourse were related to their socio-economic status, rather than to the fact they were students. Forty-two of the forty-four individuals reporting that they had experienced sexual intercourse before they were fifteen were multi-users. Schofield found that sexual behaviour was associated with drinking and smoking. Sexually experienced teenagers were more likely than others to use alcohol and to smoke cigarettes. Schofield's study indicated that drinking, smoking, and sex were all aspects of the general social behaviour of young people. He asserts that sexual behaviour amongst young people is influenced by the 'teenage sub-culture'. There is, he maintains, a popular image of how a young adult should behave and some young people are pressurized by their peers to conform to this image, even to the extent of having sexual intercourse against their better judgement (Schofield 1968:146–9).

Informal discussion with several groups of drugtakers corroborated this view. One professional man in his early thirties stated that when he had been a university student there had been great pressure to brag about sexual conquests and sexual prowess was assumed to be the gauge of one's masculinity: 'I was afraid to admit that I was still a virgin. I expect half the others were too.'

Sexual achievements are quite widely discussed by groups of young males. I noted this to be true amongst all of the main sub-groups, with the general exception of those with a regular female partner, who generally avoided such discussions. This could well indicate that sexual insecurity, rather than sexual fulfilment, provoked many conversations about amorous conquests. Some of those most voluble about their virility were those with little status in conventional terms. Many of the low-status unemployed and manual workers continually assured me that they were 'having it regular' and extolled the virtues of friends of theirs who were perceived as especially talented at 'pulling chicks'. Overt coarseness in statements about sex was often evident amongst the manual workers but many of the middle-class respondents regarded it as a mark of their liberalism and freedom from convention to be explicit about sexual matters and to use sexually-orientated swear words. In general those most committed to the general lifestyles of the drug scene were those with the least stable sexual relationships. Some changed their sexual partners frequently and a few individuals lived with several different people during my residence in Cheltenham.

The great majority of students and middle-class bohemians, though liberal in their opinions, were not promiscuous. The survey did not examine how many sex partners respondents had had, but my general impression was that both drugtaking and sexual behaviour were related to the general lifestyle and social position of the individual.

Early first sexual experience was associated with the use of heroin and other injected drugs. Fourteen of the forty-four individuals who reported that they had experienced sexual intercourse before they were fifteen had used heroin: a further two had injected other drugs. More than half of the twenty-four people reporting that they had used heroin also reported that they had experienced sexual intercourse before their fifteenth birthday.

Early first sexual intercourse was associated with early first drug experience. Thirteen of the forty-four reporting that they had had sexual intercourse before their fifteenth birthday also reported having used drugs before they were fifteen. Ten of these were from working-class families.

Drugs and Interest in Sex

The drugtakers interviewed were divided in their views on whether or not drugs had affected their interest in sex. Some believed there had been little link between the two. Others asserted that there had been an association, either as an aphrodisiac, or in reducing interest in sex. Nobody reported that drugs had made them interested in their own sex. Perhaps this result was misleading for homosexual tendencies are likely to be concealed.

Altogether, 61.5 per cent of those interviewed stated that the drugs they had used had at some time increased their interest in sex. Roughly a third of these attributed this to a reduction of inhibition and their existing mood rather than to a chemical aphrodisiac effect. A third of the study group reported noticing little, if any, connection between the drugs they had used (mainly cannabis) and sex, and nineteen individuals had found that drugs reduced their interest. Certain drugs, particularly the opiates, are generally agreed to depress sexuality. Two of the heroin users confirmed that whenever they had used heroin over a prolonged period they had become temporarily impotent.

Psychedelics present a more confused picture. Leary maintained that L.S.D. is primarily a sexual drug. Many of those who had used L.S.D. disagreed with this view. Hallucinogens are sensual drugs, they maintained, but not explicitly sexual ones. Several individuals reported having made love while under the influence of L.S.D. and mescalin and reported that their enjoyment had, in fact, been enhanced by these drugs. Many people had used cannabis in a sexual context but it was generally agreed that if one is in a good mood, or in an agreeable situation, hallucinogenic drugs are likely to increase one's general appreciation, regardless of whether it is of sex, or anything else. Hallucinogens were not claimed by anyone to be dependable aphrodisiacs. They intensified perception rather than changing it in any particular way.

The general opinion of cannabis was that it could, under the right circumstances, increase interest in sex. Many people were emphatic that hallucinogens, including cannabis, increase one's affections for a lover on an emotional as well as a purely physical level. Several people stated that L.S.D. made them fully appreciate the spiritual and intellectual virtues of others rather than increasing their sexual impulses.

Table 14
The effects of drugs on sexual interest

	students				*non-students*				*total*	
	users		*multi-users*		*users*		*multi-users*			
	males	*females*	*males*	*females*	*males*	*females*	*males*	*females*	N	%
little connection	12	5	11	2	4	4	16	4	58	26.0
depends on mood/ drug	3	1	4	1	5	–	26	4	44	22.0
some drugs increase interest	8	–	12	7	5	6	33	8	79	39.5
drugs reduce interest	–	2	4	1	2	1	8	1	19	9.5
total	23	8	31	11	16	11	83	17	200	100.0

Cannabis and the barbiturates were frequently compared with alcohol:

> '. . . Therefore much drink may be said to be an equivocator with lechery; it makes him and it mars him; it sets him on, and it takes him off; it persuades him, and disheartens him; makes him stand to; and not stand to; in conclusion, equivocates him in a sleep, and giving him the lie, leaves him.' (Shakespeare, *Macbeth,* Act II, scene III).

Cannabis may reduce one's inhibitions in a sexual situation, and so act as a catalyst to sexual behaviour, but it is as likely to induce lethargy and sleep. Barbiturates and Mandrax similarly produce intoxication, which may act in the same way, although there is a certain amount of folk lore about the aphrodisiac effects of 'randy Mandies'.

Several people reported that amphetamines were sexual stimulants. These drugs induce a surge of confidence and energy and may well be used in a sexual situation to increase alertness.

The consensus view was that drugs were only mildly related to sexual enjoyment and were mainly reducers of inhibition. It is suggested that relatively few people used drugs for specifically sexual purposes, although some had deliberately done so on occasion.

There are a few apocryphal stories about people using various solvents and dry-cleaning fluids as aphrodisiacs. Such practices are likely to be dangerous and unsuccessful. The main link between drugs and sexuality is a situational one. People tend to make love to those they are closest to emotionally. They often use drugs in a similar way and so drugtaking and sexual intercourse may occur more or less simultaneously. It is likely that most drugtakers will have sexual relations with partners who are at least aware of their drugtaking, even if they do not necessarily join in. If both partners use drugs, it is distinctly possible that eventually they will combine drugs with sex, just as many 'conventional' people combine alcohol and sex.

Drugs and Sexual Enjoyment

Forty per cent of those interviewed reported that drugs had enabled them to increase their sexual enjoyment. The opposite was reported by 57.5 per cent. Only amongst the non-student multi-users did a majority report that drugs had increased sexual enjoyment. It is suggested that this group were more attached to drugs and to the drugtaking way of life than most of the others interviewed. In my view, many of this group would report that drugs increased their enjoyment of life in general, rather than just of sex. In many ways, this group was the most hedonistic and tended to use drugs more extensively than most of the student multi-users.

Sexual Difficulties

A few people stated that they were poor at making contact with members of the opposite sex and that their drugtaking was an attempted solution to, or escape from, this problem. In some cases the individuals concerned were physically very unattractive (in my view!) and clearly felt distressed by their inability to attract partners, or to maintain permanent, or long-term relationships. One young male, very neglected physically, and acutely depressive in personality, stated that his sexual problems were steadily forcing him towards 'heavy' (dangerous) drugs. This individual felt that he was a failure in the eyes of his parents, who expected high academic attainments from him which he was unable to achieve. He was clearly psycho-neurotic and acknowledged that he used drugs to deaden his sense of sexual and academic failure. I noted half a dozen vagrants (all males) who spoke in similar terms of their sexual problems. In all cases, the people concerned appeared generally psychologically disturbed and may have been attributing this general state to sexuality. Some of these had few friends, and only fleeting sexual episodes, since they were difficult to communicate or live with.

Sexual Behaviour and Drugtaking

The results of the study indicate that most of the drugtakers interviewed were sexually experienced and, in comparison with Schofield's survey, unusually so.

The evidence leads towards the conclusion that sexual behaviour was considered a normal part of the lifestyle of the groups observed. There was certainly considerable sexual competition amongst groups of young males, to the extent that virginity had a stigma in some circles where it was regarded as a sign of immaturity. There were some casual sexual liaisons amongst many groups of young people. This was true of some of the low-status drugtakers observed, but most respondents were basically monogamous in their habits.

The individuals most likely to exhibit promiscuous behaviour were observed to be the low-status group, many of whom were very experienced drugtakers and who reported that sexual and drugtaking activities started simultaneously, at an early age. One classic illustration of this was given by a drugtaker who at the time of the survey, was working and fairly well-established economically:

> 'When I was fourteen I ran away from home because I wanted to be a hippy . . . I finally met some people by the seaside. My initiation was a good one. I made it for the first time with a chick in a cave. That was also the first time I used dope. I didn't take much notice of the drug though, because I was too interested in the sexual bit.'

Entry into the drug-using sub-culture involves a revision of one's values and definitions concerning behaviour. People with rigid orientations are unlikely to have a psychological need to do this. In some ways drugtakers adopt an agnostic, short-term pragmatism. New experiences are welcomed and assessed individually. Sexuality is another form of pleasure-seeking and is compatible with the (anti-Puritan) ethos of the sub-culture. There is an emphasis on being human and spontaneous and drugtakers generally choose to take some of their values from the peer-group instead of from their parents. Most of the students and middle-class bohemians interviewed emphasized that they only valued sex in conjunction with sincere relationships but, in the same way, thought sex a natural corollary of being in love. I believe that in a college or university situation drugtaking and sexual experience are likely correlates of sociability and involvement with other people.

Erich Goode in the United States found greater sexual opportunities and maturity amongst cannabis smokers than amongst non-users:

> 'American University students who use marihuana are far more likely to have engaged in pre-marital sex; and the more frequently any given undergraduate used marihuana, the greater would be his sexual experience.'

Goode concluded that drug use and sexual behaviour were more influenced by social factors than personality (Goode 1972b).

One interesting fact was the apparent absence of homosexual relationships. This may be due to my failure to investigate this as a separate topic. Many individuals lived with peers of the same sex but none were obviously homosexual. Amongst the low-status unemployed and manual workers a few individuals stated that they had had occasional homosexual experiences, but that these had been without any emotional involvement and they did not consider themselves to be homosexual. Similar instances of homosexuality by 'heterosexual' males were reported by Humphreys in his participant observation study in America (Humphreys 1970).

During my field-work I noted that the 'gay scene' or homosexual fraternity frequented rather different haunts from most of the drugtakers I encountered. The two milieux seemed fairly separate, and while some drugtakers were doubtless homosexual, the ethos of the drug scene, as of youth culture in general, was overwhelmingly heterosexual. Because of this heterosexual behaviour tended to be far more conspicuous than any homosexual liaisons, which were more likely to have been concealed.

Was There a Uniform Lifestyle?

In this section I have examined some indicators of the lifestyle of the study group: employment, living conditions, and sexual behaviour. While it is possible from this evidence to produce a composite picture of the 'typical' drugtaker who is employed or a student, living in a flat, and sexually experienced or permissive, this would be misleading. My general conclusion in relation to the subjects of this study is similar to G. V. Stimson's impression of the 111 heroin addicts in his recent research; that the differences between the sub-groups are too great to warrant any single stereotype.

My field-work experience and the survey data support the view that there were important regularities of behaviour and life experience associated with the illegal (and legal) use of drugs. This does not imply that drug use necessarily produces a lifestyle or is produced by that lifestyle. Both may have been 'caused' by other factors, such as age, being of low-status through unemployment or manual work, or by attributes associated with being a student or middle-class bohemian. The study group nevertheless regarded themselves, in many ways, as a distinctive section within the community. As I have suggested, the behaviour of the low-status sub-group contrasted with that of other respondents.

In my discussion of the notions of sub-culture and contra culture I stated that there was great diversity within the study group, in spite of their general identity as 'radical' drugtakers. My observations of their lifestyles conform to my view that the 'sub-culture' if such exists, contains many disparate and individualistic groups, differentiated primarily by their employment patterns, self-images, and general social position.

13. Drugtaking and Social Structure

I have examined how drugtaking groups with a characteristic lifestyle developed as the crystallization of social positions. I shall attempt in this chapter to evaluate the empirical evidence I have collected in the light of theories of anomie. The variations within the study group place severe limitations upon the usefulness of many sociological theories. Most sociological theories of deviant behaviour are essentially class theories and are therefore rendered inappropriate by the fact that 60.0 per cent of the study group were from non-manual backgrounds.

One of the main sociological theories of deviant behaviour is the theory of anomie, or normlessness. The concept of anomie was originally introduced by Emile Durkheim to describe an imperfect relationship between individuals and the social structure. In *The Division of Labour*, first published in 1893, he suggested that as society develops technically, it becomes less able to provide psychological satisfaction for its members. Rapid social change leaves people in a vacuum and anomie ensues as the result of the loss of traditional expectations and usages.

Durkheim's sociological theory was extended in 1938 by Robert Merton. Merton agreed with the earlier writer that when restraints wither, certain social conditions may cause 'excessive ambition' which may break the norms of traditional interaction. Merton distinguished between the culturally prescribed goals of a society and the means available to attain them. He suggested that post-industrial society emphasizes the goal of monetary wealth more than the importance of legitimate ways of competing for it. He emphasized the sociological nature of his theory and distinguished the estrangement of a single personality, 'anomia' from the disjunction of goals from legitimate ways of reaching them, which causes anomie. If each role incumbent within the social structure is motivated to use conventional means of achieving common goals, deviance is unlikely unless more fruitful alternative means are available, or other goals become valued. Merton suggests that people select patterns of behaviour determined by the correspondence or dissonance between their aspirations and expectations. Strain is: 'a function of the degree of disjunction between goals and means, or of the sufficiency of means to the attainment of goals.'

Talcott Parsons contends that anomie is the antithesis of complete integration and maintains that there is a continuum between these two extreme states (Parsons 1949:377). Merton re-iterates Durkheim's view that in some societies, certain goals are inherently unlimited and have been pursued so fervently that the appropriate normative restraints have collapsed. Merton emphasized the variety of deviant behaviour, a symptom of anomie, but concedes that not all deviance is due to malintegration. Merton's views have been criticized on the grounds that individual behaviour is influenced by personality and socialization, which need not support common values and goals. A family socializes its members by transmitting to them that fragment of a culture to which it has been exposed. A. Cohen has commented upon the influence of sub-cultures within society, as being deviant, yet organized and enforcing their own forms of institutionalized behaviour on their members.

MacIver defines anomie as

> 'the state of mind of one who has been pulled up by his moral roots . . . The anomic has become spiritually sterile, responsive only to himself and responsible to no one, He lives on the thin line of sensation between no future and no past.' (MacIver 1950)

This departs from the purely sociological approach to anomie. In 1956 L. Srole produced a scale to measure the psychological dimensions of anomie, which he conceptualized as a state of mind relating to the actor and his perceptions. He tried to measure satisfaction with level of adaptation. He assumed that individuals react to their social environment. Later his scale was broadened to account for the independent personality factors. His scale revealed that individual satisfaction with one's situation was related to socio-economic status factors dependent upon position within the opportunity structure.

Anomie is partly a group or social solution or response, in some way attributable to separate psychological factors such as rigidity and hostility. Some people are better equipped to tolerate status frustration and adapt to new situations than others. Insofar as this has proved to be tenable, theories of anomie have been modified to include the psychological influences of an individual's attitude to contemporary society. Some theorists suggest that a differing incidence of 'anomic persons' in different social strata may indicate distribution of certain (psychotic) personality types rather than the effects of socialization.

Merton suggests that there are different types of adaptation to anomie. He describes five types of reaction, related to the availability and acceptance of, the prevailing values in society. He suggests that the type of deviant behaviour a person adopts will depend upon the pressure exerted upon him by the social structure.

Table 15
*Merton's theory of deviant innovations**

mode of adaptation		*culture goals*	*institutionalized means*
I	conformity	+	+
II	innovation	+	–
III	ritualism	–	+
IV	retreation	–	–
V	rebellion	±	±

(+ signifies acceptance, – signifies rejection, and ± signifies 'rejection of prevailing values and substitution of new values'.)
(*From Merton 1964: 140).

Merton assumes that, initially, people share a common set of social goals, and that their behaviour depends on the possibility of these being attained.

I *Conformity* is possible when people accept the goals and have a reasonable chance of attaining their ends.

II *Innovation* ensues when the means of achieving social goals are unevenly distributed: 'This response occurs when the individual has assimilated the cultural emphasis upon the goal without internalizing the institutional views governing ways and means for its attainment.'

High ambitions combined with unequal chances are associated with higher rates of deviant behaviour amongst the least privileged strata in society. Merton comments (1963:141) on the general pressure to succeed in the 'open-class ideology' of the United States. This puts more emphasis on goals than on the approved means of attaining them. Hence, some sections of the population use deviant ways of reaching socially approved goals.

III *Ritualism* involves the scaling-down of 'lofty cultural goals' to the point of satisfying one's aspirations without contravening the norms of society. Merton recognizes that this is scarcely a form of deviance. It is rather a 'conformist' but unambitious response of accepting the general goals of affluence and status on a reduced level. Merton asserts that ritualism is commonplace in societies where one's status depends largely on one's achievements.

> 'The syndrome of the social ritualist is both familiar and instructive. His implicit life-philosophy finds expression in a series of cultural cliches: "I'm not sticking my neck out", "I'm playing safe", "I'm satisfied with what I've got", "Don't aim too high and you won't be disappointed".' (1963:150)

This is a typical lower-class form of adaptation.

IV *Retreatism* is an adaptation by rejecting both cultural goals and institutionalized means. Merton suggests it is probably the least common form of deviance. He states that people adopting this pattern of behaviour are in society, but not of it.

> 'In this category fall some of the adaptive activities of psychotics, autists, pariahs, outcasts, vagrants, vagabonds, tramps, chronic drunkards and drug addicts . . . This is not to say that in some cases the source of their mode of adaptation is not the very social structure which they have in effect repudiated nor that their very existence within an area does not constitute a problem for members of society.'

Retreatism is likely to occur when the individual assimilates both the cultural goals and institutional practices, but fails to achieve the desired ends through approved means. Defeat and frustration lead to the 'drop-out reaction'. The realization that cultural goals are unobtainable is followed by a rationalizing 'rejection' of both goals and means. Sometimes the fantasy life is chosen as an alternative source of gratification. This is often a suggested reason for drugtaking.

V *Rebellion* leads people to try to change the social structures to create a new set of goals and means. Merton suggests that this reaction is more likely from members of a rising class than from those who are on the way down.

Merton's revaluation of 'anomie' is as much a subjective evaluation as an empirical one. He failed to emphasize the differential availability of illegitimate as well as legitimate means. A person lacking either approved or delinquent means of gaining social goals may adopt the fourth mode of deviation, retreatism. Merton's theory assumes that everyone in a society will share common goals. This is debatable. Phillipson points out that he does not explain movement into and away from deviant careers, nor the choice of any specific reaction to a state of anomie (Phillipson 1971).

The ecological studies of the 'Chicago School' of urban sociologists examined the incidence of various types of deviancy in Chicago. These studies emphasized the 'normality' of some forms of deviant behaviour in certain neighbourhoods. Most of the studies were taken to support Durkheim's view that deviancy was a symptom of disorganization.

Two studies in particular are notable: Thrasher's research into delinquent gangs (1927), and Whyte's *Street Corner Society* (1968). Both were detailed pieces of field research and questioned the assumption of deviance being 'pathological', since within their own terms of reference, deviant groups were organized and require conformity. Sutherland suggests that deviants learn their behaviour within a sub-culture, a network of other deviants. In relation to drugtaking, my own experience substantiates this view. Cloward and Ohlin (1960) maintain that all young people internalize middle-class objectives but that in working-class districts legitimate opportunities are scarcer than elsewhere, so illegitimate (deviant) alternatives are adopted if these are readily available. In some areas crime is well organized, but in others it is not, and a looser, aggressive reaction ensues instead of the pursuit of material gain. This view was challenged by W. B. Miller (1962) who maintained that middle-class values are different from those of the lowest strata of the working class. This makes it inappropriate to evaluate the behaviour of both groups with the same criteria.

The first obvious disparity between the findings of the present study and anomie theory is the fact that many of those interviewed were from middle-class backgrounds. The students and middle-class bohemians appeared to be successful in 'conventional' terms, and seemed to seek their objectives in culturally approved ways, through education and employment. Most of the respondents appeared to be contending with the demands of their careers. The evidence supports the conclusion that the students and middle-class bohemians were not in a state of anomie as described by Merton. On the other hand, the low-status unemployed and manual workers could be interpreted as being in such a state. Referring to Merton's categories of innovation, some individuals were retreatist, that is, they had failed to achieve their aims due to lack of educational qualifications or inability to meet the demands of jobs or education. There was a continuum of involvement with the drugtaking way of life. In general those most involved with the lifestyles were the low-status individuals. This sub-group, but only this sub-group, appeared to correspond to the conditions of anomie and could well have become drugtakers as a response to thwarted aspirations.

In its most extreme form, the drugtaking way of life was incompatible with continuing work or education. This was evinced by the disdain for work expressed by several 'heads'. In general, those with access to middle-class goals, and who had been socialized to accept such goals, were unlikely to reject them, as long as their peer group supported their pursuit. Students and non-manual workers had clear career objectives and these sub-groups usually discouraged deflections from the pursuit of these goals. There seemed little chance that a person in a student or middle-class milieu would become attracted to the lifestyle of the unemployed or low-status 'head'. This was generally regarded as an undesirable identity. But it must be stressed that people can become addicted accidentally, and some addicts are members of the high-status medical professions. Availability of drugs may be an additional factor.

Much of the behaviour of the groups I observed was not instrumental, that is, intended to attain middle-class or conventional goals. Some individuals were criminal, but most were not. In relation to Merton's suggested types of innovation, the lifestyle of the low-status unemployed or manual workers appeared to be retreatist. Many of this group had not only rejected the means of attaining cultural goals by giving up work or education; they had rejected the goals themselves. As a group, they had evolved a sub-cultural response to economic privation and lack of education of ideological hostility to conventional society. This sub-group was quite distinct from the students and middle-class bohemians who were generally conformist. Those individuals who had decided to drop-out of the educational system had apparently undergone an ideological conversion away from middle-class values and goals. There is no evidence that all those from poorer working-class backgrounds ever had high levels of aspiration in conventional terms. Perhaps as W. B. Miller suggests, they never contemplated middle-class goals. While accepting Merton's assertion that deviance is most likely at times of social change (such as *rite de passage*, or trauma), I do not interpret the evidence of this study as a general substantiation of the view that all respondents had become drugtakers, or adopted their respective lifestyles 'because' of 'strains' within the social system.

Anomie is a social position or situation and it is not necessarily equated with low status or poverty. It is a collective response rather than an individual state (anomia). It has widely been assumed that anomie involves the replacement of legitimate or socially accepted behaviour by deviant or illegitimate behaviour. This, as Merton has stated, may be a response to status frustration or lack of opportunity within the conventional, workaday world. In my discussion of sub-culture and reference groups I indicated that the study group was not homogeneous. The evidence of this study suggests that the 'drug scene' contains a widely differing number of individuals and sub-groups, who have in common only a vague ideological consensus and a single pattern of behaviour, namely cannabis smoking. Some individuals were far more committed to drugtaking and its attendant lifestyles and ideologies than others, and any theoretical explanation or analysis of illegal drug use must take these important differences into account. The 'sub-culture' of drugtakers was not a whole entity separate from society and only certain groups within the drug scene appeared to approximate to a contra-culture, or to be totally beyond the goals and values of the mainstream of society.

The students and middle-class bohemians had access to, and were generally motivated to attain, middle-class or conventional goals. Most appeared to have conventional self-images and restricted their drugtaking accordingly. Even so, some could have been under stress not known to an outsider. The drug scene was a constellation of disparate groupings and sub-networks, linked in some cases only by the common factor of drugtaking. Only some of the low-status unemployed and manual workers corresponded to the retreatist mode of adaptation sometimes associated with drugtaking. Elements in this sub-group seemed to have a sense of futility and purposelessness and to believe that they could not attain their ambitions within society. The distinction between the low-status unemployed and manual workers and the students and middle-class bohemians was evident in relation to their values, patterns of drugtaking, their lifestyle, and other biographical data. My observations lead me to conclude that in many ways the low-status unemployed and manual workers most nearly approximated to the stereotype of the junkie; 'purposeless, drifting youngsters' (Willis 1973:71).

It did seem evident, however, that the drug scene was a collective response to at least a vague discontent with conventional, conservative ideals and 'straight' society. Following from the general conclusion that the study group were heterogeneous, only the most deeply committed to drugtaking as an alternative way of life and primary point of reference correspond to the situation or response known as anomie.

My judgement is that anomie theory is a useful way of characterizing the extreme form of commitment to drugtaking most evident amongst the low-status unemployed and manual workers, those with the least stake in the mainstream of society. I do not think that the drugtaking of those who seemed successful occupationally and academically, and who for the most part seemed to define their identities and ambitions within the workaday world, need necessarily be explained in terms of anomie. My examination of this topic has been largely concerned with anomie as a group solution to problems of adjustment within the social structure. In view of the extensive use of psychological research in this field, it is possible that the formation of at least some drugtaking coteries can be explained in psychological terms. It is a further possibility that drugtaking is associated with, or caused by, peculiarities of biographical experience, which may be regarded as ancillary symptoms of stress or maladaption within the social system. For this reason I shall discuss some of the relevant biographical details of the study group, which may illuminate my evaluation of the general well-being of those I interviewed.

Acknowledgement
The author and publishers wish to thank Macmillan Publishing Company, Inc. for permission to reproduce *Table 15*, taken from Robert Merton (1964), *Social Theory and Social Structure* : 140.

FIVE Some Aspects of Life Experience

14. Biographical Disturbance

It has frequently been implied that deviant behaviour may be a response to social or psychological stresses. I have evaluated the general lifestyle of the study group in relation to Merton's theory of anomie. Many of the clinical studies of drugtakers, including those I have mentioned, have indicated that a high proportion of individuals receiving medical treatment for physical drug dependence have disturbed biographies. This information has contributed to a general assumption amongst policy makers and non-drugtakers at large that drugtaking is a symptom of distress or privation. One of the main distinctive features of the present study is that it is concerned, not with in-patients or drugtakers known to 'official' agencies, but with individuals in the community. It is illuminating, therefore, to discover how the biographies of the study group compare or contrast with those of institutionalized drug dependents, who may not be typical of drugtakers in the community. The study group were most unlikely to be a representative sample of the total drugtaking population. Nevertheless, it is useful to relate the evidence of the present study to research findings collected in different ways.

Family Background

The classic sociological investigation by Isador Chein and his associates in New York came to the conclusion:

> 'In almost all the addict families (97 per cent) there was a disturbed relationship between the parents, as evidenced by separation, divorce, open hostility, or lack of warmth and mutual

> interest. In these conditions the mother was usually the important parent figure in the life of the youngster. But, whatever the vicissitudes of the relationship between the boy and his mother, one theme was almost invariably the same – the absence of a warm relationship with a father figure with whom the boy could identify.' (Chein *et al.* 1964:273–4)

Much of the research into deviance has emphasized the importance of family relationships to the subsequent development of the individual. The work of John Bowlby has been notable in this field (1957). The popular stereotype of the drugtaker depicts an individual attempting to escape from all manner of suggested social and psychological problems. This stereotype is largely based upon the case histories of in-patients attending drug treatment centres.

Intactness of natural family

One hundred and sixty-five of the 200 respondents, 82.5 per cent of the study group, had been brought up continuously by both parents. Two individuals had been born out of wedlock and did not know who their real parents were. Parental separation, divorce, or death did not appear to be associated with social class, sexual behaviour, delinquency, or drug histories. In fact, it did not seem a relevant factor.

Cockett's study of drugtaking amongst young offenders also investigated the influence of disrupted parental relationships upon drug use. He concluded that family disruption, the break-up of the relationship of an individual's natural parents by death, separation, or divorce before the individual reached the age of sixteen had no bearing on the occurrence or development of drugtaking habits: 'The drugtakers do not show any consistent difference from the controls in regard to the percentage with disrupted families' (Cockett 1971:82–3).

Cockett's study was concerned with young people who were convicted offenders. These were all 'deviant' since they were delinquent. This study hardly looked at a general cross-section of young people, since both the drugtaking and control groups were institutionalized. It is possible that the controls may have had unusually disturbed family backgrounds which concealed the fact that the drugtakers did too.

The findings of the present study are consistent with those of

Cockett's investigation and depart from the traditional notion that drugtakers are largely, or often, from disrupted family backgrounds. Only in one or two cases were individuals from disrupted family backgrounds evidently 'at risk'. One male, who had been brought up in a children's home, had a history of severe psychiatric illnesses and was deeply involved with the drug scene. In general, those individuals whose parents had separated, divorced, or died seemed no different from those whose natural families remained intact.

Relationship between parents

In view of the suggestions in the literature that impaired or disturbed family relationships are influential in the development of deviance, the perceived quality of the relationship between each respondent's parents was examined. 133 individuals, 66.5 per cent of the study group, reported that they believed both of their parents were happy together. Twenty-seven per cent stated that they believed one or both of their parents to be unhappy together, and thirteen individuals, 6.5 per cent, were uncertain about the quality of the relationship between their parents. Females were significantly more likely than males to state that they believed their parents were unhappy together, twenty out of forty-seven, compared with only thirty-four out of 153. It is possible either that the females in the study group were more psychologically disturbed than the males or that females were more sensitive than males to the quality of their parents' relationships.

Multi-users were significantly more likely than users to report that they believed their parents were unhappy together, forty-two out of 142, compared with seven out of fifty-three. Perceived parental unhappiness was not significantly associated with experience of injecting drugs. This is interesting, since many studies of addicts at treatment centres suggest drug dependence is linked with disrupted family backgrounds. It is possible, if not probable, that the individuals attending treatment centres are atypical of those in the community who use injected drugs. Those using prescribed heroin may differ from the drugtakers in this study who had generally used black market or 'Chinese' heroin. Some of those most deeply involved with the drugtaking way of life (i.e. multi-users) were deeply interested in emotional issues and the evident association between multi-use and perceived parental unhappiness may indicate that, as a group, multi-users, especially the low-status unemployed and manual workers, were preoccupied with questions of personal adjustment. Some certainly saw themselves as cut off from 'conventional' society and minimized their interest in the milieu of their parents. Possibly this was a rationalization or partial explanation of their commitment to the peer group and to the drug scene. I have already mentioned that a number of this sub-group appeared to be concerned about their emotional problems. Some told me in informal discussions that they were deeply sensitive to the perceived deficiences of their family relations. A corollary of this was the finding that perceived parental unhappiness was significantly associated with the individual having, at some time, made a parasuicidal act. Ten of the fifty-four respondents who reported that their parents were unhappy together had attempted suicide compared with only eleven of the other 140 respondents. I shall discuss parasuicide more thoroughly later in this section. This conclusion is broadly consistent with Cockett's finding in his study that the drugtakers included more individuals who had experienced nervous symptoms in childhood than did the controls (1971:97). Cockett also found that the relationship between these symptoms and the subsequent development of drug habits applied to all of the drugtakers on his scale.

My own observations support the view that several of the low-status unemployed and manual workers were prone to anxiety states and many had disturbed biographies. I witnessed a large number of personal traumas, such as broken love affairs and volatile relationships amongst the low-status sub-group. Several individuals led extremely disorganized and, in some cases, unhappy lives. Several case histories illustrated this. One girl, for example, reported that her step-mother had virtually forced her out of the family house. She attributed her involvement with the drug scene as a response to her rejection within her family. She also stated that she used cannabis as a sedative.

Relationship with parents

Another 'traditional' view is that drugtaking may be linked with relational difficulties with one or both parents, as exemplified by the case I have just mentioned. 157 respondents, 77.5 per cent, reported that they were on good terms with their mothers/stepmothers, and

66.0 per cent that they were on good terms with their fathers/step-fathers. There was no association between poor relationship with parents and either social class, drug histories, delinquency, unemployment, or sexual experience.

Altogether seven individuals, 3.5 per cent, reported that they were on poor/very poor terms with both parents/step-parents. Five of these had experience of injecting drugs. Four were females, three were males. Two of the males appeared very unhappy and insecure and seemed highly neurotic. One of these had a history of medical treatment for schizophrenia.

The evidence does not support the view that unhappy homes played an important part in the development of drugtaking behaviour. The great majority of respondents came from neither homes broken by parental divorce, separation or death, nor perceived as unhappy. On the contrary, most respondents reported that they came from happy, stable families. It is possible that the general conclusion was influenced by a tendency within the drug scene to exaggerate one's kindly disposition and to idealize parental relationships from a distance. Most of those interviewed no longer lived with their parents and some were clearly rather sentimental about the nature of their relationship with them.

Living with parents

The evidence indicates that drugtaking developed under peer group influence. I have suggested that becoming a drugtaker involves rejecting many of the preconceptions about drugs likely to be held by parents and that such a redefinition is most likely to occur when the peer group replaces the parental milieu as the dominant group for an individual.

The First Report of the National Commission on Marihuana and Drug Dependence (U.S.A.) maintained that all American studies of cannabis users indicated that cannabis use was statistically correlated with separate residence from parents (1972:42). Similarly Cockett found that in his study drugtakers were more likely than non-drugtakers to be living away from their families for various reasons (1971:86). He pointed out that this did not necessarily impute bad feeling or estrangement.

In the present study, 162 individuals, 81.0 per cent of the study group, were living separately from their parents. I suggest that becoming a drugtaker is part of a process of self-evaluation which occurs during a *rite de passage,* a change in life situation, or a 'social uprooting'. The great majority of those interviewed were living, or were in frequent close contact, with others of their own age group. Many volunteered that they preferred to live separately from their parents and valued their freedom and independence. A great number commented during interview that they had always been on affable terms with their parents but were relieved to have left home since they wanted to live in their own way and had formerly been inhibited. They had regarded the proximity of their parents as a constraint. As a corollary of this sort of comment, several stated that they had been on better terms with their parents since leaving home.

The whole lifestyle of the sub-groups I observed was an expressive, youthful one. Its components were varied and included styles of dress, language, and behaviour. The ethos was essentially one of unmarried young adults in a situation where they were cut adrift from the constraints and values of their parental homes and were asserting their own values and ideals within the peer group situation.

While the evidence suggests that in general the study group did not come from disrupted, hostile families, there were exceptions. Some of the low-status unemployed and manual workers were hostile to their parents, and had accomplished a fairly thorough-going rejection of the values and lifestyles of their parents. It was clear that in some cases, a high level of commitment to the drug scene, particularly when this included the injection of drugs, was associated with antagonism to one's parents.

Family size

184 respondents, 92.0 per cent, had at least one sibling. The average student had 2.1 siblings and the average non-student users and multi-users had 3.0 and 2.2 siblings respectively. Seven of the low-status unemployed and manual workers had at least six siblings, and one had eleven. The high incidence of respondents from large families is interesting, and is consistent with Reeves's Southern Hampshire evidence. The larger families reported were amongst the low-status respondents. Nevertheless it is interesting to note that 16.0

per cent of the overall study group were only children. This is in marked contrast to the population as a whole.[1]

It is possible that individuals from larger families had been subject to less parental restraint than those who were only children. This is merely a conjecture based on both the apparent independence of the study group in terms of lifestyles and the the reported good relations with their parents. Some of the low-status unemployed and manual workers came from very large families and my close contact with them indicated that they were used to a remarkably free-and-easy regime within the home. In general practical terms, individuals with large numbers of siblings would have received less parental attention than only children. This may have contributed to their greater involvement with peers.

Drug use within the family

Individual attitudes to drugtaking are likely to be influenced by the behaviour of significant others in relation to drugs. If the daily routine of a family includes regular alcohol or tobacco use, this may set a pattern that will be learned and imitated. Parents who use legal drugs may influence their children's use of illegal ones. In the preceding discussion I have examined factors associated with pressures from outside the family contributing to the adoption of drugtaking behaviour. I now turn to examine what role, if any, was played by respondents' families. My informal discussions with drugtakers had suggested that the general assumption that drugtaking was invariably concealed from parents was not always valid. In order to investigate this subject, respondents were asked whether or not their parents and siblings used illegal drugs under non-medical circumstances.

Drug use by siblings

Seventy-six of the 184 individuals who had siblings reported that their siblings had also used drugs. In spite of the fact that these comprised 38.0 per cent of the total study group, only 2.0 per cent of those interviewed stated that they had initially been 'turned on' by a sibling. Several of those I encountered discussed their siblings' drug use with

[1] *Social Trends*, No. 3, 1972. Table 8:64.

me at some length. In most cases they indicated that they had different friends from those of their brothers and sisters, often because of age differences. One or two had introduced younger siblings to drugtaking, but very few appeared to be on very close terms with drugtaking siblings. Most stated that they 'believed' their brothers and sisters had used drugs. My impression was that drugtaking behaviour invariably took place outside the parental home and that any connection between siblings was limited by this fact. Most of those interviewed stressed that drugtaking was compartmentalized into an 'away from home' category. Like sexual behaviour, it was generally not discussed with either siblings or parents, since certain social taboos militated against this. Many individuals stated that they hoped that their siblings did not use drugs because they were too young or too naive to benefit from this experience. Several spoke in terms of drugs being only for mature people and indicated that they disapproved of adolescents using them. In most cases those reporting the use of drugs by siblings believed that their siblings had used more or less the same range of drugs as they had. In cases where a respondent asserted that a sister had used drugs, this was almost always attributed to the influence of boyfriends or peers beyond the family.

> 'My sister started going out with guys who were on the scene. She used to be pretty straight, but now she smokes (cannabis). Last year she went out with a bloke who was against drugs. She gave them up for a bit. I think she still smokes dope. We don't talk about things like that at home.'

Two of the male respondents introduced me to their drugtaking brothers who in turn agreed to be interviewed. In general I noted little interaction between siblings in the groups I observed, mainly because most of the individuals I encountered were living away from home and many had become drugtakers since leaving their parents' residences.

Drug use by parents

Most of those interviewed reported that they were on good terms with both parents. Drugtaking is widely depicted as a form of purely youthful deviation and it is interesting to examine how the respondents reconciled their own drugtaking with their parents' presumed abstinence from illegal drugs. In fact eighteen individuals, 9.0 per cent of the study group, reported that their parents had at some time used drugs such as cannabis and opium under non-medical circumstances.

Several respondents reported that their fathers had used drugs while overseas as servicemen during the Second World War. One individual stated that his father was a merchant seaman and often smoked substances presumed to be cannabis or opium while he was in places such as Hong Kong and the West Indies. One female student had discussed her own drugtaking with her mother and had discovered that she had smoked cannabis with a group of artistic and theatrical friends in London during the 1940s. A few of the low-status unemployed or manual workers stated that they had 'turned their fathers on', but the general impression was that the great majority of respondents believed that their parents had no experience and little knowledge of drugtaking. Many were eager to point out that their parents used alcohol and tobacco and several of the low-status unemployed or manual workers stated that their fathers were often the worse for drink. Some respondents commented that their parents received regular supplies of barbiturates and tranquillizers on the National Health Service, and several suggested that this was a classic example of legal drug-dependence amongst the middle-aged.

Amongst the low-status unemployed and manual workers there appeared to be an aggressive ethos that associated 'hard drinking' with masculinity or maturity. Much of the social life of this sub-group, as of their parents, was centred upon public houses and in many ways they appeared to copy the drinking behaviour of their parents. The addition to their lifestyles of illegal drugs was compatible with their frequent practice of drinking heavily and to the point of intoxication. Many respondents argued that they were basically no more drug-oriented than their parents. Several contended that they treated cannabis as an alcohol substitute, and that they regarded it as both cheaper and less deleterious than alcohol:

> 'How can older people criticize us for smoking pot? There are half a million alcoholics in Britain and thousands of people die every year because of lung cancer caused by tobacco-smoking. Pot smokers aren't junkies, and I don't know anyone who uses "hard" drugs. My parents are hypocritical. They both drink and

> smoke (cigarettes) and would have a fit if they knew I use what they call "drugs". I don't use drugs as much as they do.'

This statement, by a male student teacher, was a fairly typical one. One of the low-status unemployed made a similar comment:

> 'My old man gets pissed (drunk) every night. He spends a fortune on booze. How he's got the cheek to moan about me using dope, I just don't know. He's like an animal when he's drunk.'

In general the students and middle-class bohemians did not have an aggressively militant attitude to their drug use. They were clearly aware of a difference of opinion with their parents on this issue but reacted to this with the long-suffering air of those who believe their rectitude is unrecognized. Drug use involved a process of redefinition whereby the 'dangerous' drugs became the conventionally accepted alcohol and tobacco. This was rather paradoxical in view of the extensive alcohol and tobacco use amongst the study group.

While the evidence indicates that few respondents had parents who had used drugs such as cannabis, many of those interviewed maintained that their parents were the 'drugtakers' in a wider sense. Nevertheless, the findings support the view that drugtaking was generally a departure from patterns of behaviour learned within the family. Even when siblings were drugtakers, or were perceived as drugtakers, this was more often associated with the peer group than the home. This conclusion is supported by the fact that 80.5 per cent of those interviewed stated that they believed their parents had been unaware of their first drug experiences and that they had generally concealed these events, fearing parental hostility or disapproval. The thirty-seven individuals, 18.5 per cent of the study group, who reported that their parents had known about their first drug experiences reported that in most cases they had been worried: 'My parents thought I was sick. They said I would go on to harder drugs and wanted to know what was wrong that drove me to drugs. They just didn't understand.'

The study group, unlike the drug users in Chein's study, did not, in general, appear to come from disturbed families. Some individuals, notably low-status unemployed and manual workers were hostile to their parents, but these appeared the exception, rather than the rule, within their sub-group.

Education

The stereotype of the junkie depicts an individual so engrossed in the pursuit of immediate pleasure that longer-term goals are rejected or ignored. It is a common traditional assumption that deviance is essentially a 'disease' of the low-status and economically underprivileged.

Three quarters of the study group, including seventy-nine of the non-students, had passed at least G.C.E. Ordinary level exams, and of these, nineteen individuals, 9.5 per cent, had a degree or some form of professional qualification. This lends no support to the view that all drugtakers are likely to be uneducated or that as a group they are 'drop-outs'. All the students interviewed were apparently contending with the demands of their courses and some of the non-manual workers were highly qualified educationally. This conclusion corresponds to R. Cockett's finding in his study of delinquents, that drugtakers were more likely than non-drugtakers to have better than secondary modern school education and to have had a slightly higher average intelligence rating than non-drugtakers (Cockett 1971:90).

Social class

The generally high educational qualifications of the study group are consistent with the large number of students and others from middle-class families who were interviewed. In contrast with the 'educated' majority, thirty-five individuals, 17.5 per cent of the study group, had no educational qualifications at all, even though thirty-two of these had left school. There was a significant association between lack of educational qualifications and low socio-economic status. Twenty-four of those without educational qualifications had fathers who were manual workers.

Users and multi-users were not significantly different in lack of educational qualifications. There was a significant association between lack of educational qualifications and the use of heroin and other injected drugs. Ten of those without educational qualifications had used such drugs, compared with only twenty-one of the other 169 respondents.

There was a significant association between lack of educational qualifications and delinquency. Eleven of those without qualifications

Table 16
Educational qualifications

	students				*non-students*				*total*	
	users		*multi-users*		*users*		*multi-users*			
	male	*female*	*male*	*female*	*male*	*female*	*male*	*female*	N	%
none	–	–	–	–	5	4	23	3	35	17.5
C.S.E.	–	–	–	–	3	4	5	1	13	6.5
G.C.E. 'O' levels	3	–	4	6	3	2	31	8	57	28.5
G.C.E. 'A' levels	16	8	25	5	2	–	16	4	76	38.0
professional qualifications	2	–	1	–	3	1	6	1	14	7.0
degree	2	–	1	–	–	–	2	–	5	2.5
total	23	8	31	11	16	11	83	17	200	100.0

had been convicted of more serious offences, compared with only twelve of the rest of the study group. In addition, lack of education qualifications was significantly associated with having had sexual intercourse before the age of fifteen; fifteen of the unqualified, compared with only twenty-nine of the rest of the study group, reported having had such early sexual intercourse.

There is a great deal of research into educational opportunity which links low social class with poor schools, low academic attainment, and lack of career motivation. It is suggested that those without educational qualifications were denied a major source of access to middle-class goals and, as a group, were of low-social status. In fact virtually all of the unqualified were classified as low-status unemployed and manual workers. Their lifestyle was, as I have stated, rather different from that of either the students or the middle-class bohemians. Those without educational qualifications were distinctive within the study group. Unlike the students and middle-class bohemians, few had career aspirations and several complained that they felt bitterly that they were handicapped by their lack of qualifications. Some were plainly jealous of the students and others whom they saw as privileged by virtue of having some form of qualifications or conventional status. Those who lacked educational qualifications were amongst the most involved with the drug scene which, as I have implied, could well have been a collective response to their common low social status and lack of prestige or motivation.

In order to arrive at some general assessment of the well-being of the study group, I shall examine the following factors that may be regarded as indications of stress, abnormality, or malaise: the production of illegitimate children, the incidence amongst females of abortions, parasuicide, delinquency in general, and drug convictions in particular, in addition to medical treatment due to drug use. I shall attempt to arrive at a general evaluation of the nature and extent of some of the main problems of the study group of the other drugtakers I encountered during my field-work.

Illegitimate Children

Twenty-one of those interviewed, nineteen males and three females, reported that they had at least one child born out of wedlock. Eight of those individuals had two illegitimate children and one working-class male reported that he had six by three different women! Only five of the nineteen males were living with their offspring. The others had 'allowed' the mothers to care for them. Few seemed to be paying any maintenance and one of the females reported that her mother was looking after her child while she was a student.

Altogether fifteen of the forty-four respondents who reported that they had experienced sexual intercourse before their fifteenth birthdays had illegitimate children. These 'early starters' were significantly more likely to have illegitimate children than those who had first experienced sexual intercourse later. Three quarters of those with illegitimate children came from working-class homes, compared with about two-fifths of the rest of the study group. This difference was statistically significant.

In many ways, the number of individuals with illegitimately born children is a useful index of sexual mishaps. Most of the putative fathers had clearly not wanted their children and in most cases had left the mothers to fend as best they could. The majority of those with illegitimate children were low-status unemployed or manual workers. As a group they were both sexually precocious and, apparently, careless. The five males living with their illegitimate children had chosen to cohabit rather than to marry. As I have stated, this was often due to an ideological rejection of marriage as 'conventional' or out-moded. This need not imply promiscuity. It was (just) an alternative view of marriage.

Cheltenham has a high illegitimacy rate,[2] but the very high proportion, 10.5 per cent of the study group, with illegitimate children confirms that the individuals included in this study were an unusual group within the community.

Amongst males, there was a significant association between having an illegitimate child and having injected drugs. Five of the nineteen putative fathers had used heroin and an additional three had injected other drugs. There was also, amongst males, an association between having an illegitimate child and having been in trouble with the police. Fourteen of the nineteen males with illegitimate children had been convicted of at least one offence. This evidence indicates that those individuals with the greatest involvement with the drugtaking lifestyle, the low-status unemployed and manual workers, were most likely to have had illegitimate children.

[2] Information supplied by the Borough Health Department, 1972.

Abortions

Twelve of the forty-seven females interviewed reported that they had had an abortion. Two of these had had two pregnancies terminated. This is a very high proportion indeed. The overall abortion rate of England and Wales (estimated) for 1971 was no more than 13 per 1,000 for females aged 16–19, and 11 per 1,000 for those aged 20–44 (Lafitte 1972:623).

One of the twelve females reported that she had her pregnancy terminated on the grounds that she and her boyfriend had both used a lot of L.S.D. and feared that this might have damaged the foetus. Two of the girls were very neurotic, but otherwise there seemed little to distinguish those females who had had an abortion from those who had not. The general impression is that most appeared psychologically normal. Eight were multi-users and a few commented that their sexual behaviour had been confined to the milieu of the drug using sub-culture.

None of the twelve females reported having had experienced sexual intercourse before the age of fifteen and only two (had had it) before they were sixteen. There is no evidence that as a group these girls were particularly promiscuous.

Two had illegitimate children in their care at the time of interview but both received financial support from the father. One was cohabiting. Only one of the twelve females had used heroin and purely experimentally. One of the two girls who had had two abortions was judged by many of those who knew her to be hypersensitive and neurotic. She was plainly a very intelligent, introspective girl who seemed to have no idea of what her role in life was to be.

The high proportion of females interviewed who had an abortion further suggests that those included in the survey were a very atypical group. Schofield found in his study that sexually experienced females were more likely than others to get on well with their fathers. No such significant association emerged in the present study, although five of the twelve females who had had an abortion reported that they were on poor terms with their fathers. It is possible that if a control group of non-drugtaking females had been used, an association similar to that in Schofield's study would have emerged, since most of the females interviewed had some sexual experience and a quarter, fourteen out of forty-seven, reported that they were on poor terms with their fathers.

Parasuicide (Attempted Suicide)

One of the popular theories put forward to account for drugtaking is that it is an escape from tensions and worries. Twenty-one individuals, 10.5 per cent of the study group, reported that they had made at least one parasuicidal act. Suicide is more common in some sections of the population than in others (Stengel 1964). Students and mobile young people are especially prone to attempt to or succeed in, committing suicide. The national rate of suicide and self-injury for the age-group is about four per 100,000 (Ryle 1973:105), although it is not possible to estimate how many unrecorded suicides and suicide attempts there are. Anthony Ryle suggests that suicides are linked with depressive illnesses (manic depressive psychoses) but that suicides also occur in individuals with no histories of mental illness. One of the standard theories about suicide attempts is that they are, in fact, gestures, or pleas for attention and help (see Kreitman *et al.* 1970).

> 'The majority of acts of self-injury or poisoning are therefore not so much attempts at self-destruction as statements and communications. As such, none should be disregarded any more than should the direct voicing of a suicidal intent. To injure oneself, even without immediate fatal intent, is an expression of hopelessness or anger, and, implicitly or explicitly, a plea or a demand for more support.' (Ryle 1973:106)

Those respondents who had attempted suicide were atypical in several respects. Nineteen out of twenty-one were multi-users, and seven had experience of injecting drugs. Females were significantly more likely than males to report that they had attempted suicide – eleven out of forty-seven compared with ten out of 153.

Medical treatment

Nine of the twenty-one with histories of parasuicide reported that they had received psychiatric treatment, either directly related to their parasuicide or at some other time. All those who had received psychiatric help were prone to acute depression and may well have been psycho-neurotic. Two individuals had made two suicide attempts and one female, acutely depressive and very unstable in her personal relationships, had made five attempts at suicide. Several respondents stated that their parasuicides had been largely gestures and all conceded that had they really wanted to succeed, they could probably have done so. I know of two or three such gestures or pleas for help that occurred during my fieldwork. In all cases the means chosen was an overdose of barbiturates, taken when help was believed to be at hand. Prolonged discussion with several respondents who had attempted suicide indicated that these individuals were often very unhappy and sometimes subject to fits of uncontrollable depression. Several stated that they smoked cannabis because it was a convenient sedative.

One girl in her twenties gave the following account of her own parasuicidal act:

> 'I was living in London. I had just started college and the work got me down. I suppose I felt lonely, living away from home. I had several unhappy relationships with men and found I was pregnant. I had an (illegal) abortion and was horribly depressed afterwards. I tried lots of things. I slep around. I drank a lot. I got in with a scene and started using acid. Nothing could snap me out of my feeling of being lost. I felt nobody cared and so I took an overdose (of barbiturates). My flat-mates found me and got me to hospital in time. I suppose I knew they would find me. It was a bit melodramatic I suppose.'

This account was fairly typical – an emotional upset, combined with a tendency to be depressed. An excellent study-in-depth of a similar suicide attempt which succeeded by accident is provided by Alfred Alvaraz's account of the death of the poet Sylia Plath (1971). This case history is consistent with the statements of those in the present study who reported that their suicide bids had been intended to attract the attentions and sympathies of others when they had been depressed or unhappy. The high incidence of parasuicide in the study group indicated a high level of severe personal disturbance and unhappiness. I suggest that in some cases individuals who were highly sensitive or depressive were attracted to the drug scene because of the tolerance and friendship they found therein. One girl, who had made two suicide bids, affirmed that she had sought refuge in the 'natural community' that has been created by drugtaking. In addition, some individuals apeared to use drugs in a quasi-medical way to alleviate depression. The evidence indicates that while the majority of those interviewed and observed were apparently happy and did not have disturbed biographies, some individuals, particularly those with a wide range of drug experience, were often acutely depressed and distressed. This is consistent with my observations that some of those most deeply involved with drugtaking, notably the low-status unemployed and manual workers, led very disorganized, and often traumatic lives.

Much of the research into deviant behaviour has been concerned with delinquency, with the prevalence of criminal convictions. Many of the attempted explanations of deviant behaviour have been largely aimed at accounting for the varying levels of known or recorded crime amongst different social strata and in different geographical neighbourhoods. It is important, therefore, in my examination of the general well-being of the study group, to consider the extent of delinquency, which is a major area of deviance and a possible index of maladjustment within the social structure.

with the greatest involvement in the drugtaking way of life. Ten of those who had been given a custodial sentence had at some time used heroin or had experience of other injected drugs. Two individuals were injecting regularly at the time of interview. Both of these appeared to be physically dependent upon illegal supplies of heroin which they bought on the black market. Both individuals (respondents 26 and 101) earned some money dealing in drugs and spent a great amount of their time travelling outside the Cheltenham area, often to procure and distribute drugs.

One individual, brought up in a poor working-class family in a delinquent district of a large city, had been delinquent since he was ten or eleven. Apparently of low intelligence, his lifestyle was that of many of those in slum areas. He stated that crime was a way of life to him. His parents both had criminal records and his father had spent protracted periods in prison. At the time of interview this respondent was sometimes earning considerable sums through the sale of drugs, although he was imprisoned for this some time after my field-work ended.

Altogether twenty-two respondents, 11.0 per cent of the study group, reported that they had been convicted of more serious offences, involving either a custodial sentence, probation, or a suspended sentence. All were low-status unemployed or manual workers and all were males.

Twelve of the twenty-two reported that they had been convicted of serious offences *before* they became drugtakers. The evidence does not support the view that drugtaking necessarily, or generally, preceded or caused criminal behaviour. Only 5.0 per cent of the overall study group, all low-status unemployed or manual workers, had become seriously delinquent after first using drugs. The survey findings suggest that delinquency, when it occurred, was a concomitant of low social status rather than of drugtaking *per se*.

My informal contact with different groups of drugtakers indicated that, in general, the students and middle-class bohemians had a conventional middle-class distaste for crime. There were notable exceptions. Some individuals (stigmatized by their peers as 'rip-off artists') frequently stole from bookshops and grocers, justifying this on the political grounds that they were only 'liberating' goods from an exploitive and evil system. In general, such individuals were regarded as extreme and were disdained by the middle-class drugtakers I encountered. By far the greatest social support for petty theft was evident amongst the low-status unemployed and manual workers. Some clearly came from traditionally delinquent backgrounds; others from middle-class homes were aliented from conventional standards and frequently engaged in shoplifting on the pretext that one could not commit crimes against a corrupt establishment and capitalist system. As I have intimated, some individuals emphasized their rejection of conventional standards. I knew one young man, 'Tony', who had been a social science undergraduate at a large provincial university. He left university after refusing to sit his final examinations (according to his statement). Clearly highly intelligent, if prone to paranoid suspicions that he was being persecuted, he was a regular shoplifter and frequently stole large numbers of books from the university bookshop in the town where he usually lived.

Several of those from economically deprived backgrounds had been delinquent since they were very young. I knew two vagrants who often stayed in the Cheltenham area, both of whom had lived by stealing for protracted periods over a number of years. They seemed very amiable and were totally amoral, stealing at times even from their own friends. One of them, affectionately known as 'Groper' by his friends, was notorious for his short-lived liaisons with a succession of young, apparently very dependent, naive females. One of his temporary female partners moved to another town leaving behind her guitar, records, and a sewing machine for Groper to send on to her new address. Without apparent qualms, he sold everything at a local second-hand shop and proceded to live it up on the proceeds. I noted that, in general, the working-class drug-using groups were very tolerant of delinquency of this type. While few of the networks I encountered were explicitly criminal in their orientation, one or two were, and most at least tolerated criminal acts by individual members. Their free and easy morality was a notable feature of those most deeply involved with the drug scene. In many cases offences against property were accepted and only crimes involving violence were deprecated. A small number of those most antagonistic to 'straight' society and values were prone to violence. I knew three males, all of whom were unemployed throughout most of my residence in Cheltenham, who were well known for their aggressive tendencies. On occasion these had to be forcibly restrained (by me sometimes) from assaulting people perceived as giving them offence. One once brandished an axe at somebody who owed him a small sum of money. Two of these males had records of treatment for major psychiatric disorders. I believe that they found in the drug scene an acceptance and tolerance of their behavioural peculiarities that would not have been available elsewhere. In no instance did my observations suggest that any crime was committed because of the effects of drugs. The commonest drugs in use were cannabis and the hallucinogens, none of which were particularly likely to promote extroverted or aggressive behaviour. As I mention in Appendix III, most of the study group spent very little on drugs. The only individuals I knew to resort to theft or other criminal activities in order to finance their drug use were those regularly injecting heroin and other drugs. I encountered no more than a dozen such individuals during my field-work in Cheltenham and only three of the study group were injecting regularly at the time of interview. Several regular cannabis smokers made enough money by dealing in drugs to pay for their own consumption, but this involved relatively small-scale transactions.

In general, theft in order to buy drugs appeared to be confined to the low-status unemployed and manual workers. Most regular drugtakers gave or sold each other drugs and many of the encounters I observed involved the exchange of cannabis and other drugs. Within the coteries a great deal of discussion and interest revolved around drugs. It would almost be true to regard drugs as a type of currency or symbols of well-being and prestige. The providers of drugs, invariably close friends, were held in high esteem, since within the drug scene cannabis and other illegal substances were important marks of common identity. I often observed that cannabis, or sometimes other drugs, were handed round or provided as goodwill gestures. There is an obvious parallel with the use of coffee, alcohol, and cigarettes in non-drugtaking circles. The emphasis placed upon drugs, and the status accorded to those able to supply them, was greatest amongst the low-status unemployed and manual workers. Several even used the American junkie expression 'the man' to denote the person from whom they hoped to, or usually did, obtain their drugs. The general behaviour of the low-status sub-group was much more clearly modelled as an imitation of the 'deviant' junkie than that of either the students or middle-class bohemians.

My observations suggested that the low-status unemployed and manual workers from working-class homes adopted drugtaking as an adjunct of their antecedent, often delinquent, lifestyles. In addition, the middle-class 'drop-outs' and those alienated from the conventional goals of middle-class society often engaged in petty crime as part of their overall alienation. Several former students justified regular shoplifting on the grounds that anything stolen from 'the system' was a blow for freedom. Merton attributed deviance to blocked opportunities for reaching middle-class objectives. To some extent, the delinquency of the low-status sub-group was consistent with this view. This sub-group was not primarily a delinquent one; rather it was a milieu where delinquency was tolerated, even regarded as prestigious, along with a range of other forms of 'unconventional' behaviour. Cloward and Ohlin suggested that the drugtaking sub-culture arose from a 'double-failure' or inability to attain culture goals (wealth, prestige) through either legitimate or illegitimate means. This view is not generally supported by the present study. The students and middle-class bohemians appeared successful in attaining their ambitions through the 'legitimate' channels of education and careers. Some of the low-status group were regularly engaged in crime and had never been convicted. A few individuals were amazingly inept in both legitimate and illegitimate attempts at attaining any goals they may have had. In relation to these, the theory of Cloward and Ohlin may be applied, but it was not generally relevant.

Most of the students and middle-class bohemians regarded the delinquent elements in the drug scene as sinister. Several people warned me to be careful of individuals they regarded as dangerous. Two of the unemployed males came round to my flat in a state of some agitation because they had heard that I intended to interview one individual they believed to be dangerous.

> 'For Christ's sake, don't get mixed up with ——. He's got part of his brain missing. Like he's had too much acid. He doesn't know the difference between fact and fantasy any more. He thinks he's a warrior-god. I've seen him pull a blade on people just for looking at him. He's a nutter, Martin. If you want to talk to him, do it in the open-air with us hiding behind a tree . . . with an axe.'

My subsequent experience substantiated some of the fears of these two solicitous respondents. Individuals like the one I was warned against were notorious amongst drugtakers I encountered and were treated with prudent distrust. Many of the students told me that they regarded many of the unskilled manual workers as 'a bit rough and "heavy" '.

The delinquents were primarily a working-class group, who were 'deviant' in a variety of ways. Only one of those who had been convicted of a serious offence had a 'good' employment record and I noted that as a group, those with criminal records were frequently ill-housed, unemployed, and often openly promiscuous.

The ethos of this sub-group was explicitly hedonistic and directed towards the attainment of immediate pleasure. The delinquents were members of a face-to-face network of friends and drug dealers and, as *Diagram VI* indicates, there was a high level of observed contact between them. Much of the time of this group was spent hanging around cafes and public houses, and few had any discernible career goals or means of attaining such.

Diagram VI

The delinquents

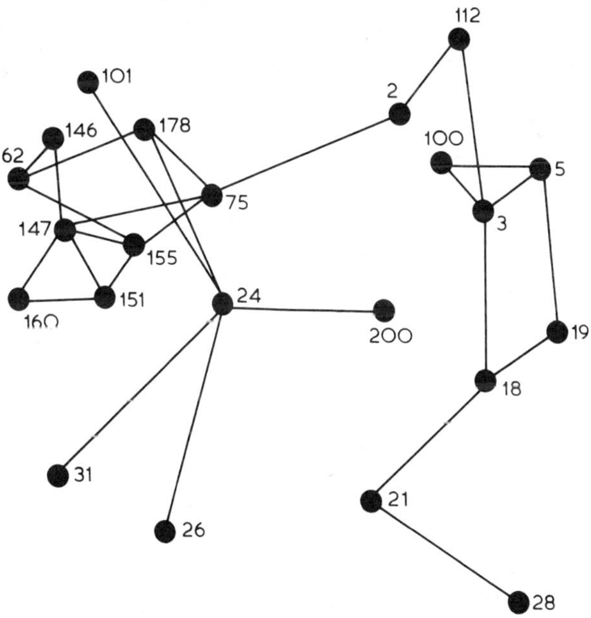

The 22 male non-student multi-users who had been convicted of more serious offences

Many of the delinquent unemployed drugtakers I encountered seemed to be intelligent under-achievers. Half of those interviewed in this category had passed G.C.E. 'O' levels and many were intelligent and articulate. Some were avid readers and gave the impression that if they had been so motivated, or given the opportunity, they could have been capable of far more than the menial jobs they had whenever they were working. Some were openly frustrated and justified their criminality by maintaining that they had never had a chance to gain educational qualifications or conventional status: 'Society never gave me anything. I can take what I want.'

While the students and middle-class bohemians were generally content to accept many of society's conventions, some of the low-status unemployed and manual workers did not and were hostile to authority in general, and to the police in particular. I heard many vitriolic statements of hatred for the police who were variously described as bourgeois, fascist pigs, and the like. As I have implied, the behaviour of some drugtakers was far removed from the 'love thy neighbour' ethic supposedly central to the hippie philosophy. As a group the students and middle-class bohemians were not prepared to step right outside the orbit of conventional values and the delinquency of some individuals was in marked contrast to the behaviour of the majority of respondents.

I found no evidence that cannabis or other drugs caused criminal behaviour, as has been suggested elsewhere (Rowell and Rowell 1939). Cannabis (the drug most widely used by the study group) generally induced drowsiness and passivity rather than extroverted or criminal behaviour. Some individuals commented that they used drugs to pacify or sedate themselves and that they were less, not more, likely to be aggressive or delinquent under the influence of drugs. There was a certain amount of unreliable hearsay evidence of the use of amphetamines by violent skinhead gangs and possibly this had some validity. My personal experience did not substantiate this view. The majority of respondents, though discontented with society, were generally law-abiding and conformist. There was no reason to surmise that becoming a drugtaker necessarily involved embarking upon a career of crime, provided one remained in the controlled milieu of the students and middle-class bohemians. In general, the reported delinquency records of the study group reflected their social class backgrounds rather than their drugtaking histories. I suggest that the relationship between intensive drug use and criminal behaviour was due to social position and economic privation (whether self-induced or inflicted) of those concerned. I knew many very heavy cannabis smokers who were not delinquent and, in general, the philosophy of middle-class drugtakers, whether drop-outs or conformists, was antithetical to crime in general, and to violence in particular.

Erich Goode comments that the cannabis users he interviewed in New York were not usually opposed to laws in general but only to specific laws they regarded as unjust (Goode 1970:238–40). My own field work broadly corroborated this view and the opinions towards the law of the drugtakers I encountered were consistent with their views about society and politics in general. Most were 'progressive' or radicals who wished to modify things and only a minority were in favour of revolution or anarchy. Goode suggests that cannabis users are more likely to commit 'crimes without victims', or private offences (such as sex acts illegal in parts of the United States), but not crimes of violence.

Cheltenham had a drug squad of its own, and throughout my residence in the town considerable local publicity was given to court proceedings and convictions related to drug offences. I shall now examine what proportion of the study group had been convicted of drug offences and consider the characteristics of those who had been convicted in comparison with other respondents.

16. Drug Convictions

One of the main disadvantages of criminal statistics is that they may not give an accurate representation of the nature or extent of crime. It is possible that those who are convicted differ from those who escape attention and are unrecorded. All of the 200 drugtakers had used illegal drugs and, theoretically, could have been prosecuted for this. In fact, only twenty-nine had ever been convicted of a drug offence: possession, cultivation, or trafficking of proscribed drugs. Twenty-seven of these twenty-nine were non-students, twenty-eight were multi-users and twenty-eight were males. These findings suggest that those who had been convicted of drug offences were not a representative cross-section of those interviewed.

Only two students had been convicted for the possession of drugs. It is possible that this was due to the fact that students are segregated from the general community by their colleges. The social life of colleges and universities is generally separated from that of non-students and the colleges are, to some extent, expected to supervise the behaviour of their own students. Some of the colleges provide accommodation and entertainments for students, which effectively reduces the number of situations in which the police have a chance to detect drugtaking or trafficking. As a group, the students apeared to me to be more discreet than many of those who had been convicted. Twenty-eight of the twenty-nine who had been convicted of drug offences were multi-users. This suggests that most cannabis (only) users were fairly unlikely to be brought to court because of their drug use. In general, the multi-users were more involved with the whole drug way of life than those who only used cannabis. Some were dealing in drugs and were more likely than the cannabis (only) users to appear a problem

Table 17
Drug convictions

	students				*non-students*				*total*	
	users		*multi-users*		*users*		*multi-users*			
	male	*female*	*male*	*female*	*male*	*female*	*male*	*female*	N	%
no convictions	23	8	29	11	15	11	58	16	171	85.5
one conviction	–	–	2	–	1	–	20	1	24	12.0
two or more convictions	–	–	–	–	–	–	5	–	5	2.5
total	23	8	31	11	16	11	83	17	200	100.0

group. Twelve of the twenty-nine individuals convicted of drug offences had been convicted of other fairly serious offences.

There was a significant association between unemployment and having been convicted of a drug offence. Altogether, sixteen of the twenty-nine offenders were unemployed, compared with thirty-six of the other 171 individuals interviewed.

Only one female reported that she had been convicted of a drug offence, and she was a multi-user.

Physical Appearance

I subjectively classified the general physical appearance of those I interviewed. There was a significant association between having been convicted of a drug offence and being classified as physically dirty or very scruffy. As a group, those who had been convicted of a drug offence were more likely than other drugtakers to be neglected or conspicuous in their appearance.

Drug Offenders and Others

The evidence suggests that those convicted of drugs offences were an atypical group of drugtakers. Those most likely to be convicted of drug offences were: males, multi-users, non-students, delinquent, unemployed, and physically dirty or untidy. This information corresponds to figures supplied by the local police, which showed that between March 6, 1970 and May 22, 1972, fifty-two people aged 17–24 were prosecuted for drug offences in the North Gloucestershire Police Division.[1] Only five of these were students and half were unemployed.

Several of the drugtakers I located reported that they had been warned about drug use by the police but had never been prosecuted. It seems that the local Drug Squad adopted a policy of only prosecuting individuals believed to be deeply involved with, or dealing in, drugs. It is clear that any attempt to prosecute all of the drugtakers in Cheltenham would have involved a large-scale purge.

The approach adopted by the police in Cheltenham appeared to be aimed primarily at drugtakers regarded as 'undesirable types'. Indi-

[1] This covers Cheltenham, Newent, Northleach, and the North Cotswolds.

viduals with previous convictions for other offences and those who were most conspicuous in their dress and behaviour were especially likely to have been prosecuted. Some of those who had been convicted of drug offences were both bizarre in appearance from a conventional, or policeman's, point of view and were noted to be exhibitionist in their public use of drugs. Certain groups openly smoked cannabis in public houses and in the gardens near Cheltenham's central Promenade. Most drugtakers regard such behaviour as risky and unwarranted. It is my view that in general, the police were particularly likely to be aware of easily observable drugtakers such as these and that this biased their choice of persons to search for drugs.

It was certainly a common occurrence for long-haired youths on the streets at night to be stopped and searched by policemen. Many students complained that this had happened to them, and in virtually all such cases reported to me, those concerned had been 'hippy' in their general appearance. Few, if any, short-haired and conventional young people reported that they had been so examined. The Deedes Report, *Powers of Arrest and Search in Relation to Drug Offences* (1970), pointed out that styles of dress alone do not constitute just grounds for a person being suspected of drug offences. This is a well-intentioned comment, but in practice, one can hardly expect those enforcing the drug laws not to be influenced by an individual's appearance. In fact, the evidence of the present study indicates that the police were fairly accurate in their prosecution of some of those most involved with drugtaking. Nevertheless, it does seem clear that certain types of drugtaker were significantly more likely than others to be apprehended. In general, those who used cannabis discreetly, in their own or friends' homes, were fairly safe from being detected. One problem is that a false picture of drugtaking results from the bias in the pattern of convictions in relation to the overall drug using group in the community. Public opinion is influenced by the fact that most of those convicted of drug offences are unemployed or of no fixed abode. I had plenty of opportunity to observe the negative reactions of non-drug users to newspaper reports such as: 'X, a labourer, of no-fixed-address, was fined £50 for possession of amphetamine sulphate . . . '

The evidence of this study indicates that most drugtakers were not delinquents and that, in many ways, those who were convicted of drug offences were an extreme and atypical group. This raises the important issue of what local police were attempting to curb: illegal drug use, or a specific type of lifestyle adopted by a minority of drugtakers. This issue is not confined to Cheltenham.

Medical Treatment

Much of the evidence about drugtakers and drugtaking is derived from studies of individuals who have come into contact with medical treatment agencies. The subjects of this study were located in an entirely different way. It is of interest, then, to discover how many of the study group had received medical treatment in connection with their drug use and whether those who had were different in any ways from those who had not. While not suggesting that the study group were 'typical' drugtakers, it is important to get some impression of how drugtakers receiving medical treatment resemble or differ from those not recorded as in-patients and drug dependents.

Twenty-five respondents had had at some time medical treatment directly related to their drugtaking. Twenty-four of these were multi-users, the exception being a student who had been using cannabis regularly and had consulted a doctor to ascertain whether or not this practice had been deleterious. Twenty of those who had sought medical advice or who had been treated in connection with

Table 18

Reasons for consulting a doctor or receiving medical treatment

reasons	N
physically dependent on heroin or amphetamines	6
L.S.D. psychosis	4
depression due to drug effects	4
psychosis caused by drugs (other than L.S.D.)	2
overdose of barbiturates	2
overdose of amphetamines and Mandrax	1
overdose of Mandrax	1
overdose of amphetamines	1
hypertension caused by drugs	1
chest pains attributed to cannabis smoking	1
headaches attributed to drugs	1
concern about the after-effects of L.S.D.	1
total	25

their drugtaking were non-students. Eleven of these came from working-class families.

One individual was generally acknowledged by his friends to have suffered long-term psychological damage after once taking several microdot tablets of L.S.D. The person concerned certainly appeared to me to be in a state of perpetual confusion, but I did not know him at the time the incident occurred. Most of the above listed reasons did not involve any major treatment. Only two of the six individuals who had ever received a prescription for drugs upon which they were dependent were regular users of such drugs at the time of interview.

During my observations I encountered several drugtakers who were clearly in need of psychiatric or other medical aid. In some cases they were not prepared to accept that they were in such need. In others, they were discouraged from contacting a general practitioner or attending a hostpital because of fear of the reception they would get.

Some drugtakers told me that on occasions when they, or friends of theirs, had gone to a hospital with a person who had taken an overdose or who was experiencing L.S.D. psychosis, they had been badly treated. Some had been told to get out, while on other occasions, hospital staff had done nothing until the local drug squad had been summoned. Incidents such as this certainly have occurred in the past and individual policemen have shown an amazing lack of sympathy. One individual case illustrates this point very clearly: one of those interviewed was arrested for his strange behaviour and placed in a police car. At this point, the drugtaker who was under the influence of L.S.D., became psychotic and very frightened. On asking his police companions, who knew he was 'tripping' where they were taking him, he was informed that they were all driving to hell!

It must be admitted that most of the stories in this vein are malicious fabrications intended to discredit the police. Nevertheless, this particular incident was widely reported by drugtakers I knew well and reflects the difficulties inherent in treating drugtaking as a police problem. Clearly, some policemen regard the drugtakers with whom they deal (that is, mainly the working-class delinquent group) as a nuisance and are unlikely to be sympathetic in a situation where the interests of these two groups of protagonists are polarized. In the same way hospital staff are likely to feel that since they are dealing with law-breakers they have a duty to notify the police. As long as this situation exists, or is believed to exist (which is more important), some drugtakers will be deterred from seeking the help that they really should have.

Shortly before the end of my field work a student came to me in a very agitated state. A girl friend of his had become very ill as the result of taking Mandrax and my advice on the matter had been sought because he was afraid to go to the local hospital. Luckily nothing serious ensued from this incident, but on other occasions such hesitation about going to the proper medical authorities could prove fatal. More people would probably seek medical aid in such cases if there was no risk of them becoming involved with the police as a result of their recourse to such help.

My general assessment of the drugtakers I encountered is that while most were well-housed, physically fit, and psychologically normal, some were not and did need help and assistance. In the medical field, help could be rendered much more effectively if it was generally known that treatment would be non-moralizing and confidential. It appears that at present, this is not so.

The Main Problems of Drugtakers

The study group was asked to give their opinions of which problems, if any, confronted drugtakers whom they knew.

Forty per cent of those interviewed acknowledged that some drugtakers had profound psychological or social problems and turned to drugs as a refuge from their difficulties. A fifth of those interviewed, mainly multi-users, asserted that as far as they were concerned, interference and harassment by the police was a major problem, if not *the* major problem. Clearly, those most tending to take this view were most likely to have been convicted of a drug offence.

Twelve individuals stated that lethargy, due to a negative and retreatist way of life, was a danger for some psychologically weak people. A further twelve were critical of the 'head' lifestyle which they saw as unconstructive and unattractive.

Other respondents suggested that the stigma of public opinion (public prejudice as they saw it) was a problem. Poor housing, impure L.S.D., insecurity, and boredom were also identified as problems. The consensus view was that drugtakers generally had no more problems than people in general, except for those who were psychologically abnormal or socially deprived *before* they started using drugs.

Improvements to Social Services

Many drugtakers believed that the main desideratum was for accurate education about the effects of drugs and people's reasons for using drugs. They resented the fact that public opinion in general, and the attitudes of those operating medical and other services in particular, were hostile to drugtakers. Few of those interviewed made detailed suggestions for improvements in social policy, apart from relaxing the existing drug legislation and treating drugs as a social or medical, rather than a legal problem. The most popular single recommendation was for the provision of more confidential counselling services, though it was pointed out that these would serve the community in general, and not solely drugtakers.

17. Summary and Discussion

A distinguishing feature of this study has been its concern with drugtakers in widely varying social positions. One of the aims was to examine possible differences between drugtakers. This was only rendered possible by locating drugtakers in the community, rather than in treatment or penal institutions, or in a single educational institution.

The study group were mainly young, unmarried, flat-dwelling, temporary residents in the Cheltenham area. Many were at early or transitional stages in their education or careers and were relatively free to establish their own lifestyle. The picture that emerges is one of great diversity. Those in the study group were not uniform in their values, behaviour, or life experiences. Great differences were apparent between individuals and sub-groups, and these were partly functions of social class and partly attributable to present career, educational, or social position.

The major differences that were evident were between the students and middle-class bohemians, on the one hand, and the low-status unemployed and manual workers, on the other. The two former sub-groups were largely comprised of people from non-manual family backgrounds who were 'conformist' in terms of their education and careers. The low-status unemployed and manual workers were primarily from manual backgrounds or were downwardly mobile individuals, with little apparent commitment to the 'work ethic' or 'conventional' values.

If those interviewed were members of a 'sub-culture' or 'contra-culture' it was a very tenuous and varied one. Most of the study group were apparently well integrated into the mainstream of society, and few individuals were totally estranged from non-drugtakers or were genuinely independent economically. Most of those observed and interviewed were in many ways similar to non-drugtakers of their own age group.

My general conclusion is that being a drugtaker was more important to many of those observed and interviewed than were the effects of the drugs they used. First, drugtaking experiences had usually been fostered by contact with, and encouragement by, friends who were held in high regard. Such contact with drugtakers and the apparent peer support for drug use in effect provided a 'neutralization' of any fears or doubts concerning drug use, and it re-socialized individuals to regard drugtaking as harmless, pleasant, or desirable. It seemed that, in general, individuals had become drugtakers in order to affirm values they believed to be important.

Many of those interviewed and encountered during my field-work emphasized that drugtaking was an overt token of commitment to a lifestyle and an ideology. Even so, some of those most deeply involved with drugtaking and with other drugtakers did not seem to have any profound ideological commitment to a 'counter philosophy'. Many of the low-status unemployed and manual workers were uninterested in political and religious issues, though some paid lip service to the 'subterranean values' I have discussed. Many of the study group seemed idealistically to repudiate some of the less attractive aspects of industrial society: materialism was rejected, and generosity, fraternity, peace, and creativity were held in high esteem. This ideology was expressed mainly by the middle-class individuals in the study group, and the proponents of radical or revolutionary views, often not themselves 'middle-class' figures, had been adopted as cult heroes within the drug scene. Few of those interviewed had great commitment to right-wing political views and few identified themselves with the 'conventional' churches. The general pattern was that the students and middle-class bohemians were radical in their beliefs and wished to improve and modify society, whereas the low-status unemployed and manual workers were either indifferent to social issues, or revolutionary in their views.

There was a general recognition that drugtakers, as such, shared a common identity through their drug use. The many differences seemed to be reflected by the views of the drugtakers themselves. Very few stated that they regarded all drugtakers as being alike.

Many of the students and middle-class bohemians appeared to participate in the activities of the drugtaking milieu almost as an apology for their general social conformity. Several stated that they were not really as 'straight' as they might seem, as if to say: 'I do have a heart, you know.'

It was evident that the behaviour of some people diverged from their ideal self-images. Some of the low-status unemployed and manual workers were delinquent and a few were often violent. In this respect some fell short of their professed ideals. Most of the students and middle-class bohemians were only incompletely involved with drugtaking and confined their activities in order to achieve their 'conventional' goals. Similarly some manual workers were only peripheral in their involvement with drugtakers. This ambivalence, or implicit conformity, was clearly disliked by those most deeply involved with the drug scene, particularly those out of work through choice, who openly repudiated 'straight' career aspirations.

Many of the study group stated that they rejected conventional social class distinctions. In practice, they appeared to retain them, since there was less contact across class boundaries than within them. The exceptions were those most deeply involved with the 'scene', the low-status and downwardly mobile, who appeared to interact regardless of social class origins. In general, those from middle-class backgrounds associated more with others from similar families than with those from working-class families. There were class antagonisms within the study group and those who continued with their education or careers often disliked, and were disliked by, those who did not. Far from being homogeneous, the study group contained a continuum of over-lapping sub-groups and cliques.

In view of the diversity within the sub-group it is useful to distinguish two main types of drugtaker:

a) individuals whose primary commitment was to their work or educational role, such as the students and non-manual workers;
b) individuals whose primary self-image was that of a drugtaker, such as those with poor work records, the unemployed, and those with no educational qualifications.

There were evident similarities between both types of drugtaker, as well as differences within each category. Even so the evidence of this study suggested that there were important differences between these two categories and that each should be considered, in many respects, as a separate entity.

Those in the former category, the students and middle-class bohemians, did not seem to have become drugtakers because of social or psychological strains, as has been suggested in much of the literature about drugtaking. Drug experimentation was so commonplace in certain circles that it did not necessarily constitute a dramatic step, or involve a profound motivation. Peer group pressure, curiosity, and drug availability seemed to be the main predisposing factors. Some people clearly regarded drugtaking, or membership of drugtaking groups, as a statement of an ideological position. This could be compared with the situation of people staging an anti-apartheid demonstration by illegal means, such as the disturbance of a sports match. Many drugtakers suggested such a parallel themselves.

Such reasons for becoming a drugtaker do not correspond to the 'medical model' of drug use as a form of sickness, a response to stress or profound problems. Neither do they fit sociological theories explaining deviant behaviour as a collective response to economical or social privation. Most of the existing theories of drugtaking have imputed that it constitutes a problem. It has generally been regarded as harmful or as a symptom of malaise. The evidence of this study does not support such a general verdict. The majority of the students and middle-class bohemians did not appear to have suffered any harm as the result of their drugtaking. On the contrary, most were emphatic that they had enjoyed it and regarded it as an enhancement of their lives.

Those individuals whose primary commitment was to their identities as drugtakers presented a very different picture. Their values and behaviour were attributable to the fact that, unlike most students and non-manual workers, many were from lower working-class families, or had 'dropped out' of higher or further education. I have suggested that the ideology of the study group appeared to have been mainly propounded by middle-class individuals. This was paradoxical in view of the fact that most middle-class respondents had only peripheral involvement with drugtaking. The values and behaviour of the most committed drugtakers were in many ways more 'extreme' than those of 'conventional' working-class or middle-class groups. Very few committed drugtakers had educational or career ambitions and many seemed to seek their aspirations within the framework of the drug scene. The injection of drugs was an indication of high commitment to the role of drugtaker. Many of the low-status unemployed and manual workers clearly espoused a more aggressive, delinquent self-image than the students or middle-class bohemians. The unselective and catholic use of legal and illegal drugs, evident amongst the most committed drugtakers, appeared to be compatible with a wish to seek oblivion. A few individuals even stated that their drug use was escapist and some said that their injection of drugs had, at times, been suicidal. The motivation for such drug use diverged very sharply from that of the two 'conformist' sub-groups, who were generally more casual in their approach to drugtaking.

A large number of those most committed to drugtaking had disturbed biographies. Many were unemployed and living in crowded housing. Several had attempted suicide and an important minority were delinquent and had both drug and non-drug convictions. Some individuals reported that they had histories of psychiatric illness or drug dependence. These corresponded in many respects to the traditional stereotype of the junkie, 'head', or 'problem drugtaker' and many of the study group conceded that some individuals used drugs in response to serious social or psychological problems.

The general social position of the low-status unemployed and manual workers was significantly different from that of the students and middle-class bohemians. The self-images, values, and behaviour of the two main types of drugtaker appeared to reflect their social class backgrounds, or present social positions (twenty of the eighty-seven low-status respondents were drop-outs from colleges or universities, and an additional twenty had been downwardly socially mobile since becoming drugtakers). The downwardly mobile group included drugtakers with the most disturbed biographies, with histories of psychiatric illness, attempted suicide, and other 'pathological' traits.

The evidence supports the view that many of those who appeared to regard themselves primarily in terms of their drugtaking roles were, or had been, beset by serious social problems. Some may well have been psychologically disturbed, but such a judgement is beyond the brief of the present study.

It is important to distinguish between two types of individuals within the low-status sub-group; those from lower working-class families and those who had been downwardly mobile. The situation of the former individuals was 'sequential', that is to say, the result of their lifelong social or economic privation as members of low-status groups; the downwardly mobile individuals had originally embarked upon middle-class careers, further and higher education, or were from 'respectable' working-class families, but had, at a definite and relatively late stage in their careers, changed direction and had fallen in terms of 'conventional' social status. Some of the downwardly mobile group had histories of mental illness, others appeared to have made a philosophical decision to reject conventional status goals. These had transferred their allegiance from the student and middle-class bohemian milieu to the more extreme and 'deviant' low-status sub-group. My observations suggested that the working-class and downwardly mobile low-status individuals were closely associated and shared a common social position. Many of those from working-class families seemed intelligent and articulate and had much in common with those who were downwardly mobile.

My impression was that thoroughgoing commitment to the role of drugtaker constituted a very different phenomenon from partial or casual commitment. In part these differences were attributable to social class: those most committed to the 'drug scene' were from both working-class and middle-class backgrounds, and were deviant in relation to the 'conventional' work values of either class. During my field-work I met plenty of manual workers just as dedicated to the 'work ethic', and just as hostile to drugtaking, as were some middle-class non-drugtakers. It is important to emphasize that many 'respectable' working-class individuals regarded some of those most deeply implicated with the drug scene as 'rough', and as deviant from conventional working-class norms. My field-work further indicated that many of those from lower working-class families had never been socialized to accept 'conventional' values and goals; these were regarded, both by other working-class and by middle-class individuals as, in effect, 'lumpen proletariat' or as reprehensible nonconformists. Similarly some of those who had been downwardly mobile were regarded as deviant from the conventional norms of their middle-class backgrounds. Both groups within the low-status sub-group were deviant in relation to their working-class or middle-class origins, and so one cannot attribute their behaviour, values, or other characteristics solely to low social status. As one student commented, the 'hard core' of the drug scene was, 'a repository for those from all social classes who rejected the work ethic'.

Many differences between those most involved with the drug scene and those with a lower level of commitment were linked with educational attainments. 'Drugtaking' covered a wide range of behaviour, much of which was not apparently motivated by any notable factors. The important consideration, from the point of view of this study, was the extent of personal commitment to one's role as a drugtaker in relation to other roles. This appeared to be influenced by the availability of other social opportunities. The two 'conformist' sub-groups, the students and middle-class bohemians, had attractive alternatives open to them and they identified only partially with the drug scene. The low-status sub-group either lacked access to or had failed within, or rejected, the conventional work and educational system. Many may have become drugtakers in order to escape their privation in other respects – as an escape from status frustration or genuine discontent with the social system.

The study group was so varied that no single theory adequately explains their behaviour. Most did not seem problematic in terms of the factors examined. Often, drugtaking was simply a leisure activity or a token of idealism. Nevertheless, those most deeply committed to their identities as drugtakers included many with disturbed biographies or from underprivileged backgrounds. These individuals seemed to have become drugtakers as a collective response to a wide range of social and psychological problems, either associated with their general life experience and class backgrounds or at a specific time in their lives. They could have been in a state of anomie. Such individuals had clearly experienced considerable difficulty and the evidence suggested that this was the sub-group towards which social policies should be primarily directed.

This study was concerned with a specific group observed and interviewed at a specific time. It must be emphasized that drug use and other forms of behaviour, for example, sexual behaviour, are in a state of flux. The drug scene is highly volatile:

> 'The significance of marihuana to a small deviant group will obviously be considerably altered when marihuana use becomes (as it may well have) a commonplace drug amongst students and I.B.M. executives' (Jock Young, personal communication).

In spite of the limitations of this study, drugtaking must clearly be considered as a new, but widespread form of social behaviour amongst young people in Britain, as in other industrialized centres. Cheltenham did not appear to be unique in any important way. It was part of a much more general pattern and drugtaking is an aspect of social and ideological change that certainly is not confined to a single Cotswolds town.

My general conclusion is that to achieve a realistic approach to the problems sometimes associated with drugtaking, one must distinguish between drugtakers. Many did not seem to have been harmed by their drug use and did not become drugtakers for any reasons that need demand social, including legal, intervention. My secondary conclusion is that drugtaking did not, in itself, constitute a problem. The problems were generally separate, often antecedent to drug use, and must be assessed in relation to the general well-being of each individual at any given social position. In this respect, certain types of drugtaking may have been symptomatic of underlying distress. It would be more constructive to help solve the root problems; to provide assistance to those individuals who need it rather than to attempt, as the law does at present, to control and penalize a wide range of drugtaking which, on the face of a great deal of evidence, seems an innocuous form of private, social behaviour.

Suggestions for Future Research

The present findings suggest that in future research it will be fruitful not to examine drugtaking in general, but to concentrate upon those drugtakers who seemed to be problematic in terms of the factors already examined. One finding of the present study was that individual drug use is more influenced by peer behaviour than by the pronouncements of strangers. It would be interesting, therefore, to evaluate the usefulness of existing drug education and propaganda, which the present study implies may be either futile or counter-productive.

It is concluded that the 'problem' drugtakers in this study were either from economically and socially underprivileged homes or had for some reason fallen from their original social positions. It is important to assess which pressures cause such commitment to the drug scene and which social or psychological factors distinguish individuals who do become downwardly mobile from those who do not. In addition, it is crucial to differentiate between drugtakers and non-drugtakers from deprived backgrounds; which factors are attributable to, or associated with drug use and which are functions of deprived backgrounds?

The Misuse of Drugs Act (1971) came fully into force on the 1 July, 1973. It would be valuable to assess the effects of this legislation in view of the findings that individuals convicted of drug offences may not be typical of the general drugtaking population. In particular, what are the effects of conviction upon individual career patterns, lifestyles, and drug use? Is conviction of a drug offence a form of deviancy amplification, an enhancement of personal commitment to the role of drugtaker, or a deterrent against drug use?

Appendix I
The Interview Schedule

The Interview Schedule

During field-work a thirty-page document was used. For the sake of brevity, this Appendix simply lists the questions included in the interview schedule.

Questions marked * were previously used by Charles Reeves in Southern Hampshire. Those marked † were used by Peter Willmott in his study of adolescent boys in East London (1966)

Q1 How long have you lived in the Cheltenham area?
Q2 Why did you come to the Cheltenham area?
Q3 How much longer do you expect to stay in the Cheltenham area?
Q4 How long have you lived at your present address?
Q5 How many places have you lived in during the last five years?
Q6 Where did you last live before you came to Cheltenham?
Q7 Where were you born?
Q8 In which year were you born?
Q9 How many people live in your household?
Q10 How many rooms does your household have?
Q11 Record respondent's tenure of housing.
Q12 How many households live in this building?
Q13 How many people live in this building?
Q14 a) Has your household the use of a working lavatory inside the building?
b) (If 'yes') Is it shared with another household?
Q15 a) Has your household the use of a bath inside this building?
b) (If 'yes') Is it shared with another household?

Q16 Classify type of respondent's dwelling (e.g. flat, digs, etc.).
Q17 Are you on the waiting list for a Council house?
Q18 Are you satisfied or dissatisfied with your accommodation?
Q19 (If answer to Q18 was 'dissatisfied') Why is this?
Q20 Do you want to move?
Q21 (If answer to Q20 was 'yes') Where would you like to move?
Q22 Are you likely to apply for a Council house?
Q23 What hobbies or pastimes are you active in, and where do you do them?
Q24 Do you own or have the use of any of the following (car, bicycle, etc.)?
Q25 a) Are your parents still both alive?
b) (If no) How old were were you when he/she/they died?
Q26 Record which parents/relatives/guardians respondent is living with.
Q27 Where do your parents live?
Q28 Are (were) your parents divorced or separated?
Q29 (If parents were divorced or separated) How old were you when their marriage broke up?
Q30 How old were you when you left your parents' home?
Q31 Record marital status of respondent.
Q32 a) Do you have any children?
b) (If 'yes') How many do you have?
c) Is he/she/are they living with you?
d) (If 'no') Why not?
Q33 a) Do you have any brothers or sisters living?
b) (If 'yes') How many do you have?
Q34 What sort of work does your father do?
Q35 What sort of work do you do?
Q36 a) Do you like or dislike your work/college etc.–?
b) Why do you say that?
Q37 a) Have you ever been out of work?
b) (If 'yes') How long were you out of work?
c) Why were you out of work?
d) Did you get unemployment or other State Benefits?
e) (If 'no') Why not?
Q38† At what age did you leave school?
Q39 a) Have you passed any exams?
b) (If 'yes') Give details.

Q40 a)* (If respondent is at school) What sort of job do you hope to go on to after you leave school?
b) (For those at school or college) Do you hope to go to University?
Q41* What would be your ideal job?
Q42 a) How much money did you bring home last week?
b) How much money did you bring home the week before last?
c) What is the main source of your income at present?
d) (If respondent is on Social Security) How long have you been out of work?
e) How many people do you have to support at present?
f) Does your husband/wife/person you live with earn any money at present?
Q43 a) How do you get on with your father/step-father?
b) How do you get on with your mother/step-mother?
Q44 a)* Would you say that your father/step-father is happy with your mother/step-mother?
b) Would you say that your mother/step-mother is happy with your father/step-father?
Q45 Would you describe your political views as (left wing, right wing, etc.)?
Q46 What are your religious beliefs?
Q47 Have you ever suffered from severe depression or unhappiness?
Q48 Have you ever attempted suicide?
Q49 a) Do you smoke cigarettes?
b) (If 'yes') How many do you smoke each day?
Q50 a) Do you drink alcohol?
b) (If 'yes') Are you a heavy drinker, and if so, do you have a drinking problem?
Q51 Which was the first drug you ever used?
Q52 Which drugs have you tried?
Q53 How old were you when you used (lst drug)?
Q54 I see you have not used (drugs not mentioned). Is there any reason for this?
Q55 You started on (1st drug used). What made you move on to try (other drugs used)?
Q56 Are there any other drugs you would like to use?
Q57 (If 'yes') Why would you like to use these?

Q58 What were the circumstances of the first time you ever used drugs?

Q59 Who introduced you to drugtaking?

Q60 a) Did your parents know about it?

b) (If 'yes') What was their reaction?

Q61 a)* To your knowledge, do either of your parents take drugs?

b) (If 'yes') Specify.

Q62 a)* Do any of your brothers or sisters take drugs?

b) (If 'yes') Specify.

Q63 a) At what age did you first marry?

b) (Where appropriate) How old were you when you re-married?

Q64 Has your husband/wife/person you live with known you use drugs?

Q65 a)* Does your Wife/husband/person you live with use drugs too?

b) (If 'yes') Specify type of drugs.

Q66 a) What is your main source of friends?

b) Are most of your friends drugtakers or non-drugtakers?

Q67 Have your parents ever been aware of your drugtaking?

Q68 a) Have your ever used drugs whilst you were still living with your parents?

b) (If 'yes') Specify type of drugs.

Q69 a) Have your ever had any medical treatment because of your drugtaking?

b) (If 'yes') Specify.

Q70 What do you think could be done to help any drugtakers you know?

Q71 What do you think are the main problems of the drugtakers you know?

Q72 What do you think should be done to make treatment or social services for drugtakers more effective?

Q73 Why did you first start using drugs?

Q74 Why are you using drugs now?

Q75 What do you think your future drugtaking will be? Do you intend to continue using drugs?

Q76 What do you think your future will be? Do you have any plans for the next few years?

Q77 What is your main aim in life?

Q78* Some people say drugs:
a) reduce interest in sex
b) increase interest in sex
c) divert interest to your own sex
d) other
Which has been true in your case?

Q79* How old were your when you first had sexual intercourse?

Q80* Is there anything in life you get a kick out of more than sexual intercourse?

Q81 Have drugs helped you to get more out of sex?

Q82 How has your way of life or attitude to people and to the world, changed since you started using drugs?

Q83 a) (to females) Have you ever had an abortion?
b) (If 'yes') Give details of legality, type of clinic, etc.

Q84 What jobs have you had since you started using drugs?

Q85 a) Have you ever had any dangerous drug arrests?
b) (If 'yes') Give details.

Q86 a) Have you ever been in trouble with the police?
b) (If 'yes') Give details.

Record sex of respondent.
Add comments on appearance, housing, etc.

In addition to the main schedule, the following supplementary questions were asked about each type of drug used by the respondent:

Drug Data Sheet

Name of drug
How old were you when you first used this drug?
How many times have you used this drug?
Why did you first use it?
Do you still use it?
How do you get the drug into your body?
Are you usually alone or with others when you use it?
What effect do you get from this drug?
What are the dangers (if any) of this drug?
Will you use it in future, and if so, why?
Would you find difficulty in going without this drug for a month?

Appendix II
Case Histories

Case Histories

The following case histories are based upon close personal contact with the individuals concerned. Details have only been omitted or changed to preserve the anonymity of those to whom they refer.

Case A

'Tiny' is twenty-two years old. Born in a village in the Cotswolds, he has always lived near Cheltenham and attended local schools. His parents own a general stores and hoped that he would help them run the family business. This was not to be. From an early age Tiny has been on poor terms with his father who regarded him as effeminate. He associated with a delinquent group at school and, like most of his friends, left school early without passing any exams. As a member of a 'rough' working-class peer group he dissociated himself from the work ethic that his parents extolled and engaged in petty crimes from a fairly early age.

He experienced his first sexual intercourse soon after puberty and his associates were similarly precocious. Some were blatantly promiscuous. The group as a whole was working class and tried to live up to an image of aggressive masculinity. Sexual exploits, heavy drinking, and delinquency were equally supported within the group, and Tiny found in group membership a pleasant alternative from the perceived constraints of his parental home.

His lack of educational qualifications severely restricted his job opportunities and he disliked the menial jobs he was able to get. On starting work, as a warehouse assistant, he moved away from his parental home into a squalid flat with some people he knew. Having no interest whatever in his boring work, he sought an emotional outlet through leisure. Rock music, sex, and drugtaking all became important aspects of his life. He had always had a horror of 'hard' drugs and never injected any himself. He used cannabis and alcohol in large amounts, drinking and smoking frequently. He was a member of a circle of low-status males who were catholic in their drugtaking habits. Several were unemployed and dealt in drugs, so that there was usually quite a variety available. Amphetamine sulphate, cannabis, opium, cough linctuses, and inhalers were all regularly ingested and Tiny finally became very deeply involved with the drugtaking way of life. He gave up work and slept rough for a while, sometimes staying with people he knew through the drug scene. Since he had no fixed address he was not eligible for Social Security. This prompted him to take a series of temporary labouring jobs, but these were too much for him physically and he obtained a nominal address at a semi-derelict cellar and gave up work. His poor physical state, combined with an apparent hypochondria ensured that sufficient medical notes were forthcoming to justify his continued dependence on Social Security payments.

He earned some money by dealing in amphetamine sulphate powder and often sold L.S.D. and cannabis. A fairly conspicuous character, he was well known to the police and was widely reputed to have given them information about other drugtakers. He was not popular in the scene for this alleged duplicity and was treated with caution and disdain. At the time I encountered him he was living with a girl who was working and relied on her income for considerable periods. He had no intention of returning to a 'straight' job: 'Too fucking boring man. I'd rather be on the dole.'

Much of his time was spent reading about and listening to rock music and he constantly commented that he hoped to 'get a band together'. He had no musical ability and busied himself by trying to find people who had such ability to play for him. His dress was that of a conventional 'head', broad-bottomed 'loon' pants, T-shirt, and colourful leather jacket. His physical appearance, as well as his accommodation, were dirty and neglected, and he seemed indifferent to personal hygiene.

Tiny's case is a fairly typical one of a locally born, low-status, drugtaker. Without career aspirations, he attempts to compensate for this through the hedonistic way of life of his peer group. Drugtaking was seen as another form of kick. He used drugs for their 'buzz' or the sensations they produced. Most of his friends were drugtakers too, and many were criminal. He liked to picture himself as part of the criminal underworld and clearly relished the idea that he was in conflict with the police. I suggest that such cases correspond to the classic theory of 'anomie', or unfulfilled aspirations.

Case B

'Tripper' is in his mid-thirties. He had a grammar school education and used to be a clerk in the Civil Service. He has always been deeply interested in art and the occult and became interested in drugs through reading about peyote cults and oriental religions. He gave up work during the mid 1960s and became a hippy for a while. He spent two years on the road and managed to get as far as India on his travels. On his return (the girl he was travelling with became homesick) he began to work as a painter and managed to sell enough of his work to support himself. Over the years he has lived with a few girls. These relationships collapsed and were soon replaced by others, since he is an amiable man and appears to attract women.

He clearly has a mystical, elitist view of drugtaking and believes that it is not for the masses to dabble in. He believed that drugs can help to attain higher levels of consciousness and, if combined with the correct philosophies, can be beneficial. Tripper regards himself as a father figure in the local drug scene, and states that he is worried about widespread use of drugs such as L.S.D. by people he regards as immature and unsuitable. Tripper suggested that his use of psychedelic drugs was the mental equivalent of my own enthusiasm for rock-climbing: 'The idea is to push experience, and thereby understanding, to the limit.'

He was very well read on religious and philosophical topics and was a good example of middle-class 'bohemianism'. He was working in an artistic job, which allowed him to be independent and he believed that work should be expressive and not oppressive. This view was quite widely held by middle-class drugtakers and was really a romantic reaction to the worst aspects of the industrial division of labour.

Tripper was careful to avoid any drugtakers he regarded as 'uncool' or careless and indiscreet. He described Tiny and his associates as 'lumpenproletariat' – 'they will drop anything, drink anything, and sleep with anything'. In contrast to the indiscriminate hedonism of the majority of manual workers observed, Tripper and his associates were rather older, most were working, and all tended to be very philosophical and more sophisticated in the ways they spoke about drugtaking. Many of this group had close friends who used heroin and a few had tried it themselves but, in general, they avoided such drugs and preferred hallucinogens which they regarded as compatible with their desires to expand their intellectual awareness. Tripper had an encyclopaedic knowledge of hallucinogens and had experimented with several little-known types of British herbs, together with an amazing array of substances from health food shops.

My first impression of Tripper was that he was a man of great self-assurance, very sage in his countenance and demeanour. He took me under his wing as a novice for instruction into meditation and mysticism and was deeply absorbed in these doctrines. He was keen to suggest sociological theories to account for drugtaking and stated that heads were an ethnic group whom he believed were a clear-seeing group of mystics in a materialistic society. He believed that many idealistic young people go through a period of self-evaluation and searching for an explanation:

> 'Many may appear to go off the rails, and trip all the time, or smoke themselves stupid. I did for a while. It's important to keep the doors open so that when they finally get their heads together, they can come back into society, and not be treated like vermin.'

He confided that he had been helped through such a phase himself by sympathetic parents and employers, who had made it much easier for him to return to a more settled way of life after a protracted period of continuous drug use.

Tripper quoted John Stuart Mill's famous dictum that private behaviour was not the business of the law. He clearly believed that his drugtaking (he smoked amazing amounts of cannabis) was his business alone and he was highly critical of the cannabis laws, which he believed intruded into the area of private behaviour.

He and his friends were quite discreet in their behaviour, but their dwellings bore all the marks of an interest in psychedelic drugs. Eastern prints, Bhuddas, records of sitar music, joss-sticks, and an assortment of pipes littered their homes. This group were not delinquent and appeared highly literate and idealistic. In the eyes of conventional society, they may have been eccentric but they did not appear to be problematic in terms of the factors examined in this study.

Case C

Ruth is an introspective, rather pretty girl. When I first met her she talked at length about her life and her hopes for the future. Conventional and neat in her appearance, she lives on Social Security so that she can concentrate on caring for her two-year old son. She has a regular boyfriend and hopes to marry in the near future, since her boyfriend is prepared to accept the responsibility of her child. Her parents live abroad and she rented a flatlet in a large house also occupied by students and young professional people.

Everyone in the house smoked cannabis quite regularly and my impression was that of a very friendly, happy group of people. Ruth had smoked cannabis for three or four years and had also used L.S.D., mescalin, and D.M.T. She found some of these psychedelic experiences disturbing and had discontinued using L.S.D., which she believed accentuated her tendency to feel depressed. She often felt unhappy about the illegitimate child, but was fiercely devoted to him and made him the focus of her hopes and ambitions. She looked forward to marriage and intended to stop using cannabis then because her fiancé disapproved of drugs. She smokes alone quite a lot, using cannabis as a sedative to sooth her to sleep at times of depression or stress. She believes this is preferable to using any of the drugs her doctor might prescribe.

Ruth commented that she thought excessive drug use could accentuate lethargy and that she was worried about getting too involved. She thought that in general drugs were over-rated and that the mass media and the law had created a false mystique which was attractive to impressionable adolescents. Her main concern was that young children or immature people should not use drugs, because she believed this would harm them and intensify their problems. She conceded that she used drugs as an escape and would prefer to face reality without their aid.

Ruth was just one of many 'middle-class' individuals I encountered who used drugs socially and, occasionally, for a sedative. Her background was, if anything, rather prim and she had been deeply distraught upon becoming accidentally pregnant. She was supported and comforted by her neighbours, all middle-class cannabis users, and she had a clear view of the sort of future she wanted for her child. She was no more a social problem than any intelligent, unmarried mother and her association with a group of drugtakers provided her with understanding friends and intellectual stimulus when her boyfriend was away from the area.

Case D

Frank is a research student in the natural sciences. He comes from a professional background and is nearing the completion of his PhD at a large, urban university. He was a keen Scout while he was at school and is deeply interested in all forms of music, literature, and politics. He considers himself a liberal-socialist and has attended a few demonstrations on matters of conscience, such as apartheid and the Vietnam war. He dresses conservatively and has short hair.

He became interested in drugs when some of his undergraduate friends began using cannabis and L.S.D. a few years earlier. He, a non-smoker, was reluctant to join in, but he read several books about cannabis and decided that it was innocuous and has smoked, socially, for two years now. He finds cannabis a pleasant alternative to alcohol and has also used L.S.D. three times. He was wary of L.S.D. at first, but decided that if he could ensure that he was in congenial, safe surroundings, it would be safe. He persuaded his girfriend to 'guide' him through his first trip, which was in Richmond Park on a sunny day, and found the experience stimulating and enjoyable. He nevertheless, regards L.S.D. as a potent drug and doubts that he will use it again.

Frank is ambitious and intends to make a successful career for himself, possibly in North America. He believes the 'underground' to be a sanctuary for social misfits and psychotics and is highly critical of the drug way of life which he believes is negative, parasitic, and non-productive. He is radical, believes in a permissive, tolerant society, and regards drugtaking as one of many new experiences he has at different times tried with enthusiasm.

Case E

Edward is a student teacher. He was brought up in a large industrial town where his father was an office worker. He left school with three 'A' levels and spent a year working in an insurance office before coming to Cheltenham to attend college. He first experimented with drugs while in the sixth form at school, smoking cannabis at weekends with a group of youths with whom he played rugby football. This behaviour was regarded as 'cool' or mature and he was attracted to the philosophy of the 'underground' which emphasized immediate experiences and political radicalism.

On entry into college he found he had more freedom than before to dress and behave as he pleased. He grew his hair longer and soon discovered a few other students who had used cannabis and other drugs. He took L.S.D. several times and reported that this was pleasant, though he discontinued on the grounds that he found these experiences rather repetitive after a while.

His chief academic interests were sociological and he was politically militant and active in college politics. He generally did well academically and appeared to be a brighter than average student. After his first year in a hall of residence he moved into a flat with a fellow student and was shortly joined by his girlfriend, another student.

His drugtaking was limited, in order not to interfere with his college commitments, and consisted mainly of communal cannabis smoking with other students. He asserted that cannabis was not more dangerous, if used carefully, than alcohol and that drug abuse resulted from antecedent social or psychological problems. He was hostile to the idea of using opiates or injecting drugs and anticipated that he would finish smoking cannabis when he became a teacher, since he considered the risks of detection to be too great to justify using the drug. He was critical of individuals he knew who were deeply involved with drugs. He regarded such preoccupation as unhealthy and negative. His varied interests included sailing and canoeing and he was emphatic that his general commitment to drugtaking was low.

The preceding case histories reveal considerable differences between individual drugtakers. It is one of the main conclusions of this study that there was no uniform pattern of drugtaking.

Appendix III
A Note on the Cost of Drugs

A Note on the Cost of Drugs

In America there is no legal supply of heroin and users have to buy their supplies on the black market. The average daily expenditure on heroin of nearly 1,000 New York addicts in 1965 was $14.35. It was estimated that to obtain this much, roughly fifty dollars worth of goods had to be stolen by each individual daily (Task Force Report 1967). It is popularly thought by the non-drugtaking public that the use of all illegal drugs is costly. In general, this is not so. The mainstay of the drug scene is cannabis and this is fairly cheap. Some tobacco, cigarette papers (skins), and a piece of cannabis resin costing £1 will be sufficient to get half a dozen people 'high' or intoxicated. In comparison to alcohol this is not expensive.

L.S.D. and the stronger hallucinogens are usually taken infrequently. Prices vary, but at the time of writing a microdot tablet of L.S.D. costs fifty pence. Amphetamine sulphate powder is sold in small amounts for about twenty pence.

In practical terms, illegal drugtaking need cost no more to the participants than social drinking and may cost less than regular cigarette smoking. Some drugs, such as cocaine, are expensive but are regarded as rare luxuries.

Drugtakers tend to be eager to 'convert' others to adopt their behaviour and most people probably do not pay for their first experiments with drugs. I encountered many people who offer a joint (cannabis cigarette) as readily as their parents might offer a glass of sherry. Within the sub-culture cannabis is regarded as a token of goodwill and friendship and it is often available free of charge to people who cannot afford to buy a smoke.

experimenting: first time.

It must be emphasized that most drugtakers use drugs in moderation and spend relatively little. Probably the 'average' regular user may buy a 'quid deal' every week or so, but may buy less and only purchase stronger psychedelics occasionally. Some individuals certainly spend far more than this. I encountered several who smoked regularly throughout the day and probably spent at least £5 each week on their personal cannabis. Most were working or augmented their income by dealing to their friends. The majority of regular users do a certain amount of dealing and this is regarded as a useful service and a legitimate way of paying for one's own drug use.

There was relatively little narcotic use in the Cheltenham area. Those individuals who were regularly injecting opiates were mainly vagrants and did a certain amount of dealing to pay for their drugs. One dealer I knew sometimes earned over £250 in a week if things went well, but this was a risky way of earning a living and the detection rate for large-scale dealers is probably quite high. In practical terms, there are little financial barriers to becoming a drugtaker. Drug use is generally no more expensive than many other youthful interests. Most of the drugtakers I encountered had left school and had some form of income and most of those still at school had at least £1 each week to spend on drugs, if they so desired.

Appendix IV
Police Discretion in Enforcing the Drug Laws

Police Discretion in Enforcing the Drug Laws

The difficult task of enforcing the drug control laws falls to the police. All of the drugtakers I encountered were clearly aware that they ran at least some risk of being apprehended. As one person who had just begun to smoke cannabis said:

> 'I was walking along the road with a quid deal (of cannabis) in my pocket. A policeman came round the corner towards me. For the first time in my life I thought God, I'm on the other side of the fence. In a few seconds my whole conception of life changed. I realized I was a criminal, and felt hostile and scared. My heart didn't stop pounding until I was safely back home. You see, I used to think of the police as people who gave me directions when I was lost, or who helped me if I had anything stolen. Since I started smoking I feel rather paranoid about them. Even if I'm clean (not carrying drugs) I feel guilty every time I see a cop. I am sure that real freaks (people more involved with drugtaking) are a lot more antagonistic towards the police than I am. I think it's all wrong, because I'm a law-abiding bloke, usually.'

These sentiments were echoed by many middle-class cannabis users. In general, those who were 'conventional' in their appearance believed that they were fairly safe from being stopped and searched, but nevertheless many felt uneasy about their relations with the police.

Some of those most deeply involved with the drugtaking way of life were fiercely hostile to the police and were eager to repeat rumours of police corruption, especially allegations that members of the drug squad smoked cannabis themselves or actually dealt in drugs.

My conversations with individual policeman at various times suggested that many were very hostile to the idea of drugtaking, which they saw as an unmitigated social evil. My general impression was that there was a rather ambivalent relationship between the police and drugtakers. The interests of both groups were clearly polarized and both viewed each other with prejudice and animosity. In spite of this many drugtakers were on familiar terms with drug squad officers and the police appeared to get much of their information directly from drugtakers. This situation inevitably lead to rumours of 'grassing' by drugtakers in return for personal immunity from arrest. This dubious situation is a feature of the criminal world in general.

The police appeared to spend most of their time scrutinizing the low-status, delinquent group of multi-users. These were generally the most conspicuous and extreme drugtakers. My observations suggested that, in general, the discreet private use of cannabis was widely tolerated. Perhaps the police realized that it was so widespread that any more than token action to enforce the law would not have been feasible.

Several policemen intimated that they believed in a policy of concentrating on those drugtakers they regarded as a 'nuisance', or as 'undesirable types'. The evidence of this study suggests that those drugtakers who had been convicted of a drug offence were not a representative group of the drugtakers in the community. My personal impression was that an individual's general appearance, social status, and demeanour had a lot to do with whether or not he was likely to be stopped and searched for drugs. I knew several long-haired students who never used drugs who reported to me that they had often been frisked by the police if they were out on the streets late at night. The chances of a long-haired or 'hippy' youth being stopped and searched would seem to exceed those of a shorter-haired, conventionally dressed individual.

I discussed this tendency with individual policemen who, correctly, pointed out that it is hard to ensure a completely objective, impartial implementation of their wide powers to stop and search. There are undoubtedly much malicious and unfounded rumours about police. I knew several people who had been caught in possession of drugs but had never been brought to court on the grounds that they seemed to be 'decent types'. It certainly seemed that middle-class drugtakers were much less likely to be prosecuted than unemployed or working-class drugtakers. This may well be true of offenders in general.

It is clear that the police are in a difficult position in relation to the drug laws. I suggest that individual officers have very considerable discretion about whether to tolerate an individual's drugtaking or to bring the matter to court. In general, the types of people who are formally charged with drug offences are those who correspond to the policeman's idea of a 'bad' drugtaker, preferably someone who is low-status, long-haired, and dirty. This means that the Home Office statistics on drug convictions record drugtakers who have been selected by the police.

One of the common assertions made by the police is that their policy is to 'go for the pushers', to concentrate not on drug users, who are seen as victims, but to apprehend drug suppliers. In fact the great majority of people arrested and convicted are in possession of small amounts and are not drug dealers.

I believe that the drug laws, as they stand at present, are subject to abuse because of the great power they give to the police. It would be interesting to know what the public reaction would be if middle-aged people were subject to arbitrary searches by the police. As it is, an incalculable number of young people are regularly stopped and searched and, sometimes, harassed on the pretext that they might possess drugs.

The existing law is unenforceable and no attempt is made to enforce it. In general, students and non-manual workers are not likely to be brought to court and those who are seem to be a very biased selection, who give a false impression to the judiciary, and to the public at large, of the nature of the drugtaking fraternity and perpetuate the unfavourable stereotype of drugtakers held by the police.

In practice, we seem to have a situation in which the drug control laws are interpreted not to penalize the possession, trafficking, or production of proscribed drugs, but to select certain types of drugtaker on the convenient pretext that they infringe these laws.

Appendix V
Tables

Table 19
Length of residence in Cheltenham area

	students				*non-students*				*total*	
	users		*multi-users*		*users*		*multi-users*			
	male	*female*	*male*	*female*	*male*	*female*	*male*	*female*	*N*	*%*
less than 1 month	3	1	2	1	1	1	16	2	27	13.5
5 weeks–6 months	3	1	1	1	1	3	3	–	13	6.5
13 weeks–1 year	1	1	6	2	1	1	5	–	17	8.5
53 weeks–2 years	8	4	6	3	–	1	9	2	33	16.5
105 weeks–3 years	5	–	6	1	1	2	12	1	28	14.0
157 weeks–4 years	–	1	6	–	3	–	7	3	20	10.0
209 weeks–5 years	1	–	1	–	2	–	5	–	9	4.5
261 weeks–10 years	–	–	1	2	3	–	3	2	11	5.5
10 years or longer	2	–	2	1	4	3	23	7	42	21.0
total	23	8	31	11	16	11	83	17	200	100.0

Table 20
Socio-economic status
(users and multi-users)

	students				*non-students*				*total*	
	users		*multi-users*		*users*		*multi-users*			
	male	*female*	*male*	*female*	*male*	*female*	*male*	*female*	*N*	*%*
I higher managerial and professional	1	–	3	–	3	2	3	1	13	6.5
II lower administrative and professional	6	4	6	1	3	1	11	2	34	17.0
III skilled supervisory non-manual	2	2	8	7	2	–	8	1	30	15.0
IV lower non-manual	6	–	4	1	1	6	16	8	42	21.0
V skilled manual	8	2	9	2	6	2	33	4	66	33.0
VI unskilled manual	–	–	1	–	1	–	11	1	14	7.0
VII residual, State Pensioners, etc.	–	–	–	–	–	–	–	–	–	0.0
don't know	–	–	–	–	–	–	1	–	1	0.5
total	23	8	31	11	16	11	83	17	200	100.0

Table 21
Socio-economic status
(the sub-groups)

	students	middle-class bohemians	low-status unemployed and manual workers	total	
				N	%
I higher managerial and professional	4	6	3	13	6.5
II lower managerial and administrative	17	11	6	34	17.0
III skilled supervisory non-manual	19	4	7	30	15.0
IV lower non-manual	11	8	23	42	21.0
V skilled manual	21	8	37	66	33.0
VI unskilled manual	1	2	11	14	7.0
VII residual, State Pensioners, etc.	–	–	–	–	0.0
don't know	–	1	–	1	0.5
total	73	40	87	200	100.0

Table 22
Cohabitation and marital status
(users and multi-users)

	students				*non-students*				*total*	
	users		*multi-users*		*users*		*multi-users*			
	male	*female*	*male*	*female*	*male*	*female*	*male*	*female*	*N*	*%*
single	20	5	22	9	14	6	57	8	141	70.5
married and living together	–	1	3	–	1	2	9	2	18	9.0
separated	–	–	–	–	1	–	4	–	5	2.5
divorced	–	–	–	–	–	–	1	–	1	0.5
widowed	–	–	–	–	–	–	1	–	1	0.5
cohabiting	3	2	6	2	–	3	11	7	34	17.0
total	23	8	31	11	16	11	83	17	200	100.0

Table 23
Cohabitation and marital status
(the sub-groups)

				total	
	students	*middle-class bohemians*	*low-status unemployed and manual workers*	*N*	*%*
single	56	29	56	141	70.5
married and living together	4	6	8	18	9.0
separated	–	–	5	5	2.5
divorced	–	–	1	1	0.5
widowed	–	–	1	1	0.5
cohabiting	13	5	16	34	17.0
total	73	40	87	200	100.0

Table 24

Changes in lifestyle or outlook associated with becoming a drugtaker

	students				*non-students*					
	users		*multi-users*		*users*		*multi-users*		*total*	
	male	*female*	*male*	*female*	*male*	*female*	*male*	*female*	*N*	*%*
became more tolerant	3	2	4	2	2	1	17	4	35	17.5
no effect at all	7	2	5	2	8	–	7	–	31	15.5
became more 'aware'	2	2	5	1	2	1	15	3	31	15.5
not due to drugs, but I have changed	4	1	7	1	2	2	4	3	24	12.0
more relaxed and friendly	1	–	2	2	2	1	5	3	16	8.0
I reject outward values	1	–	–	1	–	2	9	2	15	7.5
more tolerant of drugtakers	5	–	2	–	–	2	–	–	9	4.5
mix daily with drugtakers	–	–	1	–	–	–	3	2	6	3.0
less violent	–	–	–	–	–	–	5	–	5	2.5

more introverted and passive	–	1	–	1	–	–	3	–	5	2.5
more radical	–	–	2	–	–	–	2	–	4	2.0
more humane	–	–	1	–	–	–	3	–	4	2.0
less materialistic	–	–	–	1	–	–	2	–	3	1.5
less interested in people	–	–	–	–	–	–	3	–	3	1.5
more ambitious	–	–	–	–	–	–	2	–	2	1.0
mix less with drugtakers	–	–	–	–	–	2	–	–	2	1.0
ceased working	–	–	–	–	–	–	1	–	1	0.5
more broadminded and interested in nature	–	–	1	–	–	–	–	–	1	0.5
more hostile to drugtaking	–	–	1	–	–	–	–	–	1	0.5
don't know	–	–	–	–	–	–	2	–	2	1.0
total	23	8	31	11	16	11	83	17	200	100.0

Table 25
Religious beliefs
(users and multi-users)

	students				*non-students*				*total*	
	users		*multi-users*		*users*		*multi-users*			
	male	*female*	*male*	*female*	*male*	*female*	*male*	*female*	*N*	*%*
Atheists	1		6	1			4		12	6.0
Agnostic	11	3	12	2	7	3	37	5	80	40.0
Humanist	5	2	5		2	1	10	2	27	13.5
Church of England				1	1		3	1	6	3.0
Non-conformist		1			1				2	1.0
Roman Catholic				1		1		1	3	1.5
Divine Light Mission	1		2		1	2	7		13	6.5
Jesus Movement								1	1	0.5
Oriental Mysticism		1	1	1			10	1	14	7.0
Spiritualist		1		3			2		6	3.0
'Christian'	2		2			2	4		10	5.0
'I believe in God'	2		3	2	3	2	5	6	23	11.5
Existentialist					1				1	0.5
Quaker	1								1	0.5
Pentecostal							1		1	0.5
total	23	8	31	11	16	11	83	17	200	100.0

Table 26
Religious beliefs
(the sub-groups)

	students	middle-class bohemians	low-status unemployed and manual workers	total N	total %
Atheist	8	3	1	12	6.0
Agnostic	28	18	34	80	40.0
Humanist	12	6	9	27	13.5
Church of England	1	–	5	6	3.0
Non-conformist	1	1	–	2	1.0
Roman Catholic	1	–	2	3	1.5
Divine Light Mission	3	3	7	13	6.5
Jesus Movement	–	–	1	1	0.5
Oriental Mysticism	3	4	7	14	7.0
Spiritualism	4	–	2	6	3.0
'Christian'	4	–	6	10	5.0
'I believe in God'	7	4	12	23	11.5
Existentialist	–	1	–	1	0.5
Quaker	1	–	–	1	0.5
Pentecostal	–	–	1	1	0.5
total	73	40	87	200	100.0

Table 27
Political beliefs
(users and multi-users)

	students				*non-students*				*total*	
	users		*multi-users*		*users*		*multi-users*			
	male	*female*	*male*	*female*	*male*	*female*	*male*	*female*	*N*	*%*
very left wing	4	2	6	1	1	1	6	2	23	11.5
left wing	11	5	13	1	8	1	19	4	62	31.0
middle of the road	1	1	4	2	3	1	8	1	21	10.5
right wing	2		–	–	–	–	1	–	3	1.5
very right wing	1	–	1	–	–	–	–	–	2	1.0
not interested in politics	4	–	7	6	4	7	45	9	82	41.0
don't know	–	–	–	1	–	1	4	1	7	3.5
total	23	8	31	11	16	11	83	17	200	100.0

Table 28
Political beliefs
(the sub-groups)

	students	middle-class bohemians	low-status unemployed and manual workers	total N	total %
very left wing	13	1	9	23	11.5
left wing	30	23	9	62	31.0
middle-of-the-road	8	3	10	21	10.5
right wing	2	—	1	3	1.5
very right wing	2	—	—	2	1.0
interested in politics	17	11	54	82	41.0
don't know	1	2	4	7	3.5
total	73	40	87	200	100.0

Table 29
Age of first drug experience

	students				*non-students*					
	users		*multi-users*		*users*		*multi-users*		*total*	
age	*male*	*female*	*male*	*female*	*male*	*female*	*male*	*female*	*N*	*%*
13	–	–	–	1	–	–	3	1	5	2.5
14	–	–	2	2	–	1	9	2	16	8.0
15	–	1	6	2	3	4	12	4	32	16.0
16	4	1	5	4	–	1	12	2	29	14.5
17	4	–	9	1	2	2	19	3	40	20.0
18	5	3	5	1	5	2	10	3	34	17.0
19	6	2	3	–	2	–	6	–	19	9.5
20	1	–	–	–	1	–	4	1	7	3.5
21	1	1	1	–	1	–	4	1	9	4.5
22	–	–	–	–	1	–	2	–	3	1.5
23	1	–	–	–	1	–	–	–	2	1.0
24 or older	1	–	–	–	–	1	2	–	4	2.0
total	23	8	31	11	16	11	83	17	200	100.0

Table 30
First drug used

	students		*non-students*		*total*	
	male	*female*	*male*	*female*	*N*	*%*
Cannabis	45	18	72	23	158	79.0
Amphetamines	6		15	4	25	12.5
L.S.D.		1	4		5	2.5
Barbiturates			3	1	4	2.0
Amyl Nitrate	1		1		2	1.0
Mandrax			2		2	1.0
Librium			1		1	0.5
banana skins	1				1	0.5
aspirins in Coca Cola	1				1	0.5
Heroin			1		1	0.5

Table 31
Setting of the first drugtaking experience

	students				*non-students*				*total*	
	users		*multi-users*		*users*		*multi-users*			
	male	*female*	*male*	*female*	*male*	*female*	*male*	*female*	*N*	*%*
friends home or flat	11	6	14	5	10	3	36	10	95	47.5
school			11	1	1	2	10	3	28	14.0
party	4		1	2	1	1	9	2	20	10.0
dance	1		2				7	1	11	5.5
college/university		1	2		1	1	2		7	3.5
at home with friends	1					2	4		7	3.5
alone at home							6	1	7	3.5
public house		1			1	2	2		6	3.0
in the country with friends	3			2					5	2.5
pop festival	3						1		4	2.0
abroad							4		4	2.0
on holiday					2				2	1.0
cafe			1				1		2	1.0
youth club				1					1	0.5
at work							1		1	0.5
total	23	8	31	11	16	11	83	17	200	100.0

Table 32
Type of housing

	students		non-students		total	
	users	multi-users	users	multi-users	N	%
flat	14	19	10	53	96	48.0
bedsitter	4	7	3	19	33	16.5
hostel	—	—	—	1	1	0.5
hall of residence	4	1	—	—	5	2.5
digs	3	1	1	1	6	3.0
owner-occupied		3	3	4	10	5.0
parental house	2	6	10	14	32	16.0
rented house	3	5	—	8	16	8.0
other-temporary	1	—	—	—	1	0.5
total	31	42	27	100	200	100.0

Table 33
Subjective classification of housing
(based on observations made during field-work)

	students				*non-students*				*total*	
	users		*multi-users*		*users*		*multi-users*			
	male	*female*	*male*	*female*	*male*	*female*	*male*	*female*	*N*	*%*
acceptable	21	7	30	9	15	10	35	12	139	69.5
very untidy/drab			1		1	1	3		6	3.0
very dirty				1			8		9	4.5
unfit for human habitation							3	1	4	2.0
no fixed address	1						1		2	1.0
temporary		1		1			12	1	15	7.5
no record	1						21	3	25	12.5
total	23	8	31	11	16	11	83	17	200	100.0

Table 34
Separation from parents

	students				*non-students*				*total*	
	users		*multi-users*		*users*		*multi-users*			
	male	*female*	*male*	*female*	*male*	*female*	*male*	*female*	*N*	*%*
living with parent or guardian	3	—	4	3	8	4	11	5	38	19.0
living away from parent or guardian	20	8	27	8	8	7	72	12	162	81.0
total	23	8	31	11	16	11	83	17	200	100.0

Table 35
Self-reported delinquency

	students				*non-students*				*total*	
	users		*multi-users*		*users*		*multi-users*			
	male	*female*	*male*	*female*	*male*	*female*	*male*	*female*	*N*	*%*
delinquent	5	—	11	—	3	1	50	1	71	35.5
non-delinquent	18	8	20	11	13	10	33	16	129	64.5
total	23	8	31	11	16	11	83	17	200	100.0

Glossary of Terms

One feature of the drugtaking milieu was the fast-changing nature of the argot or jargon used. Many expressions soon passed into disuse and were replaced by others. For example the term 'reefer' has long since been outmoded as a name for a cannabis cigarette. Some of the following terms are used in this book and others were in vogue at the time of field-work:

acid	Lysergic acid diethylamide-25
bummer	bad trip or unpleasant experience
busted	raided or arrested by the police
chillum	a hollow receptacle in which drugs are smoked
cool	adjective denoting wisdom and self-control
crash (verb)	to sleep on somebody's floor
crash pad	a temporary dwelling
dealer	a person who sells drugs
dope	cannabis
downer	a depressant drug
fix (verb)	to inject drugs
freak (noun)	a drugtaker
goof-balls	barbiturates
grass	marihuana or cannabis
head (noun)	a drugtaker
high	intoxicated by drugs
jack (verb)	to inject drugs
joint (noun)	a cannabis cigarette
rip-off (verb)	to steal
score (verb)	to buy or obtain drugs
smack	heroin
speed	stimulant drugs
straights	ordinary cigarettes, or non-drugtakers

Bibliography

The following bibliography includes the main references I found useful in preparing this book. Not all have been referred to directly in the text.

1. Drugtaking

Alarcon see De Alarcon.

Addiction Research Unit, see Kosviner.

Adler, N. 1970. Drug Abuse as the Manipulation of Body Image, Sensibility and Self: The Antinonian Personality as Tuned Orgasm. Paper presented at Conference on Drug Use and Drug Subcultures, San Francisco, February 17.

Andrews, G., Vinkenoorg, S., and Owen, P. 1972. *The Book of Grass: An Anthology of Indian Hemp.* Harmondsworth: Penguin.

Ausubel, D. P. 1964. *Drug Addiction: Physiological, Psychological and Sociological Aspects.* New York: Random House.

Ball, J. C. 1967. Marijuana Smoking and the Onset of Heroin Use. *British Journal of Criminology* 1953. 7: 408–13.

Bean, P. 1974. *The Social Control of Drugs* London: Martin Robertson.

Becker, H. S. 1953. Becoming a Marihuana User. *American Journal of Sociology*: 235–42.

——— 1967. History, Culture and Subjective Experience: An Exploration of the Social Bases of Drug-Induced Experiences. *Journal of Health and Social Behaviour* 8: 163–76.

Beckett, D. 1967. Should we Legalize Pot?. *New Society* 18 May: 720–21.

Benusiglio, D., Kosviner, A., Pixner, S., Stimson, G. V., and Zacune, J. 1967. *Soft Hard and Psychedelic.* Unpublished report, L.S.E.
Bestic, A. 1966 *Turn Me On Man.* London: Tandem.
Bewley, T. H. 1966. Recent Changes in the Pattern of Drug Abuse in the United Kingdom. *Bulletin of Narcotics,* **28**: 1–13.
Bewley, T. H., Ben-Arie, O., and James, I. P. 1968. Morbidity and Mortality from Heroin Dependence. 1: Survey of Heroin Addicts Known to the Home Office. *British Medical Journal* **1**: 725–32.
Binnie, H. L., and Murdock, G. 1969. *Attitudes to Drugs and Drugtakers of Students at the University and Colleges of Higher Education in an English Midland City.* University of Leicester, Vaughan Papers, No. 14.
Birdwood, G. 1969. *The Willing Victim.* London: Secker and Warburg.
Bloomquist, E. R. 1968 *Marijuana.* New York: Collier-MacMillan.
Blum, R. H. 1965 *The Utopiates.* New York: Atherton Press.
——— 1969. *Drugs and Students.* San Francisco: Jossey-Bass.
Bradshaw, S. 1972, *Drug Misuse and the Law.* London: MacMillan.
Bromberg, 1939. Marihuana: a Psychiatric Study. *Journal of the American Medical Association* **113** (1), 4–12.
Burroughs, W. 1959. *The Naked Lunch.* Paris; Olympia.
——— 1966. *Junkie.* London: New English Library.
——— 1970. *Dead Fingers Talk.* London: Tandem.
Burroughs, W., jnr. 1971 *Speed.* London: Sphere.
Castaneda, C. 1968. *The Teachings of Don Juan: a Yacqui Way of Knowledge.* Berkeley: University of California Press.
——— 1971. *A Separate Reality: Further Conversations with Don Juan.* New York: Simon and Schuster.
Chapple, P. 1973. *The Guardian*, 31 January
Chein I., Gerard, D. L., Lee, R. S., and Rosenfeld, T. 1964. *Narcotics, Delinquency and Social Policy: The Road to H.* London: Tavistock.
Claridge, G. 1972. *Drugs and Human Behaviour.* Harmondsworth: Pelican.
Cockett, R. 1971. *Drug Abuse and Personality in Young Offenders.* London: Butterworths.
Cohen, S. 1965. *Drugs of Hallucination.* London: Secker and Warburg.
Connell, P. H. 1964. Amphetamine Misuse. *British Journal of Addiction* **60** (1): 9–27.

Crow, I. C. 1973. Two groups of Cannabis Users in South London. *Drugs and Society,* 2 (9) June: 10–14.

Crowley, A. 1972. *Diary of a Drug Fiend.* London: Sphere.

Davis, F., and Munoz, L. 1968. Heads and Freaks: Patterns of Drug Use Among Hippies. *Journal of Health and Social Behaviour* **9** (June): 156–64.

Dawtry, F. (ed.) 1968 *Social Problems of Drug Abuse.* London: Butterworths.

De Alarcon, R. 1969. The Spread of Heroin Abuse in a Community. *Bulletin of Narcotics* **21**: 17–22.

—— 1973. *The Guardian,* 9 April.

De Alarcon, R., and Rathod, N. H. 1968. Prevalence and Early Detection of Heroin Abuse. *British Medical Journal* 1 June: 549–53.

De Alarcon, R., Arroyave, F., Little, D., Letemendia, F. 1973. Misuse of Heroin and Methedrine in the City of Oxford. *British Journal of Addiction* **68** (2) June: 137–44.

De Quincy, J. 1950. *Confessions of an Opium Eater.* London: Cresset.

De Ropp, R. S. 1958. *Drugs and the Mind.* London: Gollancz.

Deedes, W. 1970. *The Drug Epidemic.* London: Tom Stacey.

Easton, K. 1965. Clinical Studies on the Pathogenesis and Personality Structure of Male Narcotic Addicts. *Journal of Hillside Hospital* **14**: 36–53.

Eddy, N., and Isbell, H. 1965. Drug Dependence: its Significance and Characteristics. *Bulletin of the World Health Organisation* **32** (5): 721–33.

Egozcue, J., and Irwin, S. 1970. L.S.D. – 25 Effects on Chromosomes: A Review. *Journal of Psychedelic Drugs* **3** (1) September: 10–12.

Eysenck, H. J., Casey, S., and Troughton, D. S. 1957. Drugs and Personality II, the Effect of Stimulant and Depressant Drugs on Continuous Work. *Journal of Mental Science* **103**: 645–49.

Forrest, J. A. H., and Tarala, R. A. 1973. Abuse of Drugs 'For Kicks': A Review of 252 Admissions. *British Medical Journal* **4**: 136–39.

——— 1973. 60 Hospital Admissions Due to Reactions to Lysergide (L.S.D.). *Lancet,* 8 December: 1310–13.

Friedenberg, S., and Camden, N. J. 1940. Addiction to Amphetamine Sulphate. *Journal of the American Medical Association* **144**: 956.

Gagnon, J. H., and Simon, W. 1970. *The End of Adolescence: The College Experience.* New York: Harper and Row.

Gilbert, J. C., and Lombardi, D. M. 1967. Personality Characteristics in Young Male Narcotic Addicts. *Journal of Consultant Psychology* **31**: 536–8.

Glatt, M. 1967. Drug Treatment Centres. *British Medical Journal* **3**: 242.

Goode, E. 1969. *Marihuana.* New York: Atherton Press.

——— 1969, Multiple Drug Use Amongst Marijuana Smokers. *Social Problems* **17** Summer: 54–62.

——— 1970. *The Marijuana Smokers.* New York: Basic Books.

——— 1972a. *Drugs in American Society.* New York: Alfred A. Knopf.

——— 1972b. Paper in *Sexual Behaviour* 2 (8): 45–51.

——— 1973. *The Drug Phenomenon: Social Aspects of Drugtaking.* New York: Bobbs-Merrill.

Gordon, A. 1971. *Patterns of Delinquency in Drug Addiction.* M. Phil. dissertation, University of London.

Green, J. 1972. *The International Times Book of Drugs.* London: Bloom.

Harms, E. (ed.) 1965. *Drug Addiction in Youth.* London: Pergamon.

Harms, E. 1972. The Heroin-Marijuana Relationship: A Basic Aspect of Drug Management. *British Journal of Addiction* **67**: 287–90.

——— 1972. The Three Types of Marijuana Dependencies. *British Journal of Addiction* **67**: 290–96.

Hekimian, L. J., and Gershon, S. 1968. Characteristics of Drug Abusers Admitted to a Psychiatric Hospital. *Journal of the American Medical Association* **205**: 125–30.

Hindmarch, I. 1970. Patterns of Drug Use in a Provincial University. *British Journal of Addiction* **64**: 395–403.

——— 1972. Adolescent Drug Use. *Synapse,* Journal of Edinburgh University Medical School **21** (3) April.

Huxley, A. 1972a. *The Doors of Perception and Heaven and Hell.* Harmondsworth: Penguin.

——— 1972b. *Island.* London: Chatto and Windus.

James, I. P. 1969. Delinquency and Heroin Addiction in Britain. *British Journal of Criminology*: 108–24.

——— 1973. Drug Abuse in Britain. *Medicine, Science and the Law* **13** (4) October: 246–51.

Johnson, B. D. 1973. *Marihuana Users and Drug Subcultures.* New York: John Wiley.

Jones, T. 1968. *Drugs and the Police.* London: Butterworths.

Kosviner, A., Mitcheson, M. C., Myers, K., Ogborne, A., Stimson, G., Zacune, J., and Edwards, G. 1968. Heroin Use in a Provincial Town. *Lancet,* June: 1189–92.

Larner, J., and Tefferteller, R. 1966. *The Addict in the Street.* Harmondsworth: Penguin.

Laurie, P. 1967. *Drugs.* Harmondsworth: Penguin.

Leary, T., Metzner, R., and Alpert, R. 1964. *The Psychedelic Experience.* New York: University Books.

Leech, K., and Jordan, B. 1967. *Drugs for Young People: Their Use and Misuse.* Oxford: Religious Education Press.

Lennard, H. L., Epstein, L. J., Bernstein, A., and Ransom, D. C. 1971. *Mystification and Drug Misuse.* San Francisco: Jossey-Bass Inc.

Lindesmith, A. R. 1968. *Addiction and Opiates.* Chicago: Aldine.

Linken, A. 1963. *Psychological Aspects of Student Drugtaking.* London: Pergamon.

Masters, R. E. L., and Houston, J. 1966. *The Varieties of Psychedelic Experience.* London: Turnstone.

McGrath, J. H., and Scarpitti, F. R. 1970. *Youth and Drugs.* Glenview, Illinois: Scott, Foresman and Co.

Meares, A. 1973. *Dialogue with Youth.* London: Fontana.

Mitchell, A. R. K. 1970. *Drugs: The Parents' Dilemma.* Royston, Hertfordshire: Priory.

Mott, J. 1973. London Juvenile Drug Offenders. *British Journal of Criminology* **13** (3) July: 209–17.

Murray, N. 1962. Covert Effects of Chlordiazepoxide Therapy. *Journal of Neuropsychiatry* **3**: 168–70.

Noble, P. J. 1970. Drugtaking in Delinquent Boys. *British Medical Journal* **1**: 102–5.

Noble, P. J., and Barnes, G. 1971. Drugtaking in Adolescent Girls: Factors Associated with Progression to Narcotic Use. *British Medical Journal,* 12 June: 620–23.

O'Callaghan, S. 1970. *Drug Addiction in Britain.* London: Robert Hale.

Phillipson, R. V. (ed.) 1970. *Modern Trends in Drug Dependence and Alcoholism.* London: Butterworths.

Plant, M. A. 1973. *Young People at Risk: a Study of the 17–24 Age Group.* Cheltenham Youth Trust Report, May.

Plant, M. A. 1974. Assessing Drugtaking as a Problem: An English Observation Study. *British Journal of Psychiatry* **124** February.

—— 1974. The Escalation Theory Reconsidered: Drugtakers in an English Town. *British Journal of Addiction* **69**: 309–13.

Plant, M. A. Drugtakers in an English Town; Factors Associated with the Use of Injected Drugs. *British Journal of Criminology* (in press).

Plant, M. A. What is the Drug Problem? *Social Work Today* 5 (9): 277–9.

Plant, M. A., and Reeves, C. E. 1973. Social Characteristics of Drug-Takers in Two English Urban Areas. *Drugs and Society* 2 (11): 14–18.

Plant, M. A., and Reeves, C. E. The Group Dynamics of Becoming a Drugtaker. *Interpersonal Development* (in press).

Reckless, W. C. 1967. *The Crime Problem.* New York: Appleton-Century-Crofts.

Reeves, C. E. 1972. Motivation for Changing Patterns of Drugtaking, Paper presented to 30th International Congress on Alcoholism and Drug Dependence, Amsterdam, Netherlands.

—— 1973. Sociological Aspects of Drug Taking in Southern Hampshire. Paper presented to 2nd International Conference on Alcoholism and Drug Dependence, Liverpool.

Ritson, E. B. 1971. Drug Use in the Provinces. *Drugs and Society* 2: 19–24.

Ritson, E. B., Toller, P., and Harding, F. 1973. Drug Abuse in the East Midlands. A Study of 139 Patients Referred to an Addiction Unit. *British Journal of Addiction* **68**: 65–71.

Rockwell, D. A. 1973. Alcohol and Marijuana – Social Problem Perspective. *British Journal of Addiction* **68**: 209–14.

Rollings, E. J. 1938. *Marihuana – The Weed of Woe.* Wichita, Kansas: Defender Club Tract.

Rowell, E. A., and Rowell, R. 1939. *On the Trail of Marihuana: The Weed of Madness.* Mountain View, California: Pacific.

Schofield, M. 1971. *The Strange Case of Pot.* Harmondsworth: Pelican.

Schur, E. M. 1966. *Narcotic Addiction in Britain and America.* London: Tavistock.

Scott, P., and Willcox, D. R. 1965. Delinquency and Amphetamines. *British Journal of Addiction* **61** November: 9–27.

Seymour, W. N. jnr. 1972. *The Young Die Quietly.* New York: William Morrow.

Smart, R. G., and Fejer, D. 1973. Marihuana Use amongst Adults in Toronto. *British Journal of Addiction* **68** (2) June: 117–28.

Solomon, D., (ed.) 1972. *The Marihuana Papers.* London: Panther.

Solomon, D., and Andrews, G. (ed.) 1973. *Drugs and Sexuality.* Herts: Panther.

Spear, H. B. 1969. The Growth of Heroin Addiction in the United Kingdom. *British Journal of Addiction* **64**: 245–55.

Speck, R. V., Barr, J., Eisenman, R., Foulkes, T., Goldman, A., and Lincoln, J. 1972. *The New Families.* New York: Basic Books.

Stafford, P. G., and Golightly, B. H., (eds.) 1967. *L.S.D. The Problem-Solving Psychedelic.* London: Tandem.

Stimson, G. V. 1973. *Heroin and Behaviour.* London: Irish University Press.

Symonds, J. 1973. *The Great Beast, the Life and Magick of Aleister Crowley.* London: Mayflower.

Taylor, N. 1963. *Narcotics: Nature's Dangerous Gifts.* New York: Delta.

Thompson, H. 1972. *Fear and Loathing in Las Vegas.* London: Paladin.

Toll, A. M. 1970. Case Study on the Attitudes of Drug Addicts to Treatment. *British Journal of Addiction* **65**: 139–58.

Trocchi, A. 1966. *Cain's Book.* London: Calder.

Tylden, E., (ed.) 1970. *A.B.C. of Drug Addiction.* Bristol: John Wright.

Waldorf, D. 1973. *Careers in Dope.* New Jersey: Prentice Hall.

Walsh, M.G.T. 1969. *Cannabis Use in a Student Population.* M. Phil. dissertation, University of London.

Walton, R. P. 1938. *Marihuana: America's New Drug Problem.* Philadelphia; Lippincott.

Wells, B. 1973. *Psychedelic Drugs.* Harmondsworth: Penguin.

Whitehead, P. 1970. The Incidence of Drug Use Amongst Halifax Adolescents. *British Journal of Addiction* **65**: 159–65.

Wiener, R. S. P. 1970. *Drugs and Schoolchildren.* London: Longman.

Willis, J. 1973. Addicts: *Drugs and Alcohol Re-Examined.* London: Pitman.

Wilson, C. W. M. (ed.) 1968. *Adolescent Drug Dependence.* London: Pergamon

Wolfe, T. 1971. *The Kool-Aid Acid Test.* New York: Bantam.

Wolff, P. O. 1949. *Marihuana in Latin America: The Threat it Constitutes.* Washington: Linacre.

Wood, A. J. 1967. *Drug Dependence.* Bristol Corporation and the British Council of Social Services.

Woodside, M. 1973. The First 100 Referrals to a Scottish Drug Treatment Centre. *British Journal of Addiction* **68** 231–41.

Wright, J. D. 1968. A Survey of the Knowledge and Attitudes about Drug Misuse Amongst 4th Year Pupils at Three Wolverhampton Schools. *Health Education Journal* **27** (3): 111–14.

Yablonsky, L. 1965. *The Tunnel Back: Synanon*, New York: Macmillan.

Young, J. 1971 *The Drugtakers.* London: Paladin.

Young J., and Brooke-Crutchley, J. 1972. Student Drug Use. *Drugs and Society* **1** (2) October 11–15.

Zacune, J. 1971. A Comparison of Canadian Narcotic Addicts in Great Britain and Canada. *Bulletin of Narcotics* **23** (4): 41–9.

Zacune, J., and Hensman, C. 1971. *Drugs, Alcohol and Tobacco in Britain*. London: Heinemann.

Zinberg, N., and Weil, A. T. 1970. A Comparison of Marihuana Users and Non-Users. *Nature* **226** 119.

2. Observation Studies

Beattie, J. H. M. 1965. *Understanding an African Kingdom.* New York: Holt, Reinhart and Winston.

Becker, H. S. 1963. *Outsiders: Studies in the Sociology of Deviance.* New York: Free Press.

Festinger, L., Riecken, H. W. jnr., and Schacter, S. 1956. *When Prophecy Fails*. Minneapolis: University of Minnesota Press.

Humphreys, L. 1970. *The Tearoom Trade.* London: Duckworth.

Malinowski, B. 1954. *Magic, Science and Religion.* New York: Doubleday, Anchor Books.

Patrick, J. 1973. *A Glasgow Gang Observed.* London: Eyre Methuen.

Polsky, N., see under Methodology.

Thompson, H. 1967. *Hell's Angels.* Harmondsworth: Pelican.

Whyte, W. F. 1968. *Street Corner Society.* Chicago: University of Chicago Press.

Yablonsky, L. 1967. *The Violent Gang.* Harmondsworth: Pelican.

3 Alcoholism

Glatt, M. M. 1972. *The Alcoholic – and The Help He Needs.* London: Priory Press.

Kessell, N., and Walton, H. 1967. *Alcoholism.* Harmondsworth: Pelican.

McClelland, D. C., Davis, W. N., Kalin, R., and Warner, E. 1972. *The Drinking Man.* London: Collier-Macmillan.

Neill, A., and Hymers, J. 1972. *Alcoholism, The Ignored Illness.* Edinburgh: Alna Press

4. Deviant Behaviour

Alvarez, A. 1971. *The Savage God: A Study of Suicide.* London: Wiedenfeld and Nicholson.

Bahr, H. M., (ed.) 1970. *Disaffiliated Man.* Toronto: University of Toronto Press.

Becker, H. S. 1964. *The Other Side.* New York: Free Press.

Carson, W. G., and Wiles, P. (eds.) 1971. *Crime and Delinquency in Britain.* London: Martin Robertson.

Clinard, M. B., *et al.* 1964. *Anomie and Deviant Behaviour.* New York: Free Press.

Cloward, R., and Ohlin, L. 1960. *Delinquency and Opportunity.* Chicago: Free Press.

Cohen, A. K. 1955. *Delinquent Boys.* Chicago: Free Press.

——— 1966. *Deviance and Control.* Englewood Cliffs, N. J.: Prentice Hall.

Cohen, S., (ed.) 1971. *Images of Deviance.* Harmondsworth: Pelican.

——— 1972. *Folk Devils and Moral Panics.* London: MacGibbon and Kee.

Cressey, D. R., and Ward, D. A. 1969. *Delinquency, Crime and Social Process.* New York: Harper and Row.

De Berker, P., and De Berker, P. 1973. *Misfits.* London: Pitman.

Douglas, J. D. 1972. *Research on Deviance.* New York: Random House.

Downes, D. 1966a. *The Delinquent Solution.* London: Routledge and Kegan Paul.

——— 1966b. The Gang Myth. *Listener,* 14 April.

Durkheim, E. 1951. *Suicide.* Chicago: Free Press.

——— 1965. *The Division of Labour*, New York: Free Press.

Gibbens, T. C. N., and Ahrenfield, T. R. H. (eds.) 1966. *Cultural Factors in Delinquency.* London: Tavistock.

Goffman, E. 1968. *Stigma.* Harmondsworth: Pelican.

Hood, R., and Sparks, R. 1972. *Key Issues in Criminology.* London: Weidenfeld and Nicholson.

Kinsey, A. C., Pomeroy, W. B., and Martin, C. E. 1948. *Sexual Behaviour in the Human Male.* Philadelphia: Saunders.

Kinsey, A. C., Pomeroy, W. B., Martin, C. E., and Gebhard, P. H. 1953. *Sexual Behaviour in the Human Female.* Philadelphia: Sanders.

Kreitman, N., Philip, A. E. Greer, S., and Bagley, C. R. 1969. Correspondence, *British Journal of Psychiatry* **115** (523) June: 746–7.

Kreitman, N., Smith, P., and Tan, E. 1970. Attempted Suicide as a Language: An Empirical Study. *British Journal of Psychiatry* **116** (534) May: 46–73.

Lafitte, F. 1972. Abortion in Britain Today. *New Society,* 14 December.

McCulloch, J. W., and Philip, A. 1972. *Suicidal Behaviour.* Oxford: Pergamon.

Matza, D. 1964. *Delinquency and Drift.* New York: John Wiley.

——— 1969. *Becoming Deviant.* Englewood Cliffs, N. J: Prentice Hall.

Matza, D., and Sykes, G. M. 1957. Techniques of Neutralization: a Theory of Delinquency. *American Sociological Review* 22: 664–70.

——— 1961. Juvenile Delinquency and Subterranean Values. *American Sociological Review* 28.

Merton, R. K. 1938. Social Structure and Anomie. *American Sociological Review* 3: 672–82.

——— 1964. *Social Theory and Social Structure.* New York: Free Press.

Merton, R. K., and Nisbet, R. (eds.) 1971. *Contemporary Social Problems.* New York: Harcourt Brace Jovanovich.

Miller, W. B. 1962. The Impact of a Total Community Delinquency Control Project. *Social Problems* **10** (2): 168–191.

Miller, W. M., and Riesman, F. 1961. The Working Class Subculture: A New View. *Social Problems* **9** (1): 86–97.

Phillipson, M. 1971. *Sociological Aspects of Crime and Delinquency.* London: Routledge and Kegan Paul.

Rubington, E., and Weinberg, M. S. (eds.) 1968. *Deviance: the Interactionist Perspective.* New York: Macmillan.

Sanders, E. 1973. *The Family.* London: Panther.

Schaar, J. H., and McClosky 1965. Psychological Dimensions of Anomie. *American Sociological Review* 3 (1): 14–40.

Schofield, M. 1968. *The Sexual Behaviour of Young People.* Harmondsworth: Pelican.

Schur, E. M. 1965. *Crimes Without Victims.* New Jersey: Prentice Hall.

Schwitzgebel, R. 1965. *Street Corner Research.* Cambridge, Mass: Harvard University Press.

Shaw, C. R. 1966. *The Jackroller.* London: Phoenix.

Simmons, J. L. 1970. *Deviants.* Berkley: Glendessary.

Skolnick, J. H. 1966. *Justice Without Trial.* New York: John Wiley.

Smelser, N. J. 1962. *Theory of Collective Behaviour.* London: Routledge and Kegan Paul.

Srole, L. J. 1936. Social Integration and Certain Corollaries: An Explanatory Study. *American Sociological Review*: 709–16.

Stebbins, R. A. 1971. *Commitment to Deviance.* Westport, Conn: Greenwood.

Stengel, E., 1964. *Suicide and Attempted Suicide.* Harmondsworth: Penguin.

Sutherland, E. H., and Cressey, D. 1970. *Criminology.* New York: Lippincott.

Taylor, L., 1973. *Deviance and Society.* London: Nelson.

Thrasher, F. M. 1927. *The Gang.* Chicago: University of Chicago Press.

West, J. D. 1967. *The Young Offender.* Harmondsworth: Pelican.

Winslow, R. W. 1970. *Society in Transition.* New York: Macmillan.

Wolfgang, M. E., Savitz, L., and Johnston, N. 1970. *The Sociology of Crime and Delinquency.* New York: Wiley.

Wootton, B. 1959. *Social Science and Social Pathology.* London: Allen and Unwin.

Yinger, J. M. 1960. Contraculture and Subculture. *American Sociological Review* **25** (5): 625–35.

Young, J., Taylor, L., Walton, P. 1973. *The New Criminology: for a Social Theory of Deviance.* London: Routledge and Keegan Paul.

5. General Sociology

Andreski, s. 1973. *Social Science as Sorcery.* London: Andre Deutsch.

Berger, P. L., and Luckman, T. 1966. *The Social Construction of Reality.* New York: Doubleday.

Forde, L. S. 1942. Culture and Human Behaviour. *Scientific Monthly* **55**: 546–57.

Gouldner, A., and Miller, S. (eds.) 1965. *Applied Sociology.* New York: Free Press.

Halsey, A. H. (ed.) 1972. *Trends in British Society Since 1900.* London: Macmillan.

Harre, R., and Secord, P. F. 1972. *The Explanation of Social Behaviour.* Oxford: Blackwell.

Hoggart, R. 1971. *The Uses of Literacy.* Harmondsworth: Pelican.

Jarvie, I. C. 1964. *The Revolution in Anthropology.* London: Routledge and Kegan Paul.

MacIver, R. 1950. *The Ramparts We Guard.* New York: Macmillan.

Mills, C. W. 1970. *The Sociological Imagination.* Harmondsworth: Pelican.

Parsons, T. 1949. *The Structure of Social Action.* New York: Free Press.

Parsons, T., and Shils, E. A. 1965. *Towards a General Theory of Social Action.* New York: Harper and Row.

Rex, J., and Moore, R. 1967. *Race, Community and Conflict.* London: Oxford University Press.

6. Youth Culture

Goetschius, G. W., and Tash, M. J. 1967. *Working With Unattached Youth.* London: Routledge and Kegan Paul.

Musgrove, F. 1964. *Youth and the Social Order.* London: Routledge and Kegan Paul.

Neville, R. 1971. *Playpower.* London: Paladin.

Ryle, A. 1973. *Student Casualties.* Harmondsworth: Pelican.

Veness, T. 1962. *School Leavers: Their Aspirations and Expectations.* London: Methuen.

Willmott, P. 1966. *Adolescent Boys in East London.* London: Routledge and Kegan Paul.

7. Social Psychology

Bowlby, J. 1957. *Maternal Deprivation and Mental Health.* World Health Organization, Monograph Series 2. Geneva.

——— 1963. *Child Care and the Growth of Love.* Harmondsworth: Penguin.

Cartwright, D., and Zander, A. (eds.) 1968. *Group Dynamics.* London: Tavistock.

Grey, A. L. 1969. *Class and Personality in Society.* New York: Atherton.

Krech, D., Crutchfield, R. S., and Ballachey, E. 1962. *Individual in Society.* New York: McGraw-Hill.

Laing, R. D. 1967. *The Politics of Experience.* Harmondsworth: Penguin.

Secord. F. F., and Backman, C. W. 1964. *Social Psychology.* New York: McGraw-Hill.

8. Methodology

Ball, J. C. 1957. The Reliability and Validity of Interview Data Obtained from 59 Narcotic Addicts. *American Journal of Sociology* **72**: 650–54.

Becker, H. S. 1952. A Note on Interviewing Tactics. *Human Organization* **12** (4): 31–2.

——— 1970. *Sociological Work.* London: Allen Lane.

Belsen, W. A., Millerson, G. L., and Didcott, P. J. 1968. *The Development of a Procedure For Eliciting Information From Boys About the Nature and Extent of Their Stealing.* Survey Research Centre, L.S.E.

Bruyn, S. T. H. 1966. *The Human Perspective in Sociology.* Englewood Cliffs, N. J: Prentice Hall.

Clark, J. P., and Tifft, L. 1966 Polygraph and Interview Validations of Self-Reported Deviant Behaviour. *American Sociological Review* **31** (4): 516–23.

Filstead, W. J. (ed.) 1971. *Qualitative Methodology.* Chicago: Markham.

Gibson, H. B. 1968. Self-Reported Delinquency. Paper presented to the 3rd National Conference on Research and Teaching in Criminology, Cambridge, July.

Kalton, G. 1966. *Introduction to Statistical Ideas.* London: Chapman and Hall.

McCall, G. J., and Simmons, J. L. (eds.) 1969. *Issues in Participant Observation.* Reading, Mass: Addison-Wesley.

McEwen, W. J. 1963. Forms and Problems of Validation in Social Anthropology. *Current Anthropology* **4**: 155–69.

Madge, J. 1953. *The Tools of Social Science.* London: Longmans.

Miller, S. M. 1952. The Participant Observer and Over-Rapport. *American Sociological Review* **17**: 97–9.

Moreno, J. L. 1953. *Who Shall Survive?* New York: Beacon House.

Moser, C. A. 1965. *Survey Methods in Social Investigation.* London: Heinemann.

Oppenheim, A. N. 1966. *Questionnaire Design and Attitude Measurement.* London: Heinemann.

Polsky, N. 1969. *Hustlers, Beats and Others.* Harmondsworth: Pelican.

Schwartz, M. S. and Schwartz, C. G. 1935. Problems in Participant Observation. *American Journal of Sociology* **60**: 343–53.

Siegel, S. 1956. *Non-Parametric Statistics for the Behavioural Sciences.* New York: McGraw-Hill.

Williams, T. R. 1967. *Field Methods in the Study of Culture.* New York: Holt.

9. Reports

Canadian Government. 1971. *Non-medical Use of Drugs.* Interim Report of the Canadian Government Commission of Inquiry (Le Dain Report). Harmondsworth: Penguin.

H.M. Government. 1969. *Cannabis.* Report of the Advisory Committee on Drug Dependence (Wootton Report) London: HMSO.

——1970. *Powers of Arrest and Search in Relation to Drug Offences.* Report of the Advisory Committee on Drug Dependence (Deedes Report). London: HMSO.

—— 1973. *Report of the Committee on Abuse of Social Security Benefits.* Cmnd. 5228. London: HMSO.

National Commission on Marihuana and Drug Abuse. 1972. *Marihuana: a Signal of Misunderstanding.* Washington: US Government Printing Office.

Presidential Commission on Law Enforcement and the Administration of Justice. 1967. *Narcotics and Drug Abuse* (Task Force Report). Washington: US Government Printing Office.

Royal College of Physicians. 1971. *Smoking and Health Now.* A report, London: Pitman.

Select Committee on Crime, House of Representatives. 1970. *Crime in America: The Heroin Paraphernalia Trade.* Washington: US Government Printing Office.

10. Miscellaneous

Evans-Wentz, W. Y. (trans.) 1951. *The Tibetan Book of the Dead.* London: Oxford University Press.

Name Index

Subject Index